LIVING IN STYLE
LONDON

LIVING IN STYLE
LONDON

Edited by
Geraldine Apponyi and Monika Apponyi
Texts by Judith Wilson

teNeues

CONTENTS

Foreword

I came to London from Vienna in 1968 to study Interior Design. There were none of the excellent schools of today at that time – the only way to learn was to be apprenticed, a system of learning I highly recommend. There were no interior designers in Vienna when I was young, the theory being that if your house was good enough for your parents and grandparents, it should be good enough for you.

As a result the only beautiful interiors were in embassies or in the houses of the "nouveau riche" who imported interior designers usually from Paris. I had a great friend whose mother had done just that and their house was easily the most beautiful and comfortable of all. Her father had travelled in China and the house was filled with exquisite porcelain and the dining room walls hung with 18th century hand-painted Chinese paper. I remember it was a subtle shade of celadon with white cranes flying around the room.

After studying History of Art I decided to visit London since my mother had a friend who was a successful interior designer. We liked one another and she took me on as her apprentice. This meant following her around with a notebook and a large, heavy satchel filled with sample books, pulling them out when asked. It was hard work, badly paid (£3 a week) but I learnt a great deal. At the time, my "boss" was mostly decorating cruise ships – fabrics had to be flame resistant and the expected lifetime of any textile was just five years. How different that was to my next apprenticeship with a friend of hers decorating private London houses, mostly narrow and tall. I worked as an apprentice with five interior designers in all, each of them well known in the trade, until I came under the wing of the legendary John Fowler, watching as he scraped small squares of 18th century walls to find the original colour underneath, hanging on his every word and writing down as much as I could. After five years of watching, listening and note-taking, I opened my own interior design company, Szapar Designs. I loved my work until marriage and children brought an end to my life in "trade" as my profession was known, and unsuitable, it was thought, at the time, for my new position. Happily those attitudes have faded.

A number of the designers in this book started out when I did and I have both admired and envied their work for many years. They all stuck to the same rules that I imbibed – please the eye, please the mind, please the pocket, make interiors comfortable and "work". By "work" was meant – can you *see* where you sit to read? Can you move in the bathroom without bumping into your partner (one should always if possible have one's own bathroom), can you cook without having to cross the kitchen for the utensils – make the interior beautiful, but functional.

So often have I seen ravishing photographs of rooms but with one glance I can see they would not serve their function. What I like in this excellent book is that the designers chosen always bear that in mind. Their rooms "work" as well as please.

Marie Christine

Her Royal Highness Princess Michael of Kent

Vorwort

1968 kam ich aus Wien nach London, um Innenarchitektur zu studieren. Damals gab es noch keine der hervorragenden Schulen, die wir heute haben – der einzig mögliche Weg, den ich nur ausdrücklich empfehlen kann, war, bei einem Praktiker in die Lehre zu gehen. Doch zu der Zeit hatte Wien keine Innenarchitekten. Was für die Eltern und Großeltern gut genug gewesen war, so die Theorie, war auch gut genug für die Kinder.

Aus diesem Grund gab es schöne Interieurs nur in Botschaften oder den Häusern der „Nouveau Riche", die ihre Innenarchitekten meist aus Paris kommen ließen. Die Mutter einer sehr guten Freundin von mir hatte genau das getan, und ihr Haus war mit Abstand das schönste und wohnlichste, das ich kannte. Der Vater meiner Freundin hatte China bereist, sodass das Haus voll war von erlesenem Porzellan und handbemaltes Chinapapier aus dem 18. Jahrhundert die Wände des Esszimmers schmückte. Ich erinnere mich an einen zarten Hauch von Seladon und weiße Kraniche, die durch den Raum flogen.

Nach meinem Studium der Kunstgeschichte beschloss ich, nach London zu gehen, wo eine Freundin meiner Mutter erfolgreich als Innenarchitektin arbeitete. Wir mochten einander, und so begann meine Ausbildung. Bewaffnet mit meinem Notizbuch und einer großen Umhängetasche voller Musterbücher, die ich auf Anweisung hervorholte, folgte ich ihr überall hin. Die Arbeit war hart und schlecht bezahlt (drei Pfund die Woche), aber ich habe sehr viel gelernt. Zu dieser Zeit stattete meine Chefin überwiegend Kreuzfahrtschiffe aus – mit schwer entflammbaren Stoffen und Textilien, die im Durchschnitt nicht länger als fünf Jahre hielten. Was für ein Unterschied zu meiner nächsten Ausbildungsstation bei einer Freundin von ihr: Sie richtete Londoner Privathäuser ein, von denen die meisten hoch und schmal waren. Insgesamt lernte ich bei fünf verschiedenen Innenarchitekten, die in der Branche einen Namen hatten, bevor mich der legendäre John Fowler unter seine Fittiche nahm. Ich sah zu, wie er kleine Vierecke von jahrhundertealten Wänden kratzte, um die Originalfarbe zu finden, hing an seinen Lippen und machte so viele Notizen wie möglich. Nach fünf Jahren des Zusehens, Zuhörens und Notizenmachens eröffnete ich mein eigenes Büro für Innenarchitektur, Szapar Designs. Ich liebte meine Arbeit – bis Heirat und Kinder meiner Laufbahn in einem „gewerblichen" Beruf, der für Ehefrauen und Mütter damals als unschicklich galt, ein Ende setzten. Glücklicherweise gehören solche Einstellungen der Vergangenheit an.

Einige der Designer in diesem Buch begannen ihre Laufbahn zur gleichen Zeit wie ich. Seit vielen Jahren bewundere ich ihre Arbeit und beneide sie darum. Sie alle halten sich bis heute an dieselben Grundsätze, die ich damals verinnerlicht habe: Erfreue das Auge, erfreue den Geist, erfreue den Geldbeutel und sorge dafür, dass die Einrichtung wohnlich ist und „funktioniert". „Funktionieren" hieß: Hat der Lesesessel genügend Licht? Kann man sich im Bad bewegen, ohne mit dem Partner zusammenzustoßen (wenn irgend möglich, sollte jeder sein eigenes Badezimmer haben)? Kann man kochen, ohne für das Kochgeschirr die ganze Küche durchqueren zu müssen? Mit anderen Worten: Sorge für ein schönes, aber praktisches Interieur.

Nur allzu oft sehe ich hinreißende Aufnahmen von Räumen, die sich schon auf den ersten Blick als unpraktisch herausstellen. Was mir an diesem ausgezeichneten Buch gefällt, ist die Tatsache, dass die ausgewählten Designer das immer vor Augen haben. Ihre Räume „funktionieren" *und* gefallen.

Mari Christine

Her Royal Highness Princess Michael of Kent

Préface

J'ai quitté Vienne en 1968 pour aller étudier l'architecture d'intérieur à Londres. À l'époque, comme les excellentes écoles dont nous bénéficions aujourd'hui n'existaient pas encore, le meilleur moyen d'apprendre le métier était d'entrer en apprentissage, un mode de formation que je recommande vivement. Dans ma jeunesse, il n'y avait pas d'architectes d'intérieur à Vienne, car on partait du principe que ce dont vos parents et grands-parents s'étaient contentés devait vous suffire.

Ainsi, pour voir de superbes intérieurs, il fallait fréquenter les ambassades ou les demeures des « nouveaux-riches », qui faisaient appel à des décorateurs étrangers, généralement parisiens. C'est ce qu'avait fait la mère d'un de mes grands amis de l'époque, et leur maison était de loin la plus belle et la plus confortable que je connaissais. Comme son père avait été en poste en Chine, la maison regorgeait de porcelaine fine, et les murs de la salle à manger étaient ornés de papier peint à la main chinois du XVIIIe siècle. J'en ai gardé le souvenir de grues blanches volant autour de la pièce sur un fond d'un délicat vert céladon.

Après mes études d'histoire de l'art à Vienne, j'ai donc décidé de venir à Londres, où ma mère avait une amie décoratrice. Nous avons sympathisé et elle m'a prise comme apprentie. Cela consistait à la suivre dans ses déplacements, munie d'un carnet de notes et d'une lourde sacoche remplie de catalogues d'échantillons, que j'extirpais à la demande. Je travaillais dur pour un salaire de misère (3 livres sterling par semaine), mais j'apprenais une foule de choses. À l'époque, ma « chef » décorait des yachts de croisière, et ce avec des tissus ininflammables et résistants, car la durée de vie du moindre textile n'excédait pas cinq ans. C'est une expérience bien différente que j'ai faite dans le cadre de mon apprentissage suivant auprès d'une de ses amies spécialisée dans l'aménagement de maisons de particuliers londoniennes, généralement étroites et en hauteur. J'avais travaillé comme apprentie auprès de cinq architectes d'intérieur, tous reconnus dans la profession, lorsque le légendaire John Fowler m'a prise sous son aile. Buvant ses paroles et prenant un maximum de notes, je l'observais tandis qu'il mettait au jour les couches successives de revêtement sur des murs du XVIIIe siècle. Au bout de cinq années passées à observer, écouter et prendre des notes, j'ai créé ma propre agence d'architecture intérieure, Szapar Designs. J'ai exercé mon métier avec passion jusqu'à ce que le mariage et la maternité mettent fin à mon activité professionnelle, qui était alors considérée comme incompatible avec ma nouvelle situation familiale. Heureusement, les mentalités ont évolué.

Certains des architectes d'intérieur et décorateurs présentés dans ce livre ont débuté leur carrière en même temps que moi, et j'ai longtemps admiré et envié leurs travaux. Tous adhéraient aux principes dont j'étais aussi imprégnée : flatter l'œil, flatter l'esprit, plaire au porte-monnaie, créer des intérieurs confortables et qui « fonctionnent ». Par « fonctionner » on entendait permettre de répondre par l'affirmative aux questions suivantes : Là où vous êtes assis, voyez-vous suffisamment bien pour lire ? Pouvez-vous être à deux dans la salle de bain sans vous gêner (à défaut de disposer d'une salle de bain personnelle) ? Quand vous cuisinez, avez-vous tous les ustensiles nécessaires sous la main ?

Je vois très souvent de belles photos de pièces. Mais il me suffit d'un coup d'œil pour savoir qu'elles ne sont pas fonctionnelles. Dans cet excellent ouvrage, j'apprécie que les décorateurs présentés ne perdent jamais de vue que leurs pièces doivent « fonctionner » tout aussi bien que plaire.

Mari Christine

Her Royal Highness Princess Michael of Kent

Introduction

Throughout the last few decades, London has increasingly become *the* trendsetter for politics, fashion, art, theatre, music and of course interior architecture and design. It is a city renowned for being exciting, vibrant and rich in culture. This is reflected by the cosmopolitan and multi-talented people who have decided to make their homes in the quintessentially "London" roads, mews', squares and terraces. Hidden within these diverse London streets and behind familiar and unprepossessing exteriors are some of the world's most beautiful and unusual interiors. No wonder, since the designers behind these interiors, are among the best in the world. They have been inspired by the infinite creative possibilities that London has to offer, as well as by the seemingly unlimited supply of great and skilled craftsmen, textile designers, artists, antique markets and one-of-a-kind shops. Not to mention the perfectly proportioned period architecture, and the innovative and contemporary recently built.

What is so wonderful about this city is that there is no specific look associated with London's interiors. Despite its vast population, it is much a constellation of small and distinct areas, with architecture and inhabitants to match that diversity. The great talent of the designers in this book is to be able to create that perfect union between these exceptional architectural and often historical spaces, and the people who live in them.

These designers, in close collaboration with their inspiring clients, have done something truly amazing. They have created spaces that are not only extraordinarily stylish, elegant, individual, and exquisitely crafted, but interiors that work and are made for living. Places where one can retreat to and exist blissfully and harmoniously in an environment crafted from start to finish with the purpose of making life more beautiful but also more comfortable and more functional. There is a quote by the designer Albert Hadley that rings true: "The essence of interior design will always be about people and how they live. It is about the realities of what makes for an attractive, civilized, meaningful environment, not about fashion or what's in or what's out. This is not an easy job."

This book brings together a broad array of the best of these interiors, from classic continental, through mad and eccentric to contemporary eclectic, and everything in-between. Also included are some of the designers' own homes, where they have had the chance to really experiment and create some of the most varied, unusual and interesting interiors of all. This book not only takes the reader inside these exclusive addresses, rarely seen before, but also gives a glimpse inside the minds of the exceptional talent that created them.

Geraldine Apponyi

Einleitung

In den vergangenen Jahrzehnten hat London sich mehr und mehr zu *dem* Trendsetter in Sachen Politik, Mode, Kunst, Theater, Musik und natürlich Innenarchitektur im weitesten Sinne entwickelt. Die Stadt hat den Ruf, aufregend, lebendig und reich an Kultur zu sein. Das spiegelt sich auch in den Kosmopoliten und Multitalenten wider, die sich in den „Ur-Londoner" Roads, Mews, Squares und Terraces niedergelassen haben. In eben diesen Londoner Straßen, hinter vertrauten und unscheinbaren Fassaden, verstecken sich einige der schönsten und ungewöhnlichsten Interieurs der Welt. Kein Wunder, denn die Designer hinter diesen Interieurs zählen ebenfalls zu den besten der Welt. Sie haben sich von den unbegrenzten kreativen Möglichkeiten, die London zu bieten hat, und von dem scheinbar unendlichen Angebot an großartigen und erfahrenen Handwerkern, Textildesignern, Künstlern, Antikmärkten und einzigartigen Geschäften inspirieren lassen. Ganz zu schweigen von den perfekten Proportionen der historischen Architektur und den innovativen und zeitgemäßen Bauwerken jüngeren Datums.

Das Wunderbare an dieser Stadt ist, dass man mit Londoner Interieurs keinen spezifischen Stil verbindet. Trotz seiner gewaltigen Einwohnerzahl ist die britische Hauptstadt in erster Linie ein Gebilde aus kleinen, höchst unterschiedlichen Stadtvierteln, deren Architektur und Bewohnerschaft der Vielfalt dieser Viertel entsprechen. Die große Begabung der Designer in diesem Buch besteht darin, die perfekte Einheit zwischen solchen einmaligen architektonischen, oftmals historischen Räumen und ihren Bewohnern herstellen zu können.

In enger Zusammenarbeit mit ihren inspirierenden Auftraggebern haben sie etwas wahrhaft Erstaunliches geleistet: Sie haben nicht einfach Räume geschaffen, die außerordentlich stilvoll, elegant, individuell und exquisit ausgeführt sind, sondern praktische, alltagstaugliche Interieurs. Sie haben Rückzugsorte geschaffen, an denen es sich glücklich und harmonisch leben lässt – in einer Umgebung, die von Anfang bis Ende mit dem Ziel gestaltet wurde, das Leben schöner zu machen, aber auch bequemer und funktionaler. Der Designer Albert Hadley hatte recht, als er feststellte: „In ihrem Kern wird die Innenarchitektur sich immer um Menschen drehen und wie sie leben. Sie beschäftigt sich mit der realen Frage, was eine ansprechende, zivilisierte, sinnvolle Umgebung ausmacht, nicht mit Mode oder damit, was in oder out ist. Das ist kein leichter Job."

Dieses Buch stellt eine umfassende Auswahl der besten dieser Interieurs vor, von klassisch kontinental über verrückt und exzentrisch bis hin zu zeitgenössisch eklektisch, einschließlich aller Zwischenformen. Manche dieser Wohnungen und Häuser werden von den Designern selbst bewohnt, die hier die Gelegenheit hatten, echte Experimente zu wagen und einige der abwechslungsreichsten, ungewöhnlichsten und interessantesten Interieurs überhaupt zu verwirklichen. Dieses Buch lädt seine Leserinnen und Leser nicht nur ein, diese exklusiven, selten zuvor öffentlich gezeigten Adressen zu betreten, sondern liefert auch Einblicke in die Denkweise der Ausnahmetalente hinter den Interieurs.

Geraldine Apponyi

Introduction

Au cours de ces toutes dernières décennies, Londres s'est affirmée comme *la prescriptrice* en matière de politique, de mode, d'art, de théâtre, de musique et bien sûr aussi d'architecture d'intérieur et de décoration. C'est une ville que l'on sait passionnante, vivante et riche au niveau culturel. Cela se reflète dans la population cosmopolite et aux talents multiples qui a décidé de s'établir dans les rues, les places et les quartiers qui font la quintessence de « Londres ». Parmi ces rues et derrière ces façades familières et peu avenantes se cachent certains des intérieurs les plus beaux et les plus singuliers. Rien d'étonnant à cela, car les spécialistes qui les ont créés sont parmi les meilleurs au monde. Ils ont été inspirés par les infinies possibilités créatrices que Londres pouvait leur offrir, ainsi que par le choix apparemment illimité de grands et talentueux artisans, créateurs de textiles, artistes, ainsi que de marchés d'antiquités et magasins uniques en leur genre, mais aussi par une architecture d'époque parfaitement proportionnée et par les édifices contemporains et innovants récemment construits.

Ce qui est génial dans cette ville, c'est que ses intérieurs n'ont pas de look spécifique. Malgré une très forte population, c'est plus une pléiade de petits quartiers très divers, qui ont tous une architecture et des habitants différents. Le grand talent des personnalités réunies dans ce livre est d'avoir réussi à associer de façon idéale ces espaces architecturaux, et souvent aussi historiques, à leurs occupants.

En étroite collaboration avec les clients qui les ont inspirés, ces designers ont réussi une chose vraiment incroyable. Ils n'ont pas seulement créé des espaces très stylés, élégants, personnalisés et brillamment exécutés, mais aussi des intérieurs fonctionnels faits pour être habités. Ce sont des lieux où l'on peut se retirer et vivre pleinement et en harmonie, dans un cadre conçu du début à la fin pour rendre la vie non seulement plus belle, mais également encore plus confortable et plus fonctionnelle. Cette citation de l'architecte d'intérieur Albert Hadley me paraît tout à fait convenir : « L'essence de l'architecture d'intérieur réside dans les gens et la manière dont ils vivent. Ce travail concerne les réalités qui rendent un cadre attrayant, raffiné et épanouissant, et non pas la mode ou ce qui se fait ou ne se fait plus. Ce n'est pas un travail facile. »

Ce livre réunit une large gamme des plus beaux intérieurs, de l'intérieur classique d'Europe continentale jusqu'à l'intérieur insensé et excentrique ou à l'intérieur contemporain éclectique, et tout ce qui peut exister entre ces extrêmes. Quelques demeures sont celles de designers, qui ont ainsi pu expérimenter et réaliser certains des intérieurs parmi les plus variés, les plus insolites et les plus attrayants de tous. Ce livre ne se contente pas de conduire le lecteur dans ces lieux exclusifs, peu visités auparavant, il leur permet de s'introduire un bref moment dans l'esprit des exceptionnels talents qui les ont créés.

Geraldine Apponyi

Theatrical Seduction

David Carter, interior designer and creative visionary, likes to design theatrical interiors that seduce. A visitor to his home is guaranteed an emotional experience, because to walk into this early eighteenth century house is to be transported into a sensual world. Guests are indeed welcome, as under the guise of *40 Winks*, David operates his home as "the world's smallest and most beautiful boutique hotel". The rooms are a favourite with art directors, models and photographers looking for a special place in London. Walls are doused in colour, and *trompe l'oeil* confounds the eye. The four-storey East London property had fallen into disrepair and has been painstakingly restored. Panelling may look authentic, but entire sections are new, recreated using an original template. Now, the rooms provide a rich visual roller-coaster ride, some moodily dark, others classically cool. In what David terms the "opium den" drawing room, walls have a frottage finish: over a gold base, the surface has been glazed and hand-applied with tissue. The result is natural-looking crocodile skin. The bathroom glints with metallic de Gournay wallpaper, and in the drawing room, the ceiling resembles that of an eighteenth century chateau, stained by centuries of wood smoke. David has an eye for the exotic. So decorative pieces are combined with tongue-in-cheek humour, fusing old and new. A nineteenth century dog stands guard in the drawing room fireplace "because he's great fun". Beautiful antique pieces rub shoulders with works by contemporary designers, such as Oriel Harwood's exotic mirror, and a chaise, in the eighteenth century French style but cast in metal, by Matt Livsey Hammond. In David's bedroom, the walls have been repainted: once a silvery grey, they are now pistachio, the colour, says David, of a delicious Ladurée macaroon. What could be more appealing in the bedroom? It's genius.

Der Innenarchitekt und Visionär David Carter liebt theatralische Entwürfe, die verführen. Ein Besuch in seinem Haus ist eine emotionale Erfahrung. Denn dieses Gemäuer aus dem frühen 18. Jahrhundert zu betreten, heißt nichts anderes, als in eine sinnliche Welt entführt zu werden. Gäste sind stets willkommen, da Carter unter dem Decknamen *40 Winks* in seinem Haus „das kleinste und schönste Boutiquehotel der Welt" betreibt. Artdirectors, Models und Fotografen, die ein außergewöhnliches Quartier in London suchen, lieben seine Zimmer. Die Wände sind mit Farben getränkt, und Trompe-l'Œil-Malereien verblüffen das Auge. Das vierstöckige Gebäude im Osten Londons war dem Verfall nahe und wurde in mühevoller Kleinarbeit restauriert. Die authentisch wirkenden Vertäfelungen wurden zu großen Teilen nach einer Originalvorlage neu geschaffen. Ein Gang durch die Etagen gleicht heute einer erlebnisreichen Achterbahnfahrt zwischen stimmungsvoller Düsternis und klassizistischer Coolness. In einem Salon, den Carter als „Opiumhöhle" bezeichnet, sind die Wände frottiert: Der goldene Untergrund wurde mit Stofftüchern von Hand lasiert, um einen Effekt von natürlich aussehendem Krokodilleder zu erzielen. Im Badezimmer funkelt eine Metalltapete von de Gournay, und in einem zweiten Salon sieht die Decke aus wie in einem alten französischen Schloss – als wäre sie über die Jahrhunderte vom Rauch des Holzfeuers fleckig geworden. Carter hat einen Blick fürs Exotische. Mit dekorativen Einzelstücken und hintergründigem Humor verbindet er Alt und Neu. Ein Hund aus dem 19. Jahrhundert hält im Kamin des zweiten Salons Wache, „weil er viel Spaß macht". Wunderschöne Antiquitäten treffen auf zeitgenössische Designerstücke wie den fremdartigen Spiegel von Oriel Harwood oder eine Chaiselongue von Matt Livsey Hammond im französischen Stil des 18. Jahrhunderts – jetzt allerdings in Metall gegossen. In Carters Schlafzimmer wurden die Wände neu gestrichen. Ehemals silbergrau, erklärt Carter, sind sie jetzt pistazienfarben wie ein köstliches Macaron von Ladurée. Was könnte für ein Schlafzimmer verlockender sein? Einfach genial.

Architecte d'intérieur et créateur visionnaire, David Carter se plaît à concevoir des intérieurs théâtraux attachants. Visiter sa maison, c'est l'assurance de vivre une émotion car, dès le seuil de cette demeure début XVIIIᵉ, on est submergé par des sensations diverses. Les hôtes sont assurément les bienvenus : sous l'enseigne *40 Winks*, David dirige « le plus petit et le plus bel hôtel-boutique au monde » comme il se plaît à le dire. Les pièces ont un franc succès auprès des directeurs artistiques, modèles et photographes en quête d'une adresse originale à Londres. Les murs sont mangés par les couleurs et les trompe-l'œil instillent le trouble. Ce bâtiment à quatre niveaux du Nord-est de Londres en délabrement a été laborieusement restauré. Si les lambris semblent authentiques, des pans entiers ont été recréés à partir d'un modèle original. Les pièces délivrent un tourbillon d'images antagonistes allant d'une ambiance feutrée à une fraîcheur toute classique. Dans ce que David nomme le salon « fumoir d'opium », les murs ont été traités par frottage : un motif vernissé a été appliqué à la main au papier de soie sur un fond doré. Le résultat : l'imitation fidèle d'une peau de crocodile. Dans la salle de bain brille le papier peint de Gournay métallisé, et au salon, le plafond ressemble à celui d'un château du XVIIIᵉ, maculé par des siècles de fumée de feu de bois. David a le sens de l'excentrique. Les éléments décoratifs sont combinés avec un humour facétieux, amalgamant ancien et moderne. Une statue de chien du XIXᵉ monte la garde dans la cheminée du salon « juste parce qu'il est impayable ». De belles pièces anciennes côtoient les œuvres de créateurs contemporains, notamment un miroir original d'Oriel Harwood et une méridienne française du XVIIIᵉ, en fait une création en métal de Matt Livsey Hammond. Les murs de la chambre ont été repeints : le gris argenté a cédé le pas à la pistache, pour David, la couleur d'un délicieux macaron Ladurée. Qu'est-ce qui pouvait aller mieux dans cette chambre ? C'est un coup de génie.

In the "opium den" *drawing room on the ground floor, a dramatic collection of furniture is set against atmospheric forest-green walls. On one side is a pair of elegant 1930s French "liner" chairs, covered in silk satin, and the circular pouffe by Mark Brazier-Jones is upholstered in red silk velvet. The windows have been deliberately left undressed, though light is filtered through eighteenth century Chinese latticework screens. In a corner of one guest bedroom stands a lamp by Mark Brazier-Jones, with a feminine, corset-style lampshade by Sera Hersham-Loftus. A chaise longue designed by contemporary furniture designer Scott Cunningham sits in the rear half of the drawing room, covered in faux bearskin. Above a marble-topped console, a ceremonial Pygmy head-dress adds a theatrical splash of scarlet.*

Im Salon mit dem Namen „Opiumhöhle" *im Erdgeschoss präsentiert sich eine dramatische Ansammlung von Möbeln vor stimmungsvollen waldgrünen Wänden. An einer Wand steht ein Paar eleganter französischer „Schiffssessel" mit Seidensatinbezug aus den 1930er Jahren neben einem mit rotem Seidensamt gepolsterten Puff von Mark Brazier-Jones. Auf Gardinen an den Fenstern wurde bewusst verzichtet. Stattdessen filtern chinesische Fenstergitter aus dem 18. Jahrhundert das Licht. In der Ecke eines Gästeschlafzimmers steht eine Lampe von Mark Brazier-Jones mit einem feminin anmutenden Lampenschirm in Korsettform von Sera Hersham-Loftus. Eine mit Bärenfellimitat bezogene Chaiselongue aus der Werkstatt des modernen Möbeldesigners Scott Cunningham bereichert den rückwärtigen Teil des Salons. Über der Konsole mit Marmorplatte steuert ein zeremonieller Pygmäenkopfschmuck einen theatralischen Spritzer Scharlachrot bei.*

Dans le salon « fumoir d'opium » *du rez-de-chaussée, une série de meubles est mis en scène dans un décor évocateur de murs vert forestier. Dans un coin, deux élégantes chaises « de croisière » des années 1930, tendues de soie satinée côtoient un pouf circulaire de Mark Brazier-Jones en velours de soie rouge. Si les fenêtres n'ont volontairement pas de rideaux, la lumière est tamisée par des grilles de fenêtres chinoises du XVIII* siècle. Dans l'une des chambres d'hôtes, une lampe signée Mark Brazier-Jones est habillée avec féminité d'un abat-jour corset de Sera Hersham-Loftus. Dans le salon, la méridienne du créateur de meubles contemporain Scott Cunningham, visible à l'arrière-plan, est tendu d'imitation peau d'ours. Au-dessus d'une console à tablette en marbre, une coiffe de cérémonie pygmée ajoute une spectaculaire tache rouge.*

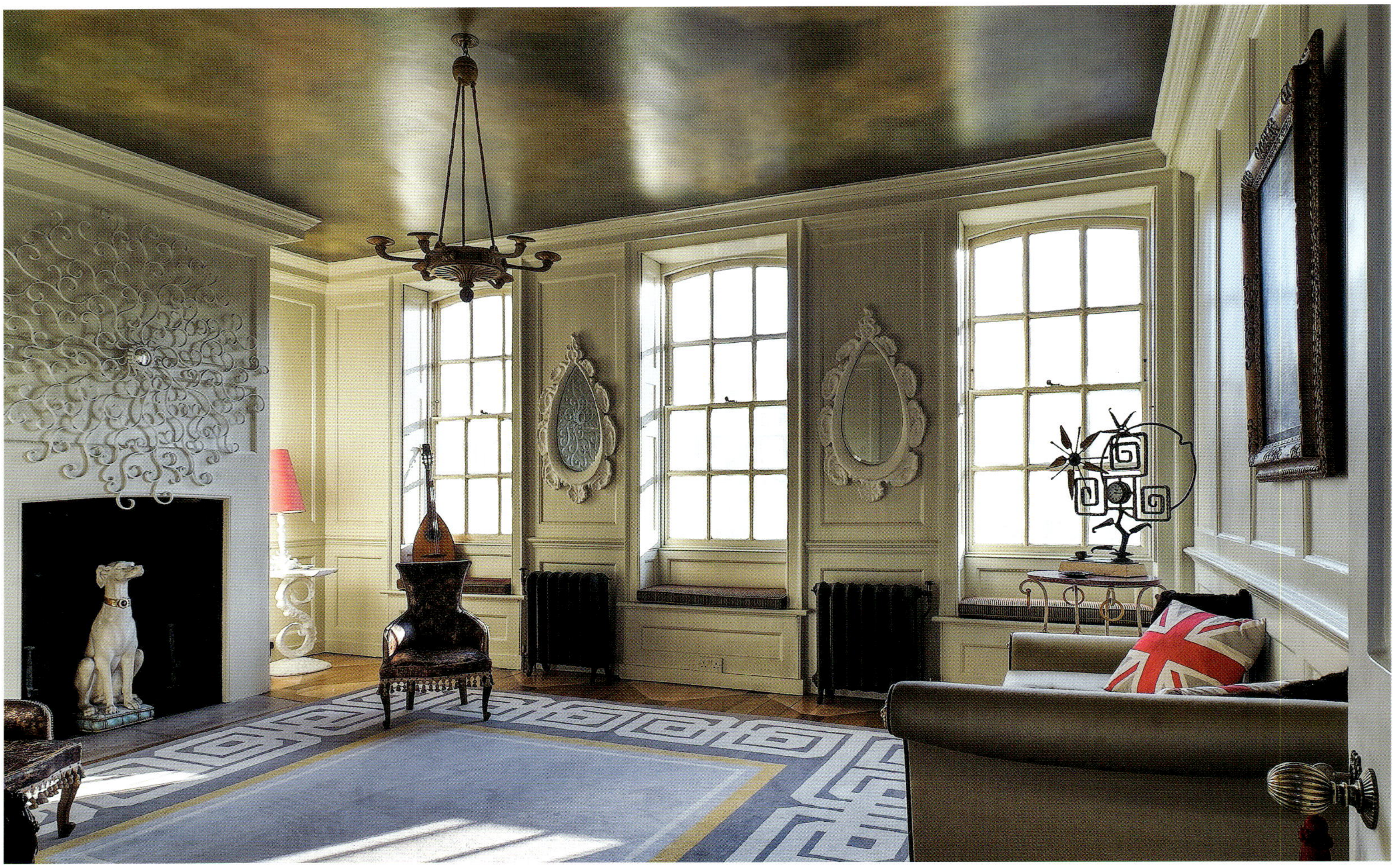

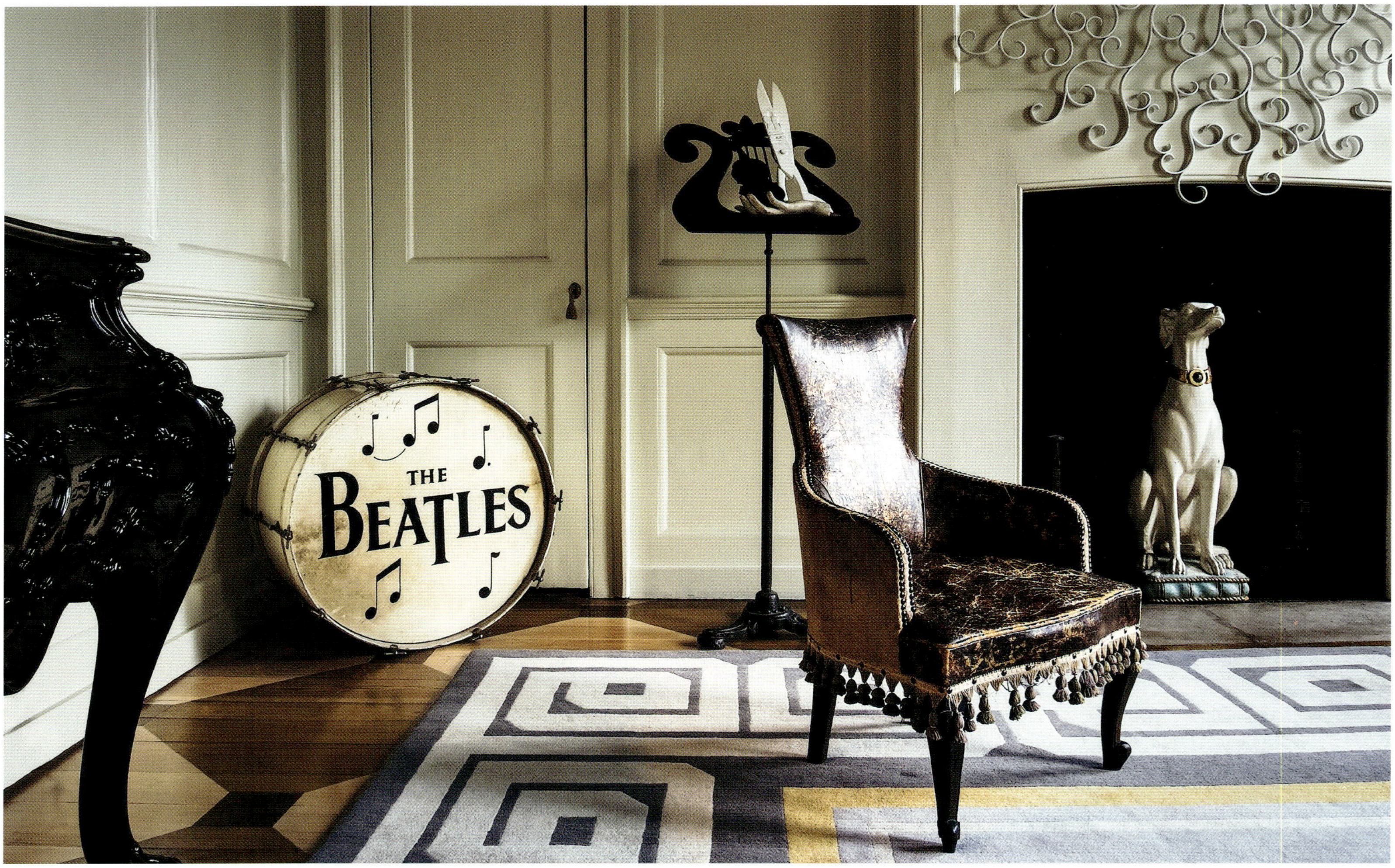
THE
BEATLES

In the "music room" drawing room, the original panelling has undergone extensive repairs. The convex mirror is by Matt Livsey Hammond. Reclaimed floorboards are covered with a bespoke wool carpet, designed by David. Above the chaise hangs a late eighteenth century portrait, and to one side is a clock by Mark Brazier-Jones. Flanking the fireplace is a pair of diminutive, early twentieth century Italian chairs in distressed gilded leather. The lower ground floor kitchen lacks natural light, so David had the walls hand-painted to resemble an Italian Palazzo. The floor is laid with 200-year-old reclaimed French oak boards, and the chairs are copies of an early eighteenth century hall chair. In the decadent gold and black bathroom, a polished aluminium bath is dramatically raised onto a pedestal.

Im als „Musikzimmer" bezeichneten Salon wurde die Originalvertäfelung großflächig saniert. Der Konvexspiegel stammt von Matt Livsey Hammond. Gerettete und aufgearbeitete Bodendielen bilden den Untergrund für einen von Carter entworfenen, wollenen Maßteppich. Ein Porträt aus dem späten 18. Jahrhundert hängt über der Chaiselongue, an deren Fußende eine Uhr von Mark Brazier-Jones platziert ist. Die zierlichen italienischen Sessel aus dem frühen 20. Jahrhundert rechts und links des Kamins sind mit vergoldetem Antikleder bezogen. Weil die Küche im Souterrain nicht vom Tageslicht verwöhnt wird, entschied sich Carter für eine in Handarbeit aufgebrachte Wandbemalung, die an einen italienischen Palazzo erinnert. Der Fußboden besteht aus 200 Jahre alten, aufgearbeiteten französischen Eichendielen, und die Stühle sind Kopien eines Brettstuhls aus dem frühen 18. Jahrhundert. Im dekadenten schwarz-goldenen Bad steht die polierte Aluminiumbadewanne dramatisch erhöht auf einem Podest.

Dans le salon « salle de musique », les anciens lambris ont été amplement restaurés et le miroir convexe est signé Matt Livsey Hammond. Les planchers réparés sont habillés d'un tapis de laine créé sur mesure par David Carter. Au-dessus de la méridienne, on peut admirer un portrait fin XVIIIᵉ et, sur l'un des côtés, une horloge de Mark Brazier-Jones. Deux délicats fauteuils italiens début XXᵉ en cuir doré vieilli encadrent la cheminée. Au niveau inférieur, la cuisine étant en lumière artificielle, David en a fait peindre les murs à la main à la manière d'un palais italien. Le sol est revêtu de planches de bois d'olivier de récupération de 200 ans d'âge, et les chaises sont des répliques de chaises de vestibule début XVIIIᵉ. Dans la salle de bain noir et or décadente, une baignoire en aluminium poli est théâtralement placée sur un piédestal.

This house is *alive with detail, and hands are a particular theme: here, a lone hand stands on the bathroom table. In David's panelled bedroom, a particularly fine and ornate example of an eighteenth century French bed is upholstered and dressed in silk, topped with an eighteenth century corona. The* trompe l'œil *design on the floor was created using wood stains and is intended to resemble a parquetry floor in the grand Russian style. In one of the guest bedrooms, hand-painted black and white stripes create a dramatic focus. In the fireplace sits a stone well cover from the Middle East.*

Dieses Haus lebt *von seinen Details, und Hände sind ein besonderes Thema – hier in Gestalt einer einzelnen Hand auf dem Badezimmertisch. In Carters vertäfeltem Schlafzimmer steht ein besonders schönes, fein verziertes Exemplar eines französischen Betts aus dem 18. Jahrhundert mit Seidenpolstern, -decken und -kissen. Die Bettkrone darüber stammt ebenfalls aus dem 18. Jahrhundert. Das Trompe-l'Œil-Muster auf dem Boden wurde mit Holzbeize erzeugt und soll ein Parkett im russischen Herrschaftsstil nachahmen. In einem der Gästeschlafzimmer ziehen kräftige handgemalte Streifen in Schwarz-Weiß die Blicke auf sich. Im Kamin thront ein steinerner Brunnendeckel aus dem Nahen Osten.*

La main constitue *l'un des thèmes décoratifs de cette maison qui fourmille de détails : ici, le moule d'une main repose sur la table de la salle de bain. Dans la chambre à coucher lambrissée de David, l'exemplaire particulièrement délicat et décoré de lit bateau XVIIIᵉ capitonné et tendu de soie, est surmonté d'un lustre couronne XVIIIᵉ. Les motifs en trompe-l'œil du sol créés à l'aide de lasure imitent la parqueterie de l'époque de la Grande Russie. Dans l'une des chambres d'amis, des rayures blanches et noires peintes à la main captent l'attention. Un couvercle de puits en pierre provenant du Moyen-Orient occupe le centre de la cheminée.*

Colour Shock

Contemporary art lovers will know David Gill, who has three London galleries and a global reputation for curating exceptional modern art and design shows. His apartment is in a 1900s building, and was formerly a handbag factory. Out of its capacious 26,000 square feet David has created not just living quarters but also a studio spanning two floors. He designed the flat himself, choosing the precise shade of poured concrete floor and working out the perfect open-plan layout. The space is jammed with surprising and exhilarating modern art. As David Gill is an art dealer one might expect pieces to come and go, but the reverse is true. David says that once he created the character of the space, key pieces had to stay central to the theme. The bright colours, he asserts, bring harmony and warmth to the interior. So while an Art Deco Eugene Printz purple daybed and a green Baroque-style Emilio Terry armchair define the living area, the star attraction in the dining area is a stunning scarlet-topped Jasmine table by Grillo Demo, featuring bronze legs. In direct contrast to the glossy velvets and zany hues here, the utility areas are deliberately spartan. The bespoke kitchen has stainless steel cupboards, and the bathroom features polished limestone walls and a granite sink, found in situ in an abandoned factory. The bedroom is soothing, with a white leather-upholstered bed made to David's design, lit from below to create a tranquil glow. Ultimately this is a flat filled with things that David loves and that have integrity for him. In the hall stands an exuberant red table, a work of art by Richard Snyder, entitled the *Venetian Magician's Chest*. Blurring the boundaries between art and furniture, it's a cue to the visitor of the colour shock to come.

Liebhaber zeitgenössischer Kunst kennen David Gill als dreifachen Londoner Galeristen und renommierten, international tätigen Kurator außergewöhnlicher Ausstellungen für moderne Kunst und modernes Design. Seine Wohnung liegt in einem Gebäude aus den 1900er Jahren und war früher eine Handtaschenfabrik. Auf mehr als 2.400 Quadratmetern hat Gill nicht nur die Wohnung selbst, sondern auch ein zweistöckiges Atelier geschaffen. Für die nach eigenen Entwürfen gestaltete Wohnung verwendete er exakt den Farbton von gegossenem Beton und einen perfekten offenen Grundriss. Der Raum ist überfüllt mit überraschender und erfrischender moderner Kunst. Von einem Kunsthändler könnte man erwarten, dass die Stücke kommen und gehen, doch das Gegenteil ist der Fall. Nachdem er den Charakter der Wohnung definiert hatte, sagt Gill, wurden bestimmte Schlüsselwerke thematisch unverzichtbar. Die leuchtenden Farben des Interieurs, versichert er, sorgen für Harmonie und Wärme. Während also im Wohnbereich eine lilafarbene Art-déco-Bettcouch von Eugène Printz und ein grüner Sessel im Barockstil von Emilio Terry auftrumpfen, ist im Essbereich ein Jasmin-Tisch von Grillo Demo mit scharlachroter Platte und Bronzefüßen der Star. Im direkten Gegensatz zu den hier überwiegenden glänzenden Samtstoffen und clownesken Farbtönen sind die Nutzbereiche bewusst spartanisch gestaltet. In der Maßküche dominieren Edelstahlfronten, im Bad polierter Kalkstein und ein Granitwaschbecken, das an Ort und Stelle in einer leer stehenden Fabrik gefunden wurde. Im beruhigend wirkenden Schlafzimmer steht ein von Gill entworfenes, mit weißem Leder gepolstertes und von unten beleuchtetes Bett, um das ein sanfter Lichtschein den Boden erhellt. Letztlich hat Gill in dieser Wohnung Dinge versammelt, die er liebt und für vollkommen hält. So steht im Flur ein überbordender feuerroter Tisch, bei dem es sich um das Kunstwerk *Venetian Magician's Chest* von Richard Snyder handelt. Diese Mischung aus Möbelstück und Kunstwerk bereitet den Besucher auf den bevorstehenden Farbschock vor.

Les amateurs d'art contemporain connaîtront certainement David Gill, propriétaire de trois galeries à Londres et organisateur d'expositions d'art et de décoration de renom international. Son appartement situé dans un bâtiment 1900 était jadis une usine de sacs à main. À partir de rien moins que 2 400 m², David Gill n'a pas seulement créé un logement mais aussi un atelier sur deux niveaux. Il a conçu l'appartement lui-même, choisissant la teinte précise du sol en béton coulé et créant le plan libre parfait. L'espace est rempli d'œuvres d'art moderne surprenantes et délirantes. Gill étant galeriste, on pourrait penser que ces pièces vont et viennent, mais c'est en fait le contraire. Pour lui, une fois le caractère de l'espace défini, les œuvres principales doivent demeurer au cœur du thème choisi. Les couleurs vives confèrent selon lui harmonie et chaleur à son intérieur. Si le séjour est défini par un divan violet Art Déco d'Eugene Printz et un fauteuil vert de style baroque d'Emilio Terry, c'est autour d'une surprenante table Jasmine à plateau écarlate et à pieds en bronze de Grillo Demo que s'organise la salle à manger. Contrastant avec les velours luisants et les teintes burlesques de cet espace, les pièces de service sont délibérément spartiates. La cuisine sur mesure est équipée d'éléments en acier inoxydable, et la salle de bain dotée de murs en pierre calcaire polie et d'un lavabo en granit, trouvé dans une usine désaffectée. Avec son lit en cuir blanc conçu selon les plans de David et éclairé par en-dessous pour procurer une sensation de douceur, la chambre apaise. En fin de compte, c'est un appartement habité par des choses que David aime et qui ont pour lui leur existence propre. C'est le cas de l'insolite table rouge de l'entrée, œuvre de Richard Snyder baptisée *Venetian Magician's Chest*. Brouillant les frontières entre art et mobilier, c'est pour le visiteur un signe avant-coureur du choc des couleurs qui l'attend.

The living area is studded with modern art. On one wall hangs Richard Prince's 1983 Untitled photograph and, beneath it, stands a sculpture by Paul McCarthy, called Chocolate Silicone Blockhead. Furniture is in a heady, glorious mix of styles, from the tufted daybed by Francis Sultana to the grey buttoned armchair and the stainless steel Ring table, both by Garouste & Bonetti. Above the L-shaped, comfortable 1930 purple daybed is a painting by Chantal Joffe. The flower emblazoned Petra lamp and the turquoise Mara side table are also by Garouste & Bonetti. On one wall in the hall hangs a 1997 photograph by Richard Prince, called Untitled (Cowboy), its orange glow suffusing the entire room with hints of colour.

Der Wohnbereich ist gespickt mit moderner Kunst. An einer Wand hängt die Fotografie Untitled von Richard Prince aus dem Jahr 1983, darunter steht eine Skulptur von Paul McCarthy mit dem Titel Chocolate Silicone Blockhead. Der Stilmix der Möbel ist prächtig und berauschend — vom gesteppten Daybed von Francis Sultana bis zum grauen, mit Polsterknöpfen kapitonierten Sessel und dem ringförmigen Tisch, beides von Garouste & Bonetti. Über der bequemen L-förmigen Bettcouch von 1930 hängt ein Gemälde von Chantal Joffe. Die Blumenschirmleuchte Petra und der Beistelltisch Mara sind ebenfalls Kreationen von Garouste & Bonetti. An einer Wand hängt eine 1997 entstandene Fotografie von Richard Prince namens Untitled (Cowboy), deren orangefarbenes Glühen den ganzen Raum mit einer Spur Farbe durchdringt.

Le séjour est constellé d'art moderne. La photographie de Richard Prince baptisée Untitled (1983) surplombe une sculpture de Paul McCarthy, intitulée Chocolate Silicone Blockhead. Le mobilier est un mélange splendide et exaltant de styles, allant du divan créé par Francis Sultana au fauteuil gris capitonné et à la table Ring en acier inoxydable, tous deux de Garouste & Bonetti. Au-dessus du confortable divan violet en L des années 1930, on peut voir un tableau de Chantal Joffe. La lampe Petra fleurie et la desserte Mara turquoise sont aussi de Garouste & Bonetti. Sur un mur de l'entrée, la photographie de Richard Prince intitulée Untitled (Cowboy) (1997) diffuse une lueur orange dans toute la pièce.

With its high ceiling, *crisp white walls and concrete floor, the hall provides the perfect backdrop for a selection of vibrant pieces. Richard Snyder's* Venetian Magician's Chest *displays a red and white plate, called* Falling Jasmine, *by Grillo Demo. On the wall, above the door, is a collage by Mike Kelley, entitled* Sex to Sexty, *and in the corner stands* Picabia Idol, *a sculpture by Paul McCarthy. The stainless steel kitchen can be glimpsed just off the hall. The dining room is fresh and modern, with a sculpture by Kendal Geers and Abigail Lane's* Ink Pad, *in aluminium and felt, twin rectangles in silver and red. The painting is* Untitled (P354) *by Christopher Wool. Set around the Grillo Demo table are 1950s Country chairs by Charlotte Perriand.*

Mit seinen hohen Decken, *den reinweißen Wänden und dem Betonfußboden bildet der Flur die perfekte Kulisse für eine Ansammlung dynamischer Stücke. Auf Richard Snyders* Venetian Magician's Chest *erhebt sich ein rot-weißer Teller von Grillo Demo mit dem Titel* Falling Jasmine. *An der Wand über der Tür hängt Mike Kelleys Collage* Sex to Sexty, *die Figur in der Ecke heißt* Picabia Idol *und stammt von Paul McCarthy. Im Hintergrund blitzt die Edelstahlküche auf. Das*

Esszimmer wirkt mit einer Skulptur von Kendal Geers und dem Ink Pad *von Abigail Lane, einem aus zwei Rechtecken bestehenden Kunstwerk in rotem Filz und silbrigem Aluminium, frisch und modern. Bei dem Gemälde handelt es sich um Christopher Wools* Untitled (P 354). *Um den Tisch von Grillo Demo stehen 1950er-Jahre-Landhausstühle von Charlotte Perriand.*

Avec son haut plafond, *ses murs et son sol en béton blancs crus, l'entrée est un cadre parfait pour une série d'œuvres pleines de vie. Sur la table rouge de Richard Snyder repose une assiette rouge et blanche de Grillo Demo, baptisée* Falling Jasmine. *Sur le mur, au-dessus de la porte, on voit un collage de Mike Kelley, intitulé* Sex to Sexty, *et dans le coin,* Picabia Idol, *une sculpture de Paul McCarthy. Depuis l'entrée, on aperçoit la cuisine en acier inoxydable. Dans la salle à manger fraîche et moderne, on trouve une sculpture de Kendal Geers, et* Ink Pad, *œuvre d'Abigail Lane, formée de deux rectangles égaux, l'un en aluminium argent et l'autre en feutre rouge. Le tableau* Untitled (P354) *de Christopher Wool trône derrière la table de Grillo Demo. Autour d'elle, les chaises campagnardes années 1950 sont signées Charlotte Perriand.*

Hanging above David's custom-made bed is *Semen,* a work by Francesco Clemente, and on the adjacent wall is an ink drawing, No. 57, by Ugo Rondinone. Set against the white leather upholstery, the bed cover, by Ulrika Liljedahl, creates a splash of contrast colour. On the bedside tables there are Three Graces lamps by Garouste & Bonetti. The study/guest room may be small, but there is room for a desk by Jean Prouvé and on one wall is Jean-Baptiste Mondino's painting of two men wrestling. The bathroom has walls in polished limestone and a granite basin. Dwarfing the staircase leading up to the flat stand two Monumental vases by Grillo Demo. The kitchen table is by Le Corbusier and the chairs are Jean Prouvé.

Über Gills spezialangefertigtem Bett hängt Francesco Clementes Werk *Semen,* an der Nebenwand die Tuschezeichnung No. 57 von Ugo Rondinone. Die Tagesdecke von Ulrika Liljedahl bildet einen kräftigen Kontrast zum weißledernen Bett. Auf den Nachttischen stehen Three-Graces-Lampen von Garouste & Bonetti. Das Arbeits- und Gästezimmer ist zwar klein, bietet jedoch genug Platz für einen Schreibtisch von Jean Prouvé und ausreichend Wandfläche für Jean-Baptiste Mondinos Porträt zweier Ringer. Das Bad hat polierte Kalksteinwände und ein Waschbecken aus Granit. Zwei Monumentalvasen von Grillo Demo stellen die Treppe in die Schatten, die nach oben in die Wohnung führt. Der Küchentisch ist ein Entwurf von Le Corbusier, die Stühle stammen von Jean Prouvé.

Au-dessus du lit personnalisé de David est suspendu un tableau de Francesco Clemente intitulé *Semen,* et sur le mur adjacent, le dessin à l'encre No. 57 d'Ugo Rondinone. Ressortant sur le capitonnage de cuir blanc, le couvre-lit d'Ulrika Liljedahl fait par contraste l'effet d'une éclaboussure de couleur. Sur les dessertes reposent des lampes Three Graces de Garouste & Bonetti. Le bureau/chambre d'amis est certes petit, mais assez grand pour accueillir un bureau de Jean Prouvé. Sur le mur, deux hommes luttent dans un tableau de Jean-Baptiste Mondino. La salle de bain, aux murs en pierre calcaire polie, comprend un lavabo en granit. Deux vases monumentaux de Grillo Demo rapetissent l'escalier qui conduit à l'appartement. Dans la cuisine, si la table est signée Le Corbusier, les chaises sont de Jean Prouvé.

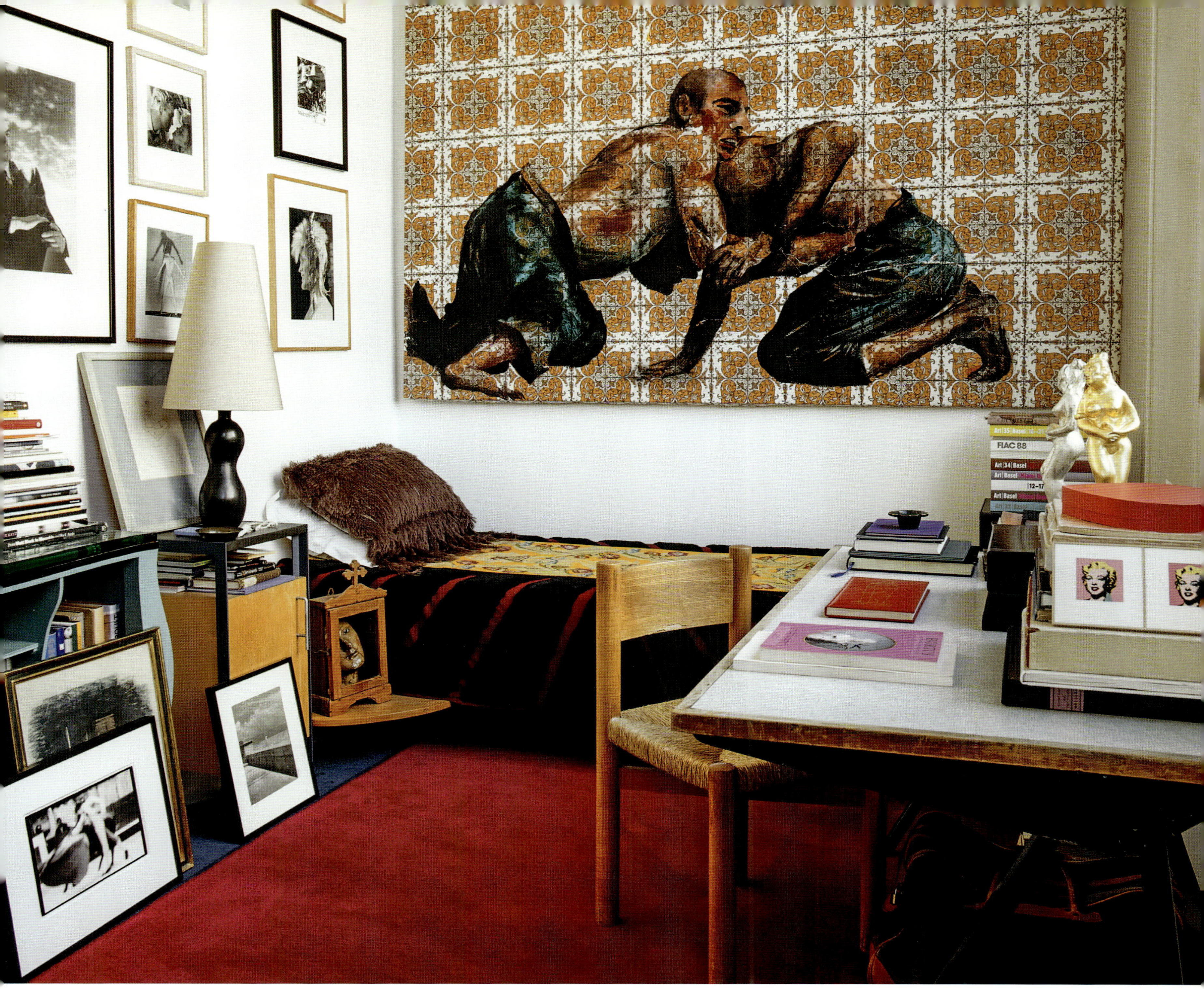
FIAC 88

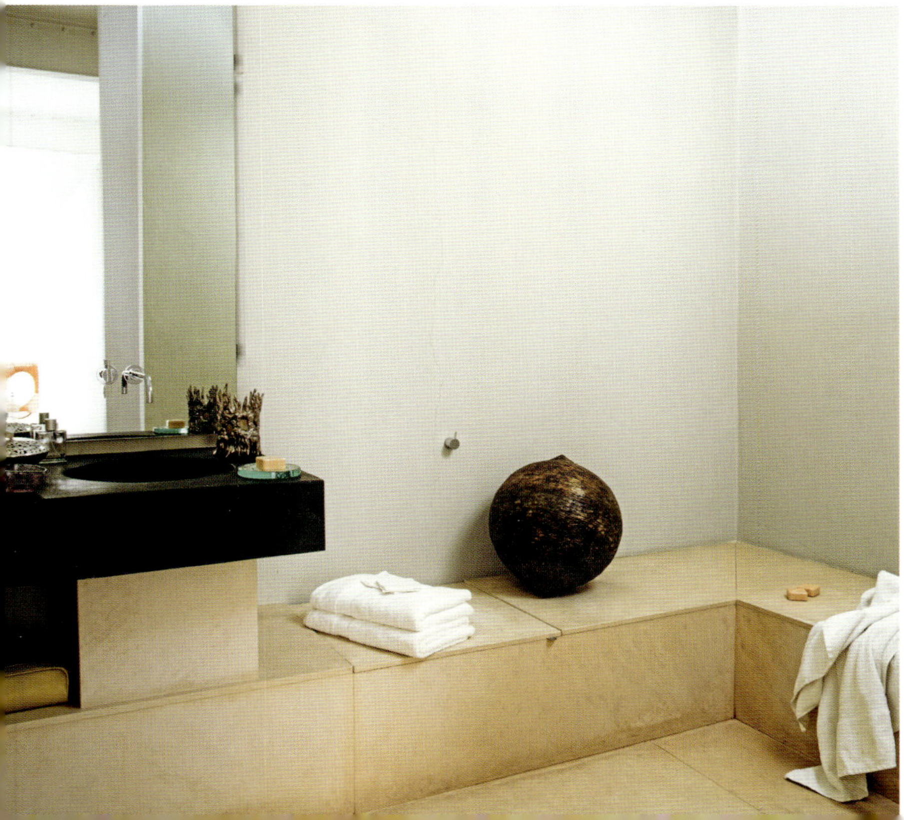

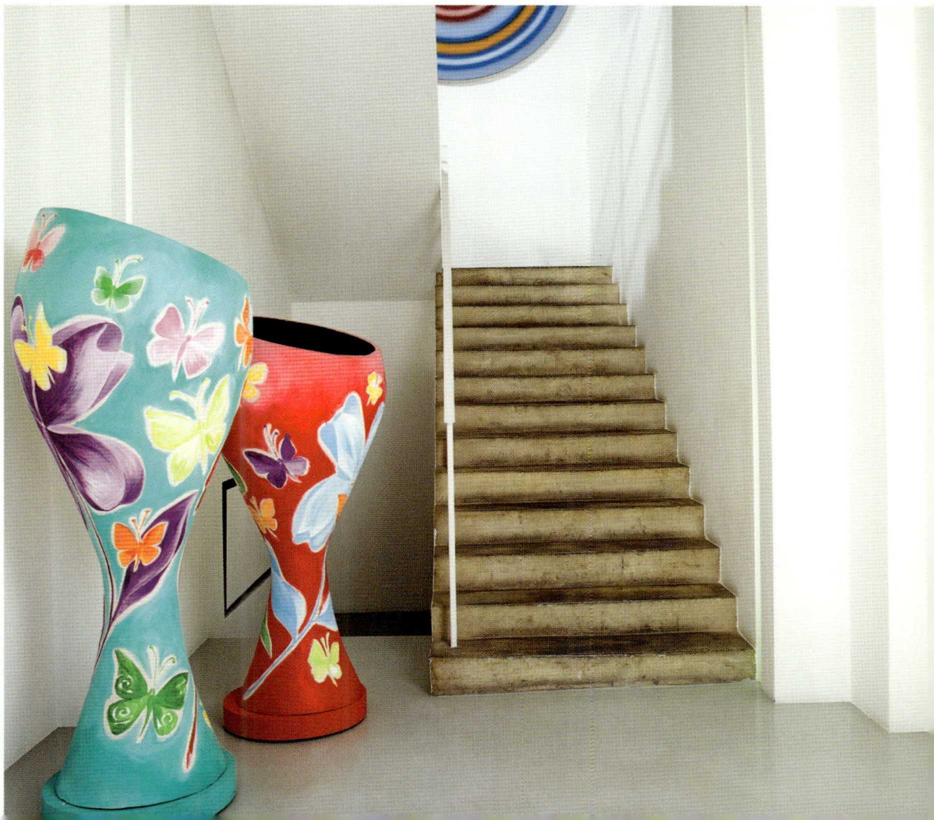

City Fusion

Behind the listed façade of a late nineteenth century building, designers Collett-Zarzycki have created a spectacular modern construction: a first and a second floor apartment, reconfigured into a new 6,000 square foot home flooded with natural light. The aim was to create a strong sense of volume and linked spaces ideal for family living. The *pièce de résistance* is a double volume living room soaring to seven metres high. It is dominated by a monolithic feature wall, clad in Roman travertine, and studded with new windows and a fireplace. Everything here is designed to flatter the property's generous proportions: bespoke furniture includes scaled up linear sofas and a stunning abstract light fitting, spanning three metres, made to order by silversmith Mark Kirkley. The neutral palette is sophisticated, yet has been punctuated with sharp saturated colour. In the living zone, twin cabinets in scarlet crackle lacquer cleverly hide speakers and contemporary glassware adds striking accents of green and aubergine. The first floor makes a dramatic statement, but with Tardis-like precision, the second floor — double stacked above the mezzanine — houses six bedrooms, a playroom and a study. The master bedroom and bathroom have been designed to share the same volume. Basins are fixed onto a freestanding unit that stops short of the ceiling, though the WC and shower are enclosed. Key materials have been used throughout to create visual unity. The first floor is laid with Jerusalem limestone slabs, and in the dining zone and study, walls and ceilings are clad in ash veneer. Textiles are cocooning, with wool column curtains in the living room and a suede-upholstered wall behind the master bedroom headboard. The designers aimed for an aesthetic of openness, and space, and rooms that link seamlessly together. The result is a breathtaking modern home tailored for twenty-first century living.

Hinter der denkmalgeschützten Fassade eines Hauses aus dem späten 19. Jahrhundert ist den Architekten von Collett-Zarzycki eine spektakuläre Konstruktion gelungen. Mit dem Ziel, die Größe des Objekts deutlich hervorzuheben und die einzelnen Räume für die Familie optimal zu verbinden, schufen sie auf rund 550 Quadratmetern aus zwei übereinander liegenden Einheiten eine moderne, lichtdurchflutete Maisonettewohnung. Das Paradestück ist das zweistöckige Wohnzimmer mit seinen bis zu sieben Meter hohen Decken. Es wird von einer monolithischen Prunkwand aus römischem Travertin mit neu eingelassenen Fensteröffnungen und einem Kamin beherrscht. Alles hier wurde entworfen, um den großzügigen Proportionen der Immobilie zu schmeicheln. Zur maßangefertigten Einrichtung gehören übergroße, geradlinige Sofas und ein atemberaubender abstrakter Deckenleuchter mit drei Metern Durchmesser aus der Werkstatt des Silberschmieds Mark Kirkley. Satte, leuchtende Farben durchbrechen die neutrale, elegante Farbgebung. Im Wohnbereich wurden die Lautsprecher geschickt in zwei offenen Schränkchen mit scharlachroter Krakelee-Lackierung versteckt. In der gesamten Wohnung setzen moderne Glasvasen und -objekte Akzente in Grün und Aubergine. Der dramatischen Aussage des unteren Stockwerks setzt das obere die Präzision einer Tardis entgegen — einer fiktiven Raum-Zeitmaschine aus der britischen Science-Fiction-Serie „Doctor Who", deren Inneres viel größer ist, als es von außen erscheint. Auf zwei Ebenen sind hier sechs Schlafzimmer, ein Spielzimmer und ein Arbeitszimmer untergebracht. Schlafzimmer und Bad der Eltern befinden sich im selben Raum. Die frei stehende Wand für die Waschbecken, die den Raum teilt, endet knapp unterhalb der Zimmerdecke, Dusche und WC sind dagegen vollständig abgeteilt. Wiederkehrende Materialien gewährleisten eine einheitliche Optik. Für den Fußboden im unteren Stockwerk wurden Jerusalemer Kalksteinplatten verlegt, Wände und Decken im Essbereich und im Arbeitszimmer sind mit Eschenfurnier verkleidet. Wohnliche Textilien wie die raumhohen Wollvorhänge im Wohnzimmer und die mit Wildleder gepolsterte Wand hinter dem Elternbett geben Geborgenheit. Eine Ästhetik der Offenheit, viel Platz und nahtlos miteinander verbundene Räume — so lautete die Zielsetzung der Architekten. Heraus kam ein überwältigendes, perfekt auf das Leben des 21. Jahrhunderts zugeschnittenes Heim.

Derrière la façade classée d'un bâtiment fin XIXᵉ, les architectes Collett et Zarzycki ont créé une spectaculaire résidence moderne : l'ancien appartement qui occupait le premier et le deuxième a été converti en un loft de plus de 500 m² inondé de lumière naturelle. L'objectif était de créer une impression de volume et d'unité entre les espaces, idéals pour la vie de famille. Au cœur du loft, le séjour double volume impressionne avec ses sept mètres de hauteur sous plafond. Ce séjour est dominé par un mur monolithique en travertin romain agrémenté de fenêtres et d'une cheminée. Tout ici est conçu pour accentuer les généreuses proportions des lieux : parmi les meubles sur mesure, on trouve de très longs canapés linéaires et un surprenant luminaire moderne de trois mètres d'envergure, commandé à l'orfèvre Mark Kirkley. La belle palette de tons neutres est ponctuée de teintes richement saturées. Dans le séjour, des petits meubles de rangement jumeaux en laque craquelée écarlate escamotent habilement des haut-parleurs alors que des articles de verrerie contemporains égrènent des nuances vert et aubergine. Si le premier niveau produit un effet spectaculaire, le deuxième niveau — avec ses étages superposés au-dessus de la mezzanine — exploite parfaitement l'espace pour abriter six chambres, une salle de jeux et un bureau. Un même volume a été attribué à la chambre et à la salle de bain de maître. Alors que les lavabos sont fixés à un élément autoportant s'arrêtant peu avant le plafond, les toilettes et la douche sont des unités fermées. Des matériaux phares ont été utilisés d'un bout à l'autre du loft pour créer une unité visuelle. Le premier étage est pavé de dalles de pierre calcaire de Jérusalem. Un placage en frêne habille les murs et les plafonds de la salle à manger et du bureau. Les textiles sont douillets, avec des rideaux de laine sans embrasses au salon et un mur tapissé en suédine derrière la tête de lit de la chambre de maître. Les architectes ont recherché une esthétique d'ouverture et d'espace, et des pièces s'enchaînant harmonieusement. Résultat : une résidence surprenante adaptée au mode de vie de notre siècle.

In the living space, *a silk rug and linen upholstery soften the imposing proportions. The dining zone is beneath the mezzanine floor, but enjoys the double volume of the main space. The furnishings are smartly contemporary, with a bespoke table in macassar ebony, linen-upholstered chairs and a bespoke stainless steel light fitting. In the hall, contemporary Italian glassware sits on a cantilevered mahogany table. The master bedroom and bathroom feature soothing pale tones, with a combination of ash flooring, bleached sycamore for the dividing wall, and marble and stainless steel for the vanity unit. The study overlooks the double volume living space. In the playroom, the TV is concealed behind a tambour door, while stained timber panels and leather beanbags add cheerful accent shades.*

Im Wohnzimmer *mäßigen ein Seidenteppich und Leinenpolster die imposanten Dimensionen. Der Essbereich liegt zwar unter dem Mezzanin, ist in der Fläche aber doppelt so groß wie der Wohnraum. Zum elegant-zeitgenössischen Mobiliar zählen ein maßgefertigter Esstisch aus Makassar-Ebenholz, Polsterstühle mit Leinenbezug und als weitere Sonderanfertigung eine Deckenlampe aus Edelstahl. Moderne italienische Glasobjekte zieren den Mahagoni-Kragtisch im Flur. Im Schlaf- und Badezimmer der Eltern überwiegen helle, wohltuende Farben in einer Kombination aus Eschendielen, gebleichtem Ahorn für die Trennwand und einem Marmor-Edelstahl-Mix für den Waschtisch. Das Arbeitszimmer überblickt den zweistöckigen Wohnraum. Im Spielzimmer verschwindet der Fernseher hinter einer Rolltür, während bunte Holzfüllungen und lederne Sitzsäcke fröhliche Farbakzente setzen.*

Dans le séjour, *le tapis de soie et les revêtements de lin atténuent les imposantes proportions. Le coin repas est situé sous l'étage en mezzanine, mais il occupe un volume deux fois supérieur à celui du salon. L'élégant mobilier contemporain comprend une table sur mesure en ébène de Macassar, des chaises revêtues de soie et un luminaire sur mesure en acier inox. Dans l'entrée, des verreries italiennes contemporaines ornent la console en acajou qui repose en porte-à-faux. Les tons pâles apaisants de la chambre et de la salle de bain de maître combinent le frêne pour le revêtement de sol, le sycomore blanchi pour la cloison, ainsi que le marbre et l'acier inoxydable pour le meuble sous vasque. Le bureau surplombe le séjour double volume. Dans la salle de jeux, un meuble à porte coulissante abrite la télévision, alors que des panneaux de bois moiré et des poufs poires en cuir agrémentent l'espace de tons gais.*

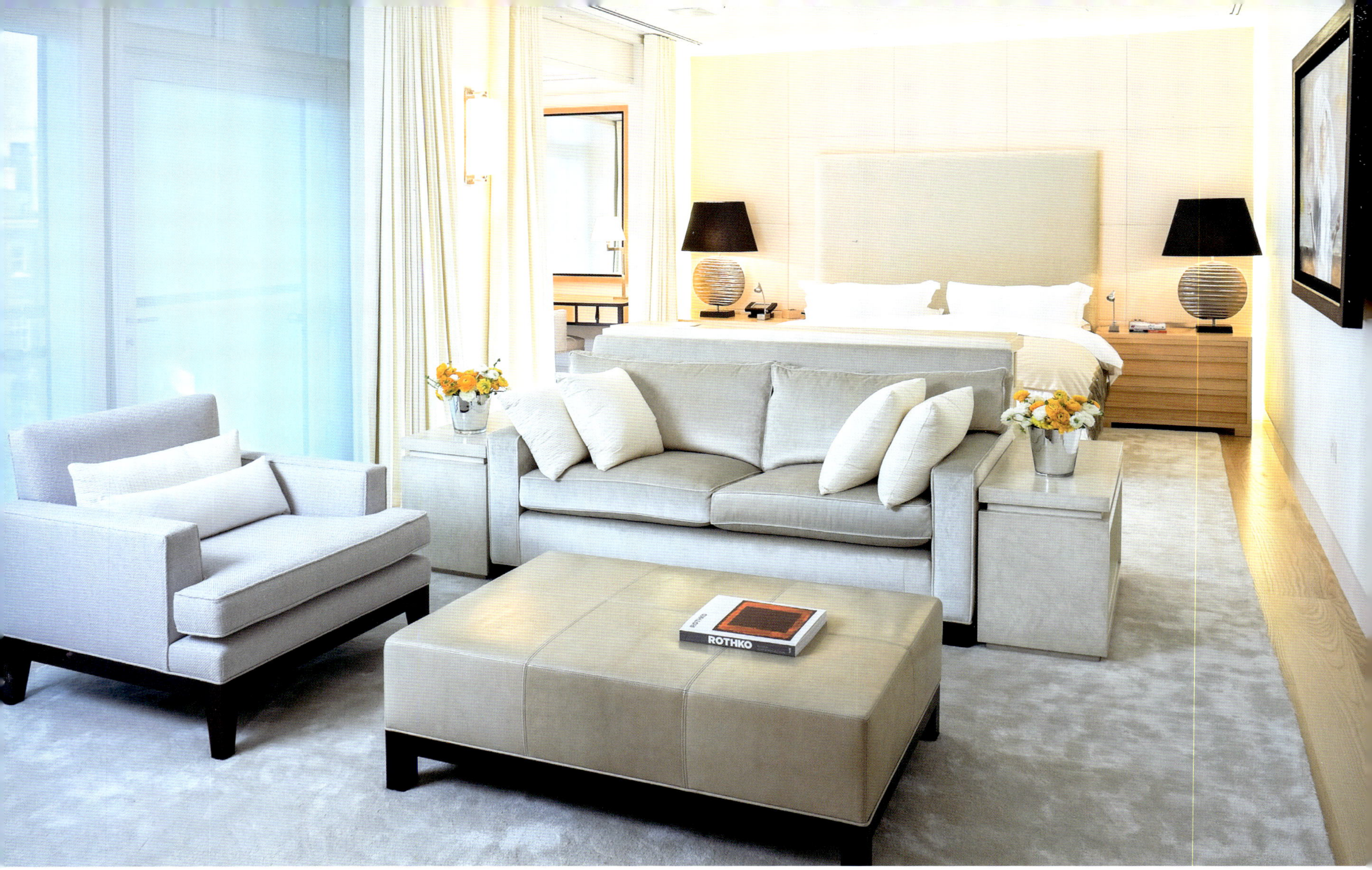
ROTHKO

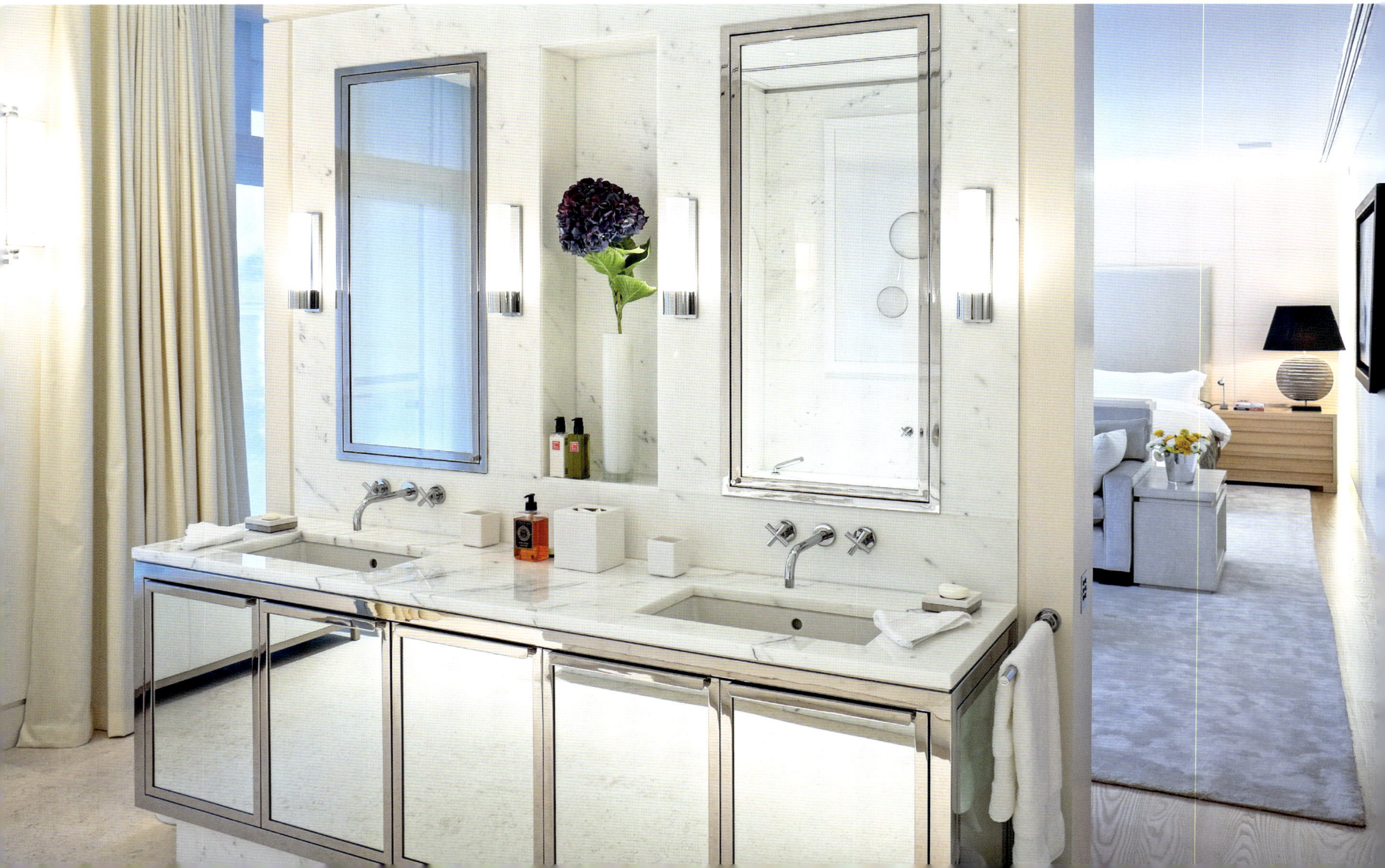

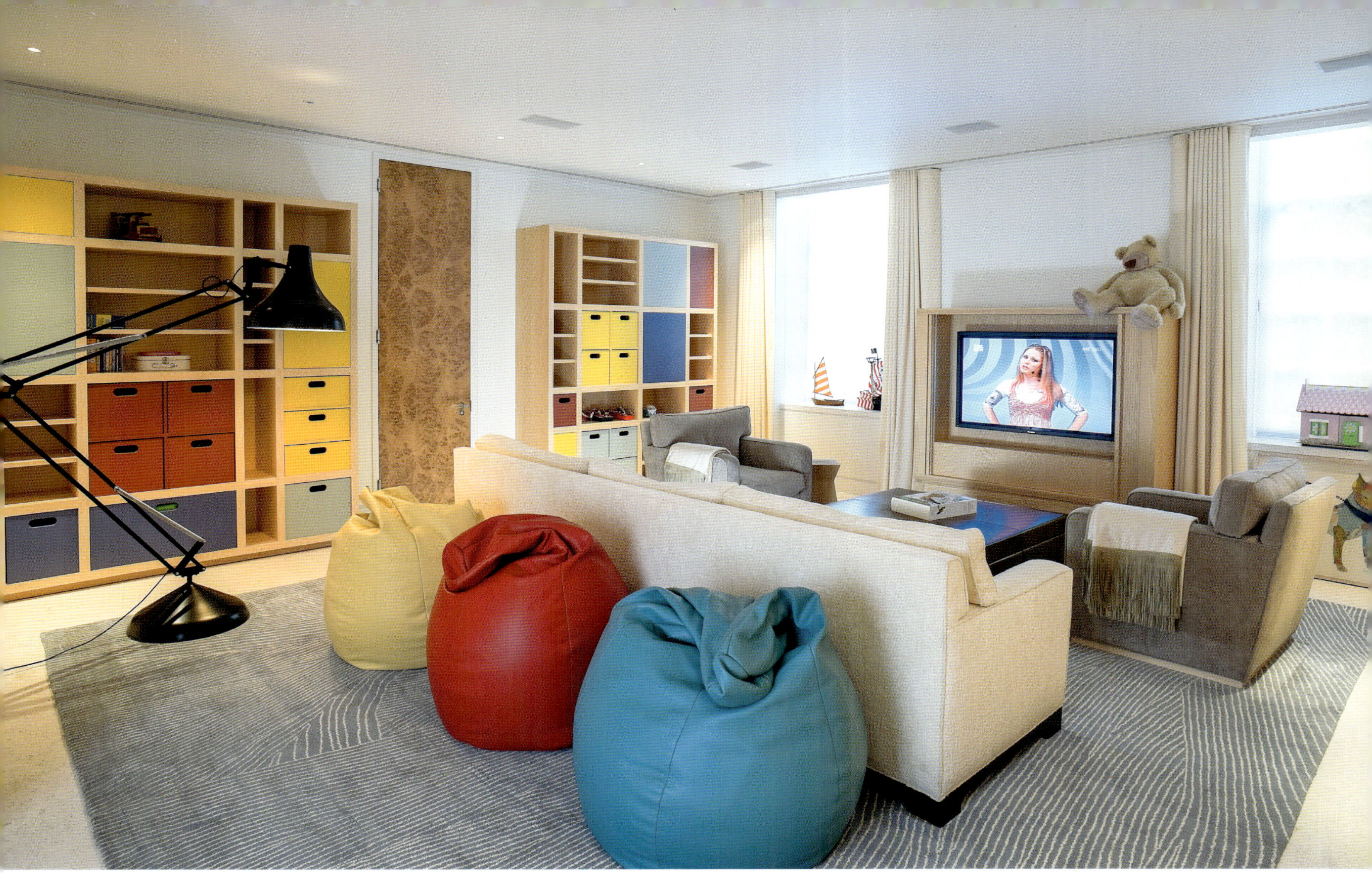

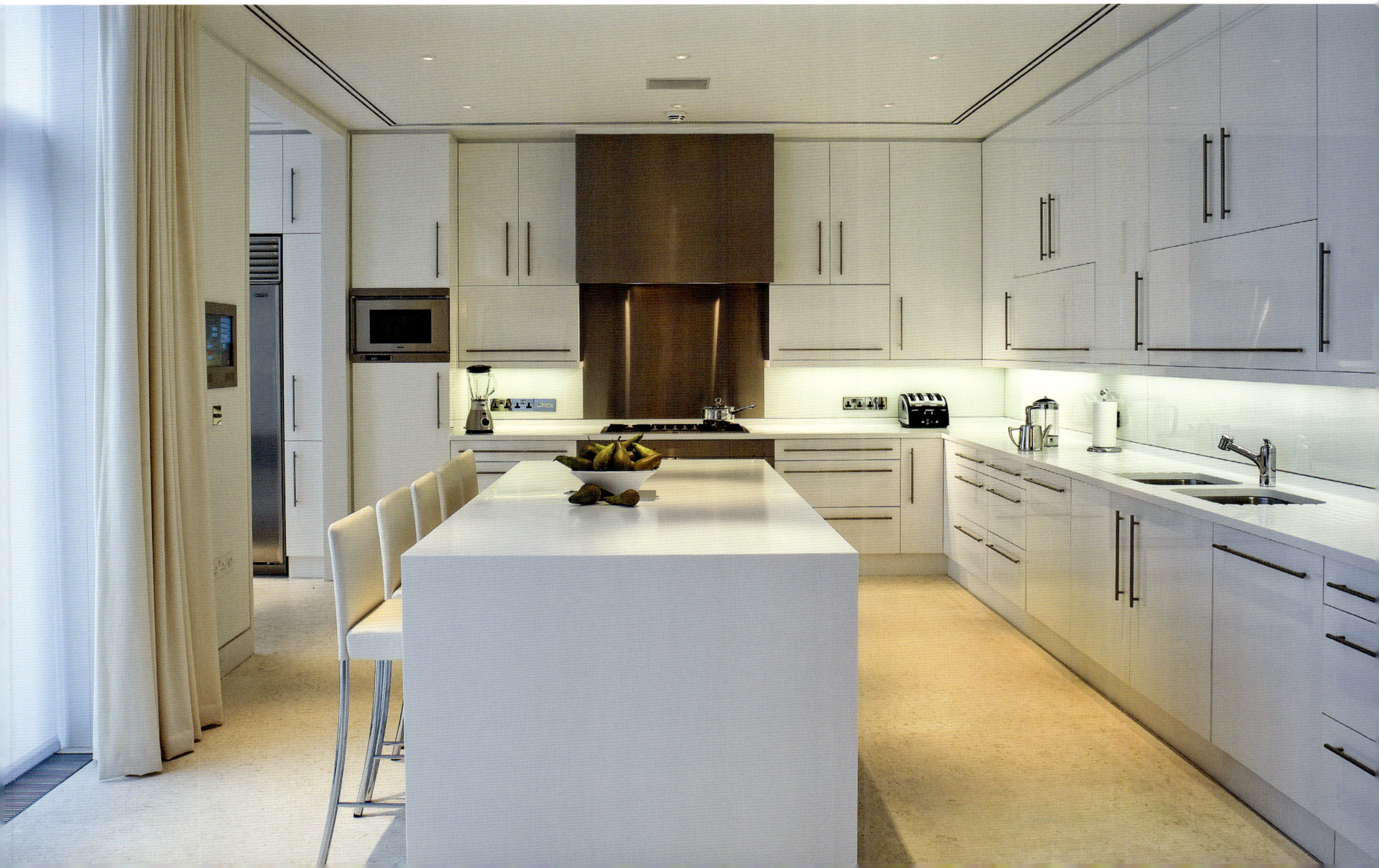

Private Luxury

For the discerning, well-heeled traveller in search of a home from home whilst staying in London, The Apartment at The Connaught offers the ultimate secret retreat. The Connaught was built in 1897, and renamed The Connaught after Queen Victoria's third son, Prince Arthur, Duke of Connaught. The visionary designer David Collins has transformed all 3,068 square feet of this penthouse suite into a chic, supremely tasteful apartment with, arguably, one of the best views across central London. For David Collins, who has decorated the world's most beautiful hotels, it was a project made in heaven, as he was given *carte blanche* to design. "I imagined a classic English interior owned by an art-loving, well-travelled relaxed guest – with deep pockets," he says. Guests enter via their own front door and are immediately enveloped in private luxury. And with its palette of Vermeer-inspired blue, grey, violet and ivory, the scheme instantly sets a serene, cool mood. The rooms may look classical, but the architecture seamlessly conceals all the twenty-first century services a sophisticated guest would expect, from temperature control to audio-visual surround sound. The space was carved out from a warren of old staff bedrooms, and little of the original architecture remains. But David designated the double height space, which previously housed the hotel's hot water tanks, as a spectacular, lofty drawing room. Without exception the furniture is bespoke, giving the mood of a tailor-made private home. And with his fictional art-loving guest in mind, David has commissioned artwork, including the X-ray photographic work in the dining room. It is the ultimate accolade when guests request a repeat commission of furniture they have seen and enjoyed here. Such requests are met with a polite, but firm "no". Like the designs in a private home, these are unique items with a capital U.

Für den anspruchsvollen, gut betuchten Reisenden, der für seinen Aufenthalt in London ein Zuhause weit weg von daheim sucht, bietet The Apartment at the Connaught das ultimative City-Quartier. Das Hotel wurde 1897 erbaut und später nach dem dritten Sohn von Königin Viktoria, Prince Arthur, Duke of Connaught, in The Connaught umbenannt. Der visionäre Designer David Collins verwandelte die etwa 280 Quadratmeter große Penthouse-Suite des Hotels in ein mondänes, äußerst geschmackvolles Apartment mit einem der wohl besten Ausblicke über die Londoner Innenstadt. Für Collins, der die schönsten Hotels der Welt eingerichtet hat, war das Projekt ein Traum: Er hatte bei der Gestaltung völlig freie Hand. „Ich stellte mir ein klassisches englisches Interieur im Besitz eines weit gereisten, entspannten Kunstliebhabers vor – mit tiefen Taschen", erklärt er. Hotelgäste betreten die Wohnung über ein separates Treppenhaus und sind augenblicklich von privatem Luxus umgeben. Dabei verbreitet die von Vermeer inspirierte Palette aus Blau, Grau, Violett und Elfenbein sofort eine gelassene, ruhige Stimmung. Die Räume mögen klassisch erscheinen, doch hinter der Fassade verbergen sich unmerklich alle Annehmlichkeiten des 21. Jahrhunderts, die ein anspruchsvoller Gast erwarten kann, von der Klimaanlage bis zum Audio-Video-Surroundsystem. Der Suite musste ein Labyrinth von Personalzimmern weichen, und auch von der ursprünglichen Architektur ist nicht viel übrig geblieben. Dort, wo früher die Wassertanks des Hotels untergebracht waren und die Decke deshalb doppelt so hoch ist wie sonst, richtete Collins ein atemberaubendes Wohnzimmer für gehobene Ansprüche ein. Das Mobiliar ist ausnahmslos auf Maß gefertigt und erweckt den Eindruck einer nach individuellen Bedürfnissen eingerichteten Privatwohnung. Mit dem Kunst liebenden Gast im Sinn gab Collins Kunstwerke wie die Röntgenfotografie im Esszimmer in Auftrag. Obwohl Anfragen von Gästen, die Nachbauten der hier gesehenen und genossenen Möbel für zu Hause bestellen möchten, für ihn die größte Auszeichnung sind, werden sie mit einem höflichen, aber bestimmten „Nein" beantwortet. Wie seine Entwürfe für Privathäuser sind auch diese Möbel Einzelstücke mit einem großen E.

Pour le voyageur aisé et exigeant en quête d'un lieu d'exception pour un séjour à Londres, « The Apartment » de l'hôtel Connaught est le refuge secret idéal. Construit en 1897, l'hôtel a été rebaptisé ainsi en l'honneur du troisième fils de la reine Victoria, le prince Arthur, duc de Connaught. Décorateur visionnaire, David Collins a fait des 285 m² de cette suite de grand standing construite sur le toit de l'édifice un appartement chic, d'une rare élégance, avec sans doute l'une des plus belles vues sur le centre de Londres. Pour David Collins, qui a décoré les plus beaux hôtels au monde, c'était un projet de rêve, car il avait carte blanche pour la décoration. « J'ai imaginé un intérieur anglais classique pour un client décontracté, amateur d'art, grand voyageur et fortuné », précise-t-il. Les clients, qui passent par une entrée privative, sont immédiatement enveloppés par le luxe d'un appartement privé. Avec sa palette de bleus, gris, violets et ivoire sortis d'un tableau de Vermeer, le cadre dégage instantanément une ambiance de sérénité et de fraîcheur. Les pièces peuvent paraître classiques, mais dissimulent habilement tous les services modernes qu'un client raffiné est en droit d'attendre, de la régulation de température aux équipements audiovisuels à son ambiophonique. Le nouvel espace a été créé à partir du labyrinthe d'anciennes chambres du personnel et il ne reste pas grand-chose de l'architecture originale. David Collins a aménagé l'espace double hauteur, qui abritait jadis les réservoirs d'eau chaude de l'hôtel, en un spectaculaire et imposant salon. Le mobilier réalisé sur mesure donne au visiteur l'impression de se trouver dans une demeure privée. Pensant à son amateur d'art imaginaire, David a passé commande d'œuvres d'art, notamment la photo prise aux rayons X dans la salle à manger. La consécration vient pour lui lorsque des clients demandent une réplique d'un meuble qu'ils ont vu et apprécié. Mais David Collins oppose à ces demandes un « non » poli mais ferme. Comme les créations d'une demeure privée, ce sont des articles uniques avec un grand « U ».

With its contemporary art and delicate hues of blue, the corridor gives a taste of the rooms to come. The corridor walls display a triptych of oil paintings by the artist Pablo Ferretti. In the private dining room, there is a limed oak buffet designed by David Collins Studio, which can be accessed both from the corridor and also from the dining room for 24-hour butler service. The smoked oak and bronze dining table is also a David Collins Studio design. The mirror above the fireplace, one of a pair, is a vintage 1930s find. Many of the accessories in The Apartment were bought by David Collins on foreign trips, at flea markets or from artisans, to give the feel of a private home.

Mit zeitgenössischer Kunst und zarten Blautönen bietet der Flur einen Vorgeschmack auf die folgenden Räume. Ein Triptychon des Künstlers Pablo Ferretti ziert die Wände des Flurs. Im privaten Esszimmer steht ein Büfett aus gekalktem Eichenholz von David Collins Studio. Für den 24-Stunden-Butlerservice ist es sowohl vom Flur als auch vom Esszimmer aus zugänglich. Der Esstisch aus geräucherter Eiche und Bronze ist ebenfalls ein Modell von David Collins Studio. Der Spiegel über dem Kamin, ein 1930er-Jahre-Vintage-Fundstück, gehört zu einem Spiegelpaar. Viele der Accessoires in The Apartment hat David Collins auf Auslandsreisen, Flohmärkten oder bei Kunsthandwerkern gekauft, um der Suite eine private Atmosphäre zu verleihen.

Avec ses œuvres d'art contemporain et ses délicates teintes bleutées, le couloir laisse augurer des pièces à venir. On peut en outre admirer sur ses murs un ensemble de trois peintures à l'huile de Pablo Ferretti. Dans la salle à manger privée, le buffet en chêne cérusé conçu dans l'atelier David Collins est accessible à la fois depuis le couloir et la salle à manger pour un service majordome 24 heures sur 24. La table en chêne fumé et bronze sort également de l'atelier David Collins. Le miroir années 1930 au-dessus de la cheminée, séparé de son jumeau, est une trouvaille. Dans The Apartment, nombre d'accessoires ont été achetés par David Collins lors de voyages à l'étranger, sur des marchés aux puces ou chez des artisans, afin de donner le sentiment d'une demeure privée.

The master bedroom has been located in the mansard space at the end of the building. The tailored bed, upholstered in Belgian linen, is also dressed with Broderie Anglaise for a soft, yet crisp finish. The relaxed, armless chairs in white lacquer, covered in lavender-coloured silk, and the pedestal table, also in white lacquer, are all designed by David Collins Studio. In the dressing room, the wardrobes are upholstered in leather and the silvered bronze and white lacquer vanity table is part of a limited edition of just six, also by David Collins Studio. The drawing room features a custom-made plaster chandelier, and the Carlos armchairs are covered in lavender mohair and silk. On the roof terrace, guests can enjoy spectacular views across the central London skyline.

Das Hauptschlafzimmer befindet sich in einer Mansarde am Ende des Gebäudes. Das Maßbett wurde mit belgischem Leinen bespannt und mit einem weichen, aber doch frischen Finish aus Lochstickereien abgerundet. Die legeren, weiß lackierten und mit lavendelfarbener Seide bezogenen Sessel und der Säulentisch mit weißem Lackfuß stammen von David Collins Studio. Die Schrankfächer im Ankleidezimmer sind mit Leder ausgekleidet, der Weißlack-Schminktisch mit

versilberten Bronzedetails wurde in einer limitierten Auflage von sechs Stück bei David Collins Studio angefertigt. Zum Deckenleuchter aus Gips, einer Sonderanfertigung für das Wohnzimmer, kombinierte Collins tiefe Sessel mit Mohair- und Seidenpolstern in Lavendel. Die Dachterrasse bietet den Gästen eine spektakuläre Aussicht auf die Skyline der Londoner Innenstadt.

La chambre de maître est située dans la mansarde, à l'extrémité du bâtiment. Le lin de Belgique et la broderie anglaise donnent au lit sur mesure un aspect à la fois doux et frais. Les chaises au style décontracté toutes de blanc laquées sont revêtues de soie lavande, ainsi que le guéridon, lui aussi laqué blanc, sont des créations de l'atelier David Collins. Dans le dressing, les penderies sont tendues de cuir et la coiffeuse laquée blanc à poignées en bronze argenté fait partie d'une édition limitée à seulement six exemplaires issue de l'atelier David Collins. Le salon est dominé par un lustre en plâtre sculpté, et les fauteuils Carlos sont tendus de mohair et soie couleur lavande. Depuis la terrasse sur le toit, les clients peuvent apprécier les vues spectaculaires sur le centre de Londres.

Baroque Bachelor Pad

Looking at the elaborate plasterwork of this early Victorian house, it's hard to imagine that the decorative process began with a complete gut job. Nicky Haslam of NH Design was asked by his client to create the "ultimate bachelor pad" and the brief was to create a modern interior "with the swagger of 1940s Baroque". The client also owned an important collection of current American art, so creating a suitable environment for these pieces became part of the plan. Nicky Haslam has spent over three decades setting his opulent stamp on grand houses around the world. His focus is always to create comfortable, practical interiors, yet he skilfully weaves in dashes of exuberance too. In this property, key architectural motifs recur throughout, including what Nicky describes as "tennis ball moulding on the doors": though not identical, the doors have a similar theme and rhythm. To shake things up a little, the dominant swirls, repeated in stone floors, on the balustrade, and on Baroque style plasterwork, have been deliberately contrasted with bold stripes. Furniture is a seamless mix of exclusive antiques and bespoke furniture. In the drawing room, for example, twin consoles flanking the doorway and a pair of lamps, cast from 1940s vases, were both specially commissioned for the room. As a designer, Nicky Haslam has always been a master of irreverent contrasts. Visitors to the drawing room may first register the deep sofas upholstered in luxurious silk velvets, yet there is also a French eighteenth century Chauffeuse chair, cheekily covered in rustic African floursack material. And perhaps it is this mix of honest simplicity and dramatic flamboyance that lies at the heart of this arresting home. The scheme is a visual feast, yet the spaces have been expertly planned to cater for the peaceful, dynamic and sociable flow of life.

Angesichts der aufwendigen Stuckarbeiten in diesem frühviktorianischen Haus ist es nur schwer vorstellbar, dass der Neugestaltung eine vollständige Entkernung vorausging. Nicky Haslam, der Kopf von NH Design, wurde von seinem Kunden um die „ultimative Junggesellenbude" gebeten – mit der Vorgabe, ein modernes Interieur „mit der Großspurigkeit des 1940er-Jahre-Barocks" zu kreieren. Außerdem besaß der Kunde eine bedeutende Sammlung zeitgenössischer amerikanischer Kunst, für die er sich eine angemessene Umgebung wünschte. Seit mehr als drei Jahrzehnten drückt Nicky Haslam prächtigen Häusern rund um den Globus seinen opulenten Stempel auf. Dabei geht es ihm immer um komfortable und praktische Einrichtungen, die er hier und da gekonnt mit einer Prise Überschwang würzt. In diesem Objekt tauchen zentrale architektonische Elemente wie das von Nicky als „Tennisballstuck an den Türen" bezeichnete Motiv immer wieder auf: Die Türen sind nicht identisch, aber thematisch und rhythmisch einander verwandt. Damit jedoch nicht zu viel Harmonie entsteht, wurden den dominanten Schwüngen, Schnecken und Voluten, die sich in den Steinfußböden, am Treppengeländer und in den barocken Stuckdekoren wiederholen, bewusst kräftige breite Streifen entgegengesetzt. Die Möbel sind eine nahtlose Mischung aus wertvollen Antiquitäten und Maßanfertigungen. Im Wohnzimmer zum Beispiel wurden die Konsolen auf beiden Seiten des Eingangs und ein Lampenpaar mit Füßen aus 1940er-Jahre-Vasen speziell für den Raum in Auftrag gegeben. Als Designer ist Nicky Haslam seit eh und je ein Meister der ausgefallenen Kontraste. Beim Betreten des Wohnzimmers fallen zuerst die tiefen, mit kostbarem Seidensamt bezogenen Sofas auf, dabei findet sich dort auch ein niedriger französischer Sessel aus dem 18. Jahrhundert mit einem frech ausgewählten Bezug aus derbem afrikanischem Sackleinen. Vielleicht ist es diese Mischung aus eleganter Schlichtheit und dramatischer Extravaganz, die das Wesen dieser faszinierenden Wohnung ausmacht. Das gesamte Projekt ist ein Fest für die Augen. Zugleich wurden die Räume virtuos geplant, um für einen friedlichen, dynamischen und geselligen Strom des Lebens zu sorgen.

En observant les délicates moulures en plâtre de cette demeure des débuts de l'ère victorienne, on a peine à imaginer que le processus de décoration a débuté par un travail d'assainissement complet. Un client de NH Design a demandé à Nicky Haslam de créer la « garçonnière idéale » et de concevoir un intérieur moderne « doté du clinquant du baroque des années 1940 ». Ce client possédant en outre une importante collection d'art contemporain américain, la création d'un cadre approprié pour ces pièces constituait un volet du programme. Depuis plus de 30 ans, Nicky Haslam imprime sa marque luxueuse dans des demeures bourgeoises du monde entier. S'il s'attache toujours à créer des intérieurs confortables et pratiques, il sait cependant adroitement y apporter des touches d'exubérance. Dans cette propriété, les grands motifs architecturaux se répètent à l'envi, notamment ce que Nicky décrit comme des « sculptures de balles de tennis sur les portes » : celles-ci ne sont pas identiques, mais partagent un thème et un rythme communs. Pour dynamiser un peu les choses, on a volontairement créé un contraste entre les volutes dominantes du dallage, de la balustrade et des moulures baroques, et les audacieuses rayures. Le mobilier combine harmonieusement meubles anciens précieux et créations sur mesure. Dans le salon par exemple, les consoles jumelles encadrant l'embrasure de la porte et les deux lampes, moulées à partir de vases des années 1940, ont été réalisées sur commande. En tant que designer, Nicky Haslam a toujours été un maître en matière de contrastes irrévérencieux. Si les visiteurs entrant au salon remarquent souvent tout d'abord les canapés profonds revêtus de luxueux velours de soie, il ne faut pas négliger la chauffeuse française XVIIIᵉ, effrontément recouverte d'une grossière toile de jute africaine. Peut-être ce mélange de pure simplicité et de spectaculaire flamboyance fait-il le charme de cette saisissante demeure. Si le plan est un régal pour les yeux, les espaces ont été organisés de main de maître afin de répondre aux besoins d'une vie à la fois paisible, dynamique et sociale.

With its creamy stone floor and striped curtains and stool, the first floor corridor works as a room. The startling artwork by Jean-Michel Basquiat is a perfect fit at one end, and above the stairs hangs a bespoke plasterwork mirror designed by NH Design. Outside the cloakroom, a grey stone floor has a decorative pattern inlaid with Corian, while in the hall, a black and white striped stone floor sets the bold decorative theme. The ornate curves of the stair rail are in keeping with the Baroque theme. The tennis ball moulding on the doors has also been repeated on the ceiling for an additional dramatic interest.

Mit seinem cremefarbenen Steinfußboden, den gestreiften Vorhängen und der im selben Stoff bezogenen Bank funktioniert der Flur im ersten Stock als eigener Raum. Das auffällige Kunstwerk von Jean-Michel Basquiat füllt ein Ende des Flurs perfekt aus, während ein maßgefertigter Stuckspiegel von NH Design die Wand über der Treppe einnimmt. Im Flur vor der Toilette ziert eine Schmuckintarsie aus Corian einen grauen Steinfußboden, im Flur nebenan gibt ein auffälliger, schwarz-weiß gestreifter Steinboden das dekorative Thema vor. Das verschnörkelte Treppengeländer fügt sich nahtlos ins barocke Grundmotiv ein. Der Tennisballstuck an den Türrahmen wurde um des dramatischen Effekts willen an der Decke wiederholt.

Avec ses dalles crème ainsi que ses rideaux et son banc rayés, le couloir du premier est une pièce à part entière. L'œuvre saisissante de Jean-Michel Basquiat est parfaitement à sa place à une extrémité et les escaliers sont dominés par un miroir à moulures en plâtre conçu sur mesure par NH Design. À l'extérieur du vestiaire, les dalles grises sont parées d'un motif de Corian® en incrustation, alors que dans le hall, le dallage rayé blanc et noir donne un ton audacieux à la décoration. Les riches courbes du garde-corps d'escalier sont en harmonie avec le thème baroque. Les sculptures de balles de tennis des portes ont été reprises au plafond afin de produire un effet encore plus saisissant.

In the formal drawing room, sofas are carefully grouped for conversation, while the small ground floor drawing room has a serpentine shaped banquette sofa. At the "library" entry into the master bedroom, there are wardrobe doors lined with olive green linen. The kitchen is smart, with black lacquer walls and stainless steel surfaces, and leading off it is the dining room, which is dominated by a scarlet artwork by Jean-Paul Basquiat, and spinach green lacquer doors. In the drawing room, the walls are covered in coffee colour ribbed cotton, alternating with panels of antiqued glass. The bathroom exudes glamour, featuring walls of antiqued glass and charcoal black and white strie marble. The bedroom is a calming haven, with walls battened in a neutral herringbone.

Während im formalen Wohnzimmer die Sofas für Unterhaltungen perfekt arrangiert sind, verfügt das kleine Wohnzimmer im Erdgeschoss über eine halbrunde Sofabank. Auf beiden Seiten des „Bibliothekszugangs" zum Schlafzimmer befinden sich Schranktüren mit olivgrünem Leinenbezug. Von der eleganten Küche mit ihren schwarzen Lackfronten und Edelstahloberflächen führt eine Tür ins Esszimmer, das von einem scharlachroten Basquiat und spinatgrünen Lacktüren dominiert wird.

Im großen Wohnzimmer wurden die Wände abwechselnd mit kaffeefarbenem Baumwollrips und antikisierten Glastäfelungen verkleidet. Diese tauchen im Bad wieder auf, wo sie in Verbindung mit schwarz-weiß gemasertem Marmor einen Hauch von Glamour verströmen. Demgegenüber gleicht das Schlafzimmer mit dem neutralen Fischgrätmuster seiner Wandbespannung einer Oase der Ruhe.

Dans le grand salon classique, les canapés sont soigneusement groupés pour la conversation alors que le petit salon du rez-de-chaussée abrite un simple canapé d'angle aux formes sinueuses. Flanquant l'entrée « bibliothèque » de la chambre de maître, on note deux portes de penderie tendues de lin vert olive. L'élégante cuisine, avec ses murs laqués noir et ses surfaces en acier inoxydable, donne sur la salle à manger, qui est dominée par une œuvre écarlate de Jean-Paul Basquiat et des portes laquées vert épinard. Aux murs du salon, le piqué de coton côtelé couleur café alterne avec des panneaux de verre au fini antique. Un pouvoir de fascination émane de la salle de bain, avec ses parois en miroir au fini antique et son marbre noir charbon veiné de blanc. La chambre est un havre de paix, avec le motif neutre à chevrons de ses murs lambrissés.

A Gentleman's Retreat

On entering this eighteenth century cottage, the visitor is enveloped in intricate texture, glowing colour and, at night, flickering candlelight. The house has been designed by Alidad, whose signature style aims to stimulate the senses. For this project, the priority was to rationalise the living space. Now, there is an intimate ground floor dining room, first floor formal drawing room and studies, and a second floor master suite. The house is Grade II listed, so the original staircase, wood panelling, and Bolection fireplaces required particular care. Alidad's glimpses of the original house, "a jewel from another time", prompted a vibrant decorative tone, weaving ruby reds, moss greens and gold. Yet texture has a star-turn, too. Antique tapestries adorn walls and tables, and fabrics are indulgent, from bespoke silk damask on a George I wing chair, to linen velvets and velvet damasks in the drawing room. To bring the house to life, Alidad has used light and shade to spark a new mood in each room. Mirrored verre églomisé panels glitter in the dining room, hand-painted wallpaper adds a light touch in the garden study, and Jerusalem sandstone in the bathroom gives a crisp, masculine ambience. Precious antiques have been cleverly used to alter scale and create focal points. In the hall, a seventeenth century Flemish portrait boldly welcomes guests, and one drawing room wall is dominated by a seventeenth century Flemish tapestry, artfully hung to enhance the room proportions. The unique, and the bespoke, are everywhere. A visitor who sinks into the sofa, will be surrounded by scatter cushions in Italian voided silk velvet, French appliqué and Flemish tapestry. And at the dining table, chairs are upholstered in cut velvet, trimmed with custom-made French gold braid. This is a home lavish with attention to detail, celebrating beauty for beauty's sake.

Beim Betreten dieses Cottages aus dem 18. Jahrhundert wird der Besucher von exklusiven Oberflächen, leuchtenden Farben und, wenn es Abend wird, von flackerndem Kerzenlicht umhüllt. Die Entwürfe stammen von Alidad, der mit seinem unverkennbaren Stil alle Sinne anregen will. Bei diesem Projekt stand die effektivere Nutzung der Wohnfläche im Vordergrund. Nach dem Umbau verfügt das Haus über ein intimes Esszimmer im Erdgeschoss, einen Wohn- und Empfangsraum und zwei Arbeitszimmer im ersten Stock und eine Schlafzimmersuite im zweiten. Da das Gebäude unter Denkmalschutz steht, mussten Originaleinbauten wie das Treppenhaus, die Holzvertäfelungen und die historischen Kamineinfassungen besonders sorgfältig behandelt werden. Nachdem Alidad das ursprüngliche Haus, „ein Juwel aus einer anderen Zeit", gesehen hatte, entschied er sich für eine pulsierende Dekoration in Abstufungen von Rubinrot, Moosgrün und Gold. Als Hauptattraktion schmücken antike Tapisserien Tische und Wände. Die opulente Stoffpalette reicht von einer Seidendamastanfertigung für einen Ohrensessel aus der Zeit Georgs I. bis zu Leinensamt und Samtdamast im Wohnzimmer. Um das Haus mit Leben zu erfüllen, tauchte Alidad jeden Raum mit Licht und Schatten in eine eigene Atmosphäre. Im Esszimmer schimmern verspiegelte Hinterglasmalereien an den Wänden, handgemalte Tapeten verleihen dem zum Garten gelegenen Arbeitszimmer einen luftigen Touch, und im Bad sorgt Jerusalemer Sandstein für ein frisches, maskulines Ambiente. Mit wertvollen Antiquitäten wurden Maßstäbe geschickt verändert und Blickfänge geschaffen. Im Eingangsbereich begrüßt ein markantes flämisches Porträt aus dem 17. Jahrhundert die Gäste, während eine flämische Bildwirkerei aus der gleichen Zeit auf beeindruckende Weise eine ganze Wand des Wohnzimmers schmückt und es größer wirken lässt. Unikate und Sonderanfertigungen sind überall präsent. Die Sofakissen im Wohnraum sind mit gemustertem italienischem Seidensamt, flämischen Tapisserien und französischen Geweben mit Applikationsstickerei bezogen, die Esszimmerstühle mit geschnittenem Samt gepolstert und mit individuell gefertigten französischen Goldborten besetzt. In so viel verschwenderischer Detailfreude feiert die Schönheit sich selbst.

Dès le seuil de cette chaumière XVIIIe, le visiteur est enveloppé par des textures sophistiquées, des couleurs chaudes et, la nuit, par la lueur vacillante des bougies. L'aménagement intérieur a été réalisé par Alidad, décorateur connu pour son style qui exacerbe les sens. Donnant la priorité à la rationalisation de l'espace de vie, il a créé une salle à manger chaleureuse au rez-de-chaussée, un salon de réception et des bibliothèques au premier étage, et une chambre de maître avec salle de bain au deuxième étage. La maison étant classée, il fallait conserver l'escalier, les lambris de bois et les manteaux de cheminée à majestueuses moulures d'époque. Ce qu'Alidad a vu de la maison d'origine, « un joyau d'une autre époque », lui a inspiré ces tons éclatants rouge rubis, vert mousse et or. Les textures sont elles aussi à l'honneur, avec des tapisseries anciennes recouvrant les murs et les tables, ainsi qu'une débauche de tissus d'ameublement, de la soie damassée qui tapisse une bergère à oreilles George Ier aux velours de lin et velours damassés du salon. Pour donner vie à la maison, Alidad a imprimé dans chaque pièce une ambiance particulière par des jeux d'ombre et de lumière. Des panneaux en verre églomisé scintillent dans la salle à manger, du papier peint décoré à la main ajoute une touche de fraîcheur à la bibliothèque donnant sur le jardin, et le grès de Jérusalem confère à la salle de bain une sobriété toute masculine. Des antiquités rares ont été judicieusement disposées pour jouer sur l'échelle et attirer le regard. Dans le hall, les visiteurs sont accueillis par un portrait flamand du XVIIe, tandis que dans le salon, un mur est investi par une tapisserie flamande du XVIIe qui souligne les proportions de la pièce. Rareté et confection sur mesure sont les maîtres mots. Le visiteur qui se laisse tomber dans le profond sofa est entouré de petits coussins habillés de velours de soie damassé, d'applications de tissus à la française et de tapisserie flamande. Les chaises de la salle à manger sont recouvertes de velours damassé orné d'un galon doré commandé tout spécialement en France. Cet intérieur traduit un sens aigu du détail, du beau pour l'amour du beau.

Glimpsed beyond the dining room, the hall sets the decorative tone for the house, a feast of texture and glowing colour. An eighteenth century wall hanging adorns one wall and tossed over the table is a seventeenth century Herat carpet. The nineteenth century console table, from Christopher Hodsoll Antiques, features a semi-precious stone inlay. In the drawing room, the listed wood panelling provides a subtle, warm backdrop for a deep, custom-made sofa in gold linen velvet, made to Alidad's specification. Accompanying furniture and lighting is ornate, with a black lacquered Chinese coffee table, and table lamps in antique bronze and ormolu and brass, with cream box-pleated silk lampshades. In the corner, an occasional table is covered in an antique Suzani textile made into a tablecloth.

Aus dem Esszimmer fällt der Blick ins Entree, das den Ton für die Einrichtung des Hauses vorgibt – ein Fest der Texturen und glühenden Farben. Zum Wandbehang aus dem 18. Jahrhundert gesellt sich ein Herat-Teppich aus dem 17. Jahrhundert als Tischüberwurf. Der Konsolentisch aus dem 19. Jahrhundert vom renommierten Londoner Antiquitätenhändler Christopher Hodsoll glänzt mit einer Einlegearbeit aus Halbedelsteinen. Im Wohnzimmer bildet das denkmalgeschützte Holzpaneel

einen dezenten, warmen Hintergrund für das tiefe, maßgefertigte Sofa, dessen goldener Bezug aus Leinensamt nach Alidads Vorgaben hergestellt wurde. Zu den ausgesuchten Beistellmöbeln zählen ein schwarzer chinesischer Lacktisch als Couchtisch und Tischleuchten in Antikbronze, Goldbronze und Messing mit cremefarbenen Schirmen aus Seidenplissee. Für die Tischdecke auf dem Beistelltisch in der Ecke wurde eine antike Suzani-Stickerei umgearbeitet.

Dans l'enfilade du salon, le hall d'entrée donne le ton : cette maison est un festival de textures et de couleurs chaudes. Une tenture XVIIIᵉ orne un mur, tandis qu'un tapis Herat du XVIIᵉ agrémente la table. La console XIXᵉ, pièce de l'antiquaire Christopher Hodsoll, est incrustée de pierres semi-précieuses. Dans le salon, les lambris classés forment une toile de fond subtile et chaude pour le sofa profond en velours de lin or, fabriqué conformément aux indications d'Alidad. Les autres meubles et les luminaires sont très riches, notamment la table basse en laque de Chine noir et les lampes mariant bronze, laiton et cuivre au fini antique, coiffées d'abat-jour plissés en soie crème. Dans un angle, une desserte est recouverte d'une nappe taillée dans du Suzani ancien.

The house has two studies: the "gentleman's study", is designed in the spirit of the eighteenth century, with walls in faux hand-painted marquetry and parquetry panelling. The William IV chair is covered in original ox blood leather, and there is a nineteenth century Ziegler carpet. In the dining room, verre eglomise panels feature paintings of Ottoman sultans, and the bespoke candleholders are in cast bronze. The bathroom has Italian marmorino walls and the washstands feature nickel-plated detailing. In the garden study, walls have been hand-painted, inspired by an eighteenth century Swedish document and the custom-made bookshelf houses a collection of antique vellum books. The formal drawing room plays up a jewel-like colour scheme, with an armless slipper chair covered in red boucle, and heavy cotton damask curtains.

Das Haus hat zwei Arbeitszimmer, von denen das „Herrenzimmer" mit Parkett und handgemalten „falschen Intarsien" den Geist des 18. Jahrhunderts atmet. Der Sessel aus der Zeit Williams IV. ist mit Originalleder in Ochsenblutrot bezogen und steht auf einem Ziegler-Teppich aus dem 19. Jahrhundert. Die Hinterglasmalereien im Esszimmer zeigen osmanische Sultane, die Bronzeleuchter sind Sonderanfertigungen. Im Badezimmer harmonieren vernickelte Waschtischarmaturen mit Wänden aus italienischem Marmorino. Die Motive der handbemalten Wände im gartenseitigen Arbeitszimmer gehen auf eine alte schwedische Vorlage aus dem 18. Jahrhundert zurück, und im maßangefertigten Bücherregal hat eine Sammlung antiker Bücher mit Pergamenteinband ihren Platz gefunden. Das Wohn- und Empfangszimmer leuchtet in Edelsteinfarben – mit einem Slipper-Sessel ohne Armlehnen in rotem Bouclé und schweren Vorhängen aus Baumwolldamast.

La maison comprend deux bibliothèques. L'une d'elles est aménagée dans l'esprit du XVIIIe, avec des murs en faux travaux de marqueterie et lambris peints à la main, un siège Guillaume IV tapissé de cuir sang de bœuf d'origine et un tapis Ziegler XIXe. Dans la salle à manger, on remarquera les panneaux de verre églomisé ornés de scènes ottomanes et les chandeliers en bronze moulé. Dans la salle de bain, les murs ont bénéficié d'un enduit Marmorino, et les meubles sous vasque sont assortis de robinetteries nickelées. Dans l'autre bibliothèque, qui donne sur le jardin, les décors muraux ont été peints à la main d'après un document suédois datant du XVIIIe, et les rayonnages sur mesure accueillent des livres anciens imprimés sur vélin. Le salon de réception arbore une palette de couleurs rutilantes, avec un fauteuil de chambre tapissé de bouclette rouge et de lourds rideaux en coton damassé.

Bank Transfer

One of the greatest delights for London dwellers is the rich choice of architectural styles that abound in the city. For Tara Bernerd, who designed this extraordinary property for herself and her husband, the chance to convert an old bank into a home was a golden opportunity. With the accommodation spanning a lower ground and ground floor, high ceilings, and original detailing from its former life as a bank, it was a completely unique space. Tara has transformed the building with a deft touch, leaving key features in place. The central sweeping staircase has been revamped with new steel handrail and oak trims, but the original wall panelling in the living area, and the bank manager's timber doors with frosted glass, were retained. In a home boasting such vast proportions, the furniture and art must be larger than life. In the main living area, a giant B & B Italia sofa sprawls in one corner, there is a pool table, and the walls are hung with original and bold Warhol art. Yet despite the flashes of jewel colour from the Philippe Starck Eros chairs, this home has been assembled with a restrained eye. Tara has chosen shades and textures to reflect the mood of a club, using deep cream and tobacco, from hounds-tooth upholstery to a battered leather armchair, and new wide oak flooring on the ground floor. Downstairs in the basement, where there was less natural light, she has played with strong, deep colours. The Parisian-inspired bathroom has burgundy-lacquered walls and black marble worktops, and the bedroom has red silk walls. The look is cocooning and dramatic, boudoir and sexy. Tara has transformed this cavernous, commercial building into a welcoming, warm entertaining space with a young, irreverent vibe. Just one question remains. Would the bank manager have approved?

Zu den größten Freuden der Londoner gehören die vielen verschiedenen Architekturstile der Stadt. Für Tara Bernerd, die dieses außergewöhnliche Zuhause für sich und ihren Mann geschaffen hat, war die Umwandlung einer Bank in eine Privatwohnung eine einmalige Chance. Das absolut einzigartige Objekt, bestehend aus Keller- und Erdgeschoss, konnte mit hohen Decken und Originaldetails seiner früheren Nutzung auftrumpfen. Wichtige Teile davon blieben nach Bernerds geschickter Umgestaltung erhalten. Die zentrale geschwungene Treppe bekam ein neues Stahlgeländer und Eichenblenden, die ursprüngliche Wandtäfelung im Wohnbereich blieb dagegen ebenso erhalten wie die Holz- und Mattglastüren des früheren Direktors. Eine Wohnung mit derart gigantischen Ausmaßen verlangt nach überlebensgroßen Möbeln und Kunstwerken. In einer Ecke des Hauptwohnbereichs macht sich ein riesiges Sofa von B & B Italia breit, es gibt einen Billardtisch, und an den Wänden hängen plakative Originale von Andy Warhol. Doch abgesehen von den edelsteinfarbenen Akzenten, die die Eros-Stühle von Philippe Starck setzen, wurde diese Wohnung eher zurückhaltend arrangiert. Die von Bernerd ausgewählten Farbtöne und Oberflächen sollten die Atmosphäre eines Klubs widerspiegeln, von Polsterbezügen mit creme- und tabakfarbenem Hahnentrittmuster über einen abgewetzten Ledersessel bis hin zu breiten neuen Eichendielen im Erdgeschoss. Ein Stockwerk tiefer, wo das Tageslicht weniger wird, herrschen dunkle und kräftige Farben vor. Mit burgunderrot lackierten Wänden und Arbeitsflächen aus schwarzem Marmor atmet das Badezimmer Pariser Flair. Rote Seide schmiegt sich an die Schlafzimmerwände. Die Optik ist umschlingend und dramatisch, edel und sexy. Bernerd hat diese höhlenartigen Geschäftsräume in einen warmen, einladenden und unterhaltsamen Raum mit junger, selbstbewusster Atmosphäre verwandelt. Nur eine Frage bleibt: Hätte der Bankdirektor zugestimmt?

L'un des plus grands plaisirs des Londoniens est d'admirer les styles architecturaux très divers qui abondent dans leur ville. Pour Tara Bernerd, qui a conçu cette fabuleuse résidence pour elle-même et son mari, la possibilité de transformer une ancienne banque en maison d'habitation représentait une chance en or. Avec ses pièces réparties sur deux niveaux, ses plafonds hauts et des détails vestiges de sa fonction de banque, cet espace était absolument unique en son genre. Tara Bernerd a su habilement transformer l'édifice, tout en en conservant les éléments clés. Tandis que le majestueux escalier central a fait peau neuve avec une nouvelle main courante en acier et des limons en chêne neufs, les lambris de bois d'origine dans l'espace de vie ainsi que les portes en bois agrémentées de verre dépoli du directeur de banque ont été conservés. Dans une habitation s'enorgueillissant d'aussi vastes proportions, mobilier et œuvres d'art doivent être plus grands que nature. L'espace de vie principal est investi par un gigantesque sofa d'angle de B & B Italia, une table de billard et d'authentiques Warhol plutôt voyants. Malgré les touches de couleurs éclatantes apportées par les chaises Eros de Philippe Starck, cet intérieur a été composé avec mesure. Pour recréer une ambiance de club, Tara Bernerd a installé un nouveau parquet à larges lattes en chêne au rez-de-chaussée et fait appel à des tons crème et tabac, auxquels font écho les tons de la garniture de sofa pied-de-poule et du fauteuil en cuir élimé. Au sous-sol, pour compenser le déficit en lumière naturelle, elle a joué sur des coloris intenses et profonds. La salle de bain d'inspiration parisienne est dotée de murs laqués bordeaux et de plans de toilette en marbre noir, tandis que dans la chambre, les murs sont tendus de soie rouge. Il en résulte un look douillet et spectaculaire, élégant et sexy. Tara Bernerd a fait de cet édifice commercial tenant de la caverne un endroit accueillant et chaleureux, à l'atmosphère jeune et irrévérencieuse. On se demande juste si le directeur de banque aurait approuvé.

The lower ground floor has been converted into a vast kitchen and dining room, dominated by a sweeping central staircase. The floor has been laid with blue-grey limestone, and the table from B & B Italia is teamed with Philippe Starck Eros chairs in bright colours. The cow was a present to Tara and she painted it herself. The main living area retains its original panelling and columns, and is home to a collection of modern art. The B & B Italia sofa is clustered with cashmere cushions, and there is a pool table for active guests. The battered leather club armchair was found in an antique shop and the brown velvet armchair is Maxalto. To complement, rather than tone with, the dark wood bank doors, Tara laid pale, wide oak flooring.

Auf der unteren Ebene entstand ein großer Essbereich mit offener Küche, in dessen Mitte die geschwungene Treppe dominiert. Die neuen Fußbodenfliesen sind aus blaugrauem Kalkstein, um den Tisch von B & B Italia reihen sich leuchtend bunte Eros-Stühle von Philippe Starck. Die Kuh war ein Geschenk für Bernerd, das sie später selbst lackiert hat. Der Hauptwohnbereich hat seine Wandtäfelungen und Säulen behalten und beherbergt eine Sammlung moderner Kunst. Das Sofa von B & B Italia ist übersät mit Kaschmirkissen, aktivere Gäste können sich am Billardtisch messen. Den abgewetzten ledernen Klubsessel entdeckte Bernerd bei einem Antiquitätenhändler, der braune Samtsessel ist ein Maxalto-Modell. Die breiten, hellen Eichendielen dienen eher als Kontrast denn als Ergänzung zum dunklen Holz der Banktüren.

Le sous-sol abrite désormais une vaste cuisine/salle à manger dominée par un majestueux escalier central. Le revêtement de sol est en pierre calcaire bleu-gris, et la table Boffi est associée à des chaises Eros de couleurs vives, signées Philippe Starck. La vache a été offerte à Tara Bernerd, qui l'a peinte elle-même en rouge. L'espace de vie principal, qui a conservé ses lambris et colonnes d'origine, abrite une collection d'art moderne. Le sofa B & B Italia croule sous les coussins en cachemire, et la table de billard est là pour les visiteurs qui ne tiennent pas en place. Le fauteuil club recouvert de cuir élimé provient d'un magasin d'antiquités, tandis que le fauteuil tapissé de velours marron est de Maxalto. En contrepoint des portes en bois sombre de la banque, Tara Bernerd a fait poser un parquet en chêne clair à larges lattes.

As a deliberate contrast to the traditional architecture of the original bank, Tara fitted a state-of-the-art Boffi kitchen with stainless steel and wenge detailing. The extra long dining table is from B & B Italia with a dark wenge wood top. In the master bedroom, there is a pleasing play of contrasts and colour. As an antidote to the strong red of the silk walls, there is plain sisal on the floor. In the corner of the bedroom stands an antique dressing table, a present to Tara from her mother. Dark wood cabinets flank either side of the bed, filled with favourite books and family photographs.

Als gezielten Kontrast zur klassischen Architektur der ehemaligen Bank ließ Bernerd eine topmoderne Boffi-Küche in Edelstahl und Wenge einbauen. Der extra lange Esstisch mit einer dunklen Platte aus Wengeholz stammt von B & B Italia. Im Schlafzimmer wird ein gefälliges Schauspiel von Kontrasten und Farbe geboten. Als Gegengift für das kräftige Rot der Seidenwände dient ein schlichter Sisalfußboden. In einer Ecke des Raums steht ein antiker Frisiertisch, ein Geschenk von Bernerds Mutter. In den dunklen Holzregalen auf beiden Seiten des Betts konkurrieren Lieblingsbücher mit Familienfotos.

Délibérément en rupture avec le caractère conventionnel de l'architecture de la banque, Tara Bernerd a agrémenté une cuisine Boffi ultramoderne de détails en acier inoxydable et en bois wengé. L'interminable table à manger à plateau en bois wengé noir est de B & B Italia. La chambre de maître se caractérise par un jeu plaisant sur les contrastes et les coloris. Le rouge vif des tentures en soie est neutralisé par le sisal uni posé au sol. La coiffeuse ancienne placée dans un angle de la pièce est un cadeau fait à Tara par sa mère. Le lit est flanqué de deux meubles en bois foncé, qui croulent sous les livres de chevet et les photos de famille.

Parallel Precision

For Stephen Ryan, it was second nature to create his own immaculate living space balancing classical proportions and modern styling. His apartment sits within a nineteenth century building of purpose-built artist studios, so architecturally he began with the benefits of original tall ceilings and floor-to-ceiling windows. Yet the flat was an empty shell, giving carte blanche to develop the ultimate layout. "I was able to devise a flow of perfectly symmetrical spaces, as I am keen on the harmony that symmetry creates," he says. Now the entrance hall sits sociably between the drawing room and the kitchen and dining room, and tucked away on the floor below are three en suite bedrooms and a dressing area. Stephen also wanted welcoming rooms for entertaining. A restrained palette of putty and gunmetal sets a laid-back mood, with flamboyant flashes of rose and raspberry as accents. Stephen actively layers textures, hard and soft, shiny and matt. So while drawing room walls are covered in herringbone taffeta, the hall is papered in flock wallpaper, and floors alternate between shiny porcelain tiles and parquet, dry-brushed for an antique finish. Precisely because Stephen enjoys a balanced layout, much of the furniture is custom-made: twin daybeds in silk velvet and linen upholstered elbow chairs in the drawing room emphasise symmetry. But to gently shake things up visually, there are one-off pieces, including an exquisite shell-encrusted 1940s chest. Stephen plays constantly with scale. In the drawing room, two giant black blown glass vases teeter on a console and adorning the alcove walls is a quartet of over-sized antique cast iron "pieces". Summing up the mood, Stephen says: "The design aesthetic is 1940s with an eclectic mix of furniture, art and objects." One might add that there is also a subtle, yet perfectly pitched, sense of theatre.

Für Stephen Ryan war es selbstverständlich, seinen eigenen makellosen Lebensraum im Gleichgewicht zwischen klassischen Proportionen und modernem Styling zu erschaffen. Seine Wohnung liegt in einem eigens für Künstler erbauten Atelierhaus aus dem 19. Jahrhundert, sodass er architektonische Vorzüge wie hohe Originaldecken und raumhohe Fenster bereits vorfand. Ansonsten aber war die Wohnung eine leere Hülle, die ihm bei der Ausarbeitung des ultimativen Grundrisses freie Hand ließ. „Ich bin begeistert von der Harmonie, die von Symmetrie ausgeht, und konnte hier einen Ablauf von absolut symmetrischen Räumen entwickeln", sagt er. Im Ergebnis liegt das Entree gesellig zwischen dem Wohnzimmer und dem Küchen- und Essbereich, ein Stockwerk tiefer sind drei Schlafzimmer mit en suite Bädern und ein Ankleidebereich versteckt. Darüber hinaus wollte Ryan Raum für die Bewirtung von Gästen schaffen. Eine verhaltene Farbpalette aus Grau- und Brauntönen mit extravaganten Akzenten in Rosé und Himbeere sorgt für eine entspannte Atmosphäre. Lebhaft schichtet der Hausherr Texturen übereinander, weiche und harte, glänzende und matte. Während die Wohnzimmerwände mit Fischgrät-Taft bespannt sind, schmückt eine Velourstapete den Eingangsbereich. Bei den Fußböden wechseln sich glänzende Porzellanfliesen mit gebürstetem Parkett im Antik-Look ab. Gerade weil Ryan ausgeglichene Grundrisse mag, sind viele seiner Möbelstücke Maßanfertigungen: Ein Paar identische Bettcouches in Seidensamt und Lehnstühle mit Leinenbezug im Wohnzimmer betonen die Symmetrie, während einige einmalige Stücke, darunter eine Kommode mit Muschelbesatz aus den 1940er Jahren, die Ruhe optisch ein wenig durcheinanderbringen sollen. Ständig spielt Ryan mit Maßstäben. Im Wohnzimmer balancieren zwei gigantische schwarze Vasen aus geblasenem Glas auf einem Konsolentisch, und vier antike gusseiserne „Stücke" zieren die Nischenwände. Ryan fasst die Stimmung so zusammen: „Die Designästhetik ist 1940er Jahre mit einem bunten Mix aus Möbeln, Kunst und Objekten." Daneben, könnte man hinzufügen, ist ein hintergründiger, aber perfekt abgestimmter Sinn fürs Theatralische zu spüren.

Pour son propre domicile, Stephen Ryan n'a guère eu de mal à parvenir à un parfait accord entre proportions classiques et style moderne. L'appartement étant situé dans un immeuble d'ateliers d'artistes datant du XIXᵉ, l'architecte a tiré parti des plafonds élevés et des baies vitrées sur toute la hauteur de la pièce. Mais cette coquille vide lui laissait carte blanche pour l'aménagement intérieur. « J'ai pu concevoir un flux d'espaces parfaitement symétriques, car je suis partisan de l'harmonie qui découle de la symétrie », explique-t-il. Le hall d'entrée fait le trait d'union entre, d'une part, le salon, et d'autre part, la cuisine et la salle à manger. Les trois chambres, avec chacune leur salle de bain, ont été concentrées au niveau inférieur avec le dressing. Dans les espaces de vie, que Stephen Ryan voulait accueillants, les tons mastic et vert-de-gris dominent, avec ça et là quelques notes flamboyantes de rose et de framboise. Stephen Ryan superpose allègrement les textures, le dur et le souple, le brillant et le mat : les murs du salon sont tapissés de taffetas à chevrons, ceux du hall d'entrée de papier peint floqué, tandis qu'au sol, les carrelages en porcelaine brillante côtoient du parquet que l'on a brossé à sec pour lui donner un aspect patiné. Toujours animé par son goût de l'équilibre, Stephen Ryan a commandé sur mesure une grande partie du mobilier : dans le salon, la symétrie est soulignée par des canapés-lits jumeaux tapissés de velours de soie et des fauteuils recouverts de lin. Mais des pièces de mobilier exceptionnelles, comme la ravissante commode des années 1940 incrustée de coquillages, viennent légèrement perturber l'harmonie ambiante. Stephen Ryan joue en permanence sur l'échelle : dans le salon, deux interminables vases noirs en verre soufflé trônent sur une console, et un quatuor de volumineuses « pièces » anciennes en fonte se détachent dans les renfoncements encadrant la cheminée. Stephen Ryan résume ainsi la tonalité générale : « Ce lieu associe l'esthétique des années 1940 à un ensemble éclectique de meubles, d'œuvres d'art et d'objets éclectiques. » Une affirmation à laquelle on pourrait ajouter qu'il y a là un sens de la mise en scène à la fois subtile et harmonieuse.

Unusual textural contrasts *abound in the apartment. While the drawing room sofa is in a tactile combination of leather, tweed and bronze, the doors to the kitchen are in alligator print embossed leather and, downstairs, one dressing room wall is covered in pink raffia. In the drawing room, blinds emphasise light flow and accentuate the ceiling height, while on the lacquer polished wood writing table, designed by Stephen, scaled up wire and chiffon lamps emphasise the lofty proportions. Sleek surfaces are the theme in the kitchen, but mirror is also a recurring decorative motif. In the master bedroom, mirrored doors lead to the bathrooms beyond. In the drawing room, above the antique marble fireplace from Lassco's, mirror panels frame fabric-wrapped cupboard doors concealing a TV.*

Ausgefallene Oberflächenkontraste *sind in dieser Wohnung reich vorhanden. Das Wohnzimmersofa besticht mit einer sicht- und fühlbaren Mischung aus Leder, Tweed und Bronze, Leder mit Alligatorprägung bekleidet die Küchentüren, und eine Etage tiefer wurde eine Wand des Ankleidezimmers mit rosafarbenem Bast überzogen. Im Wohnzimmer heben Jalousien den Einfall des Lichts hervor und betonen die Deckenhöhe, während auf dem hochglanzlackierten Holzschreibtisch, einem Entwurf von Ryan selbst, überdimensionale Leuchten aus Draht und Chiffon die erhabenen*

Proportionen unterstreichen. In der Küche gab Ryan glatten Oberflächen den Vorzug. Nicht nur hier sind Spiegel ein wiederkehrendes Einrichtungsmotiv. Im Hauptschlafzimmer führen Spiegeltüren zu den dahinter liegenden Bädern, und im Wohnzimmer umrahmen die Spiegelelemente über dem antiken Marmorkamin von Lassco, einer englischen Spezialfirma für die Bergung und Bewahrung antiker Bauelemente, dezente stoffbespannte Schranktüren, hinter denen sich ein Fernseher verbirgt.

Les contrastes de textures *inhabituels sont légion : tandis que le sofa du salon marie des touchers aussi variés que ceux du cuir, du tweed et du bronze, les portes donnant sur la cuisine sont en cuir repoussé effet croco, et au niveau inférieur, une cloison du dressing est tendue de raphia rose. Dans le salon, des stores concentrent les rayons de la lumière du jour et soulignent la hauteur sous plafond, un effet que produisent également les lampes en fil métallique et chiffon posées sur le bureau en bois laqué signé Stephen Ryan. Si les surfaces mates sont à l'honneur dans la cuisine, les miroirs sont aussi un élément décoratif récurrent. Dans la chambre de maître, des portes miroirs ouvrent sur une salle d'eau et une salle de bain. Dans le salon également, au-dessus du manteau en marbre de la vieille cheminée de chez Lassco, les portes recouvertes de tissu du placard à télévision sont entourées de miroirs.*

Perfectly Proportioned

Nina Campbell has decorated grand houses all over the world, imbuing each with easy, elegant English style. When poised to decorate her latest London home, built as an artist's studio in 1870, she was unfazed by its modest two floors. "The house didn't have much architectural style, so we gutted it," she says. Working to a personal brief, she has created two intimate gardens and two bedroom suites, and maximised the entertaining spaces. In the newly dug out basement, there is now a TV room, guest suite and utility room. With a characteristic lightness of touch, Nina has used an airy palette of shell pink, lilac and aqua for a fresh mood, yet her signature love of vibrant colour makes the sea-green hall dramatic. The focus here is not just on beauty, but comfort and practicality too. Surfaces please the senses: heavy linen drapes screen windows, walls are battened with linen, and tactile velvets and flower-sprigged cottons are used for upholstery. Every spare centimetre has been winkled out of the living space, using *trompe l'oeil* trickery and bespoke features. The drawing room is only 14 feet wide, so there is an extra slim custom-made sofa to ensure the room seats eight, and doors to the master bathroom are mirrored and folding to enhance the space. Nina is skilled at creating a relaxed interior. Combining modern artwork, such as Patricia Lombardia's abstract in the drawing room, and antiques, like the nineteenth century half moon tables in the guest room, her home appears to have evolved gradually over time. The ground floor garden is a decorative retreat, and is walled, so creates a good climate for growing plants. In it, a heady mix of lemon trees, plumbago and climbing roses make this small but perfectly formed house feel utterly complete.

Nina Campbell hat Prachtvillen auf der ganzen Welt mit ihrem lässig eleganten englischen Stil erfüllt. Als sie vor der Aufgabe stand, ihr aktuelles, 1870 als Künstleratelier errichtetes Londoner Wohnhaus einzurichten, ließ sie sich von den zwei bescheidenen Stockwerken nicht beirren. „Das Haus hatte architektonisch nicht viel zu bieten, also haben wir es entkernt", sagt sie. Nach eigenen Plänen schuf sie zwei intime Gärten, zwei Schlafsuiten und Gesellschaftsräume von maximaler Größe. Im neu ausgehobenen Keller wurden ein Fernsehraum, ein Gästebereich und ein Hauswirtschaftsraum untergebracht. Mit der ihr eigenen Leichtigkeit und einer luftigen Palette aus Muschelrosa, Flieder und Aquamarin sorgte Campbell für eine frische Atmosphäre. Die seegrüne Diele — das Ergebnis einer unverkennbaren Liebe der Innenarchitektin zu kräftigen Farben — sticht daraus dramatisch hervor. Neben Schönheit stehen bei Campbell auch Komfort und praktischer Nutzen im Fokus. Oberflächen verwöhnen die Sinne: Die Fenster sind von schweren Leinenvorhängen eingefasst, die Wände mit Leinen bespannt und die Polstermöbel mit schmeichlerischen Samtgeweben und Baumwollstoffen in Blumenmustern bezogen. Jeder Quadratzentimeter Wohnraum wurde dem Haus abgetrotzt — mit Trompe-l'Œil-Tricksereien und Maßanfertigungen. Für das nur knapp 4,30 Meter breite Wohnzimmer wurde ein extra schmales Sofa angefertigt, damit Sitzplätze für acht Personen hineinpassen, und um mehr Bewegungsfreiheit im Bad zu schaffen, wurden faltbare und verspiegelte Badezimmertüren eingebaut. Entspannte Interieurs zu schaffen, ist Campbells Spezialität. Sie kombiniert moderne Kunst wie Patricia Lombardias abstraktes Gemälde im Wohnzimmer mit Antiquitäten wie den Halbmondtischen im Gästezimmer und erweckt so den Eindruck, als sei die Einrichtung mit der Zeit gewachsen. Den Garten im Erdgeschoss sieht sie als dekorativen Rückzugsort. „Er ist von Mauern umgeben und schafft ein günstiges Klima für den Pflanzenwuchs", fasst Campbell zusammen. Mit seinem berauschenden Mix aus Zitronenbäumen, Kapwurz und Kletterrosen lässt er dieses kleine, aber perfekt gestaltete Haus absolut vollständig erscheinen.

Nina Campbell a créé dans le monde entier de superbes intérieurs empreints d'une élégance et d'une convivialité toutes britanniques. Dans sa dernière réalisation londonienne, un petit atelier d'artiste des années 1870 distribué sur deux niveaux, elle n'a reculé devant rien : « Comme la maison n'avait pas de style architectural bien défini, nous l'avons vidée de sa substance », explique-t-elle. Pour répondre à ses propres besoins, elle a aménagé deux jardins à l'abri des regards et deux chambres avec salle de bain, et elle a optimisé les espaces de vie. Elle a aussi créé un sous-sol, qui abrite un salon de télévision, une chambre d'amis avec salle de bain et une buanderie. Avec beaucoup de subtilité, la décoratrice a opté pour une tonalité générale fraîche faisant appel à du rose nacré, du mauve et du vert d'eau, sans pour autant renoncer aux couleurs vives qui sont sa marque de fabrique, comme le vert lagon saisissant de l'entrée. Ses intérieurs ne sont pas seulement beaux, confortables et pratiques, ils ravissent les sens par leurs surfaces. De lourdes toiles drapent les fenêtres, les murs sont tendus de lin, et les sièges recouverts de velours soyeux et de cotonnades fleuries. Des trompe-l'œil et des éléments personnalisés tirent parti de chaque centimètre carré. Ainsi, grâce au sofa très étroit produit sur mesure, huit personnes peuvent prendre place au salon, qui fait à peine un peu plus de 4 mètres en largeur. Et l'on accède à la salle de bain de maître par une porte miroir pliante. Nina Campbell est douée pour créer des intérieurs décontractés : mariant antiquités, comme les tables demi-lune XIXᵉ de la chambre d'amis, et art moderne, avec l'œuvre abstraite de Patricia Lombardia qui orne le salon, son logis semble s'être constitué au fil du temps. Le jardin de plain-pied porte la griffe de la décoratrice : « Les plantes grimpantes se plaisent dans cet espace clos », conclut Nina Campbell. Ce jardin, où citronniers, dentelaires et rosiers grimpants répandent un parfum enivrant, met la touche finale à ce logis certes petit, mais très bien conçu.

In the drawing room Nina has used textured fabrics from her own collections: the sofa is upholstered in a jacquard weave, and a mid-twentieth century Scandinavian chair is covered in herringbone Hardwick. The curtains are in Pencarrow linen. Nina likes to trick the eye: the hall is narrow, but seems bigger with the addition of a luxurious velvet bench, and a modern alabaster eagle by Ali Brown as a focal point. Bedrooms are in English country style, with lilac blossom wallpaper in the guest suite, and pink linen for the master bedroom. There is also glamour, with a mirrored vanity unit and a period mirror adding a flash of sharp aqua. In the walled garden, chic stripes in grey shingle and stone create a contrast to the trailing, scented plants.

Im Wohnzimmer verwendete Campbell strukturierte Stoffe aus ihren eigenen Kollektionen: Das Sofa ist mit einer Jacquardwebung bezogen, ein skandinavischer Sessel aus der Mitte des 20. Jahrhunderts mit einem Fischgrätleinen. Für die Vorhänge wurde Strukturleinen aus der hauseigenen Pencarrow-Linie verwendet. Campbell liebt die optische Täuschung: Die schmale Diele wirkt dank der luxuriösen Sitzbank mit Samtpolster und einer modernen Adlerskulptur aus Alabaster von Ali Brown als Blickpunkt deutlich größer. Die Schlafzimmer sind im englischen Countrystil eingerichtet – mit Fliedertapete in der Gästesuite und rosa Leinen im Hauptschlafzimmer. Für Glamour sorgen eine verspiegelte Schminkkommode und ein Stilspiegel, dessen Rahmen in einem kräftigen Aquamarinton aufblitzt. Im geschützten Garten bildet ein stilvoller Streifenbelag aus Stein und grauem Kiesel einen Kontrast zu den rankenden und duftenden Pflanzen.

Au salon dominent des tissus structurés signés Nina Campbell : tissé jacquard recouvrant le sofa, Hardwick à chevrons sur un siège scandinave des années 1950 et Pencarrow en lin pour les rideaux. La décoratrice adore les trompe-l'œil : l'entrée semble spacieuse car l'attention est captée par un luxueux banc tapissé de velours et un aigle en albâtre, une création moderne d'Ali Brown. Les chambres sont en style campagnard britannique, avec du papier peint à fleurs mauves dans la chambre d'amis, et de la toile saumon dans la chambre de maître. Un meuble sous vasque habillé de glaces et un miroir d'époque vert d'eau lumineux apportent une touche glamour. Dans le jardin clos, les élégantes rayures formées au sol par les galets gris et la pierre contrastent avec les plantes grimpantes odorantes.

Rooms with a View

Interior designer Veere Grenney didn't think twice when he viewed this apartment. "It was the most divine flat I had ever seen," he says. Few would argue. The apartment sits within a Grade II listed building, designed by Norman Shaw in 1875, and is located nine feet from the River Thames embankment, so has glorious views. Even better, it occupies the *piano nobile* floor, and its enfilade of three principal rooms – dining room, drawing room and master bedroom – stretches to sixty feet in width. With a characteristically elegant touch, Veere has transformed this apartment into cool, graceful living quarters. There are solid oak floors, overlaid with chunky abaca mats, and grey-white painted walls in the drawing room. Certain key materials and shapes add cohesion. Taking inspiration from the listed Art Deco fireplace in the master bedroom, Veere has added two new fireplaces, in unfilled travertine, designed in a 1930s vein. Set against the restrained backdrop of subtle colour and wonderful proportions, there is an enticing mix of furniture styles. Chic 1950s chairs, crisply upholstered in white linen, look perfectly in keeping with an early nineteenth century commode in the drawing room. And in the dining room, a new table in oak, designed by Veere, has been teamed with eighteenth century chairs, upholstered in gold strie satin. While the key living rooms share the river views, to the rear of the flat is a modern, all-white kitchen, a mirrored, 1930s style master bathroom, and two guest bedrooms. But the *pièce de résistance* is the master bedroom. Here, says Veere, he has gathered all the necessities of life: a four-poster bed, a writing desk, bookcases and a relaxing armchair. With tongue-in-cheek humour, he calls this bedsit living, but it is bedsit living on the grandest of scales.

Der Innenarchitekt Veere Grenney musste nicht zweimal überlegen, als er dieses Objekt sah: „Diese Wohnung war die göttlichste, die ich je gesehen hatte." Wer wollte da widersprechen. Die Wohnung liegt keine drei Meter vom Themseufer entfernt in einem denkmalgeschützten Gebäude von Norman Shaw aus dem Jahr 1875 – mit herrlicher Aussicht. Doch es kommt noch besser: Es handelt sich um die Beletage, deren zum Fluss gelegene Zimmerflucht aus Speise-, Wohn- und Schlafzimmer sich über eine Breite von mehr als 18 Metern erstreckt. Mit seinem typisch vornehmen Touch verwandelte Grenney die Immobilie in ein elegantes, geschmackvolles Zuhause. Auf den massiven Eichenböden im grauweiß gestrichenen Wohnzimmer liegen grob gewebte Abacá-Teppiche. Wiederkehrende Materialien und Formen sorgen für ein stimmiges Gesamtbild. Inspiriert vom denkmalgeschützten Art-déco-Kamin im Schlafzimmer, baute Grenney zwei weitere Kamine im 1930er-Jahre-Stil ein, für die er ungefüllten Travertin verwendete. Vor einer Kulisse aus gedämpften Farben und grandiosen Proportionen entfaltet sich ein verführerischer Möbelstilmix. Im Wohnzimmer bilden mondäne 1950er-Jahre-Sessel mit frisch-weißen Leinenpolstern die perfekte Ergänzung zu einer Kommode aus dem frühen 19. Jahrhundert. Und im Esszimmer stehen Stühle aus dem 18. Jahrhundert mit Bezügen aus goldenem Rippsatin um einen von Grenney entworfenen neuen Eichentisch. Hinter den Hauptwohnräumen mit Themseblick liegen eine moderne, ganz in Weiß gehaltene Küche, ein im Stil der 1930er Jahre verspiegeltes Bad und zwei Gästeschlafzimmer. Das Meisterstück aber ist das Hauptschlafzimmer. Dort, so Grenney, ist alles versammelt, was man zum Leben braucht: ein Himmelbett, ein Schreibtisch, Bücherregale und ein bequemer Sessel. Mit einem Augenzwinkern bezeichnet er den Raum als möbliertes Zimmer – ein möbliertes Zimmer im allergrößten Stil, wäre wohl die richtige Beschreibung.

L'architecte d'intérieur Veere Grenney a eu le coup de foudre à la vue de cet appartement. « C'est le plus divin que j'ai jamais vu, » a-t-il confié. Qui le contredirait ? À l'étage noble d'un immeuble classé conçu en 1875 par Norman Shaw et situé à un peu moins de trois mètres des berges de la Tamise, il bénéficie d'une vue splendide. Mieux encore, l'enfilade des trois pièces principales – salle à manger, salon et chambre de maître – s'étire sur vingt mètres. Avec la finesse qui le distingue, Veere Grenney a transformé cet appartement en une habitation élégante et décontractée. Dans le salon, les planchers en chêne massif sont couverts d'épais tapis en abaca et les murs peints en gris clair. La cohésion est assurée par des matières et des formes récurrentes. S'inspirant de la cheminée Art Déco classée de la chambre de maître, Veere Grenney a en créé deux autres, en travertin non-bouché issu d'une veine des années 1930. Contrastant sur le sobre décor composé de couleurs subtiles et de justes proportions, le mélange de styles de mobilier est séduisant. Des chaises chic des années 1950, revêtues d'un lin blanc frais semblent parfaitement en harmonie avec la commode début XIXᵉ du salon. Dans la salle à manger, une table neuve en chêne, signée Veere Grenney, a été associée avec des chaises XVIIIᵉ revêtues de Strié Satin or. Alors que les pièces principales donnent toutes sur la Tamise, l'arrière de l'appartement est occupé par une cuisine moderne d'une blancheur immaculée, une salle de bain de maître années 1930 constellée de miroirs et deux chambres d'amis. Mais c'est la chambre de maître qui tient la vedette. Dans cette pièce, Veere Grenney affirme avoir réuni tout ce qui est nécessaire pour vivre : un lit à baldaquin, un secrétaire, des bibliothèques et un fauteuil confortable. D'humeur badine, il l'a baptisée chambre meublée à vivre. Une chambre meublée certes, mais de très grande classe.

In the drawing room, pale grey satin curtains, bound with white, frame the view across the Thames, and walls are painted in soft grey-white Slate II and III from Paint Library. The 1950s chairs, designed by T H Robsjohn-Gibbings, are upholstered in white linen, and just beyond, there are glimpses of the master bedroom. All three principal rooms have French doors, featuring the original Arts and Crafts vernacular leaded lights. Against one wall in the drawing room stands a painted demi lune English Regency commode, brought by Veere from his previous home. The dining room walls are upholstered in Temple, a hand-blocked linen fabric from Veere Grenney's own collection. Above the table hangs a French 1930s Jansen chandelier.

Im Wohnzimmer rahmen hellgraue Satinvorhänge mit weißem Futter den Blick über die Themse ein. Die Wände sind in den weichen grauweißen Farbtönen Slate II und Slate III aus dem Hause Paint Library gestrichen. Hinter den mit weißem Leinen bezogenen 1950er-Jahre-Sesseln des britischen Architekten und Möbeldesigners T. H. Robsjohn-Gibbings ist ein Teil des Schlafzimmers zu erkennen. Aus allen drei Haupträumen führen Fenstertüren mit traditionell bleiverglasten Oberlichtern aus der Zeit des Arts and Crafts Movement ins Freie. Die lackierte englische Regency-Halbmondkommode an einer Wand des Wohnzimmers hat Grenney aus seiner früheren Wohnung mitgebracht. Die Esszimmerwände sind mit Temple bespannt, einem von Hand bedruckten Leinengewebe aus seiner eigenen Kollektion. Über dem Tisch hängt ein französischer Kronleuchter von Maison Jansen aus den 1930er Jahren.

Dans le salon, les rideaux en satin gris pâle à liseré blanc encadrent la vue sur la Tamise. Les murs sont peints dans des teintes douces ardoise gris blanc du nuancier Paint Library. Derrière les chaises années 1950, signées T. H. Robsjohn-Gibbings et revêtues de lin blanc, on aperçoit la chambre de maître. Les trois pièces principales ont hérité de portes-fenêtres arborant d'authentiques carreaux sertis de plomb du mouvement Arts and Crafts. La commode anglaise demi-lune peinte adossée à l'un des murs du salon provient de l'ancien domicile de Veere Grenney. Les murs de la salle à manger sont tapissés de Temple, un tissu en lin fait main de sa collection personnelle. Un lustre français des années 1930, signé Jansen, domine la table.

In the dining room, the wall-hung buffet unit, designed by Veere, has lacquered doors in donkey brown, with an unfilled travertine top. Part of its surface can be heated, to keep food warm. The table was designed by Veere specifically for the room and is in oak with gilded edges. The eighteenth century chairs were originally from a palace in Vienna, and are numbered, part of a set of 50. In the small, workmanlike kitchen, high gloss white lacquer units have been made to order, with a thick Corian worktop. The four-poster bed is hung with drapes in pale aqua Ferne Park, hand-blocked on linen, from Veere's own fabric collection. The ceilings throughout the flat are 16 feet high, so the four-poster bed balances the grand proportions.

Das wandhängende Sideboard im Esszimmer mit den eselgrau lackierten Türen, ein Grenney-Design, hat eine Platte aus ungefülltem Travertin. Um Essen warm zu halten, sind Teile der Platte beheizbar. Den Eichentisch mit der vergoldeten Eierstabkante hat Grenney eigens für diesen Raum entworfen. Die Stühle aus dem 18. Jahrhundert sind nummeriert und stammen ursprünglich aus einer 50 Stücke zählenden Wiener Palastbestuhlung. Die hochglänzenden Weißlackfronten in der

kleinen Profiküche wurden auf Maß angefertigt und mit einer mächtigen Corian-Arbeitsplatte gekrönt. Die im hellgrünen Dessin Ferne Park handbedruckten Leinenvorhänge des Himmelbetts stammen aus Grenneys eigener Textilkollektion. Bei einer Deckenhöhe von fast fünf Metern in der gesamten Wohnung bildet das Bett ein Gegengewicht zu den gewaltigen Proportionen.

Dans la salle à manger, le buffet mural aux portes laquées gris-brun conçu par Veere Grenney est coiffé d'une tablette en travertin non-bouché, dont une partie est chauffante pour conserver aux plats leur chaleur. La table en chêne à bords dorés a été spécialement conçue pour cette pièce par Veere Grenney. Anciennement propriété d'un palace viennois, les chaises XVIIIe font partie d'un lot numéroté de 1 à 50. Dans la cuisine de petite taille mais de bonne facture, les grands éléments laqués blancs ont été réalisés sur commande, ainsi que l'épais plan de travail en résine Corian®. Le lit à baldaquin est tendu de rideaux bleu pâle faits main en lin provenant de la collection Ferne Park de Veere Grenney. Les plafonds approchant les cinq mètres dans tout l'appartement, le lit à baldaquin atténue ces impressionnantes proportions.

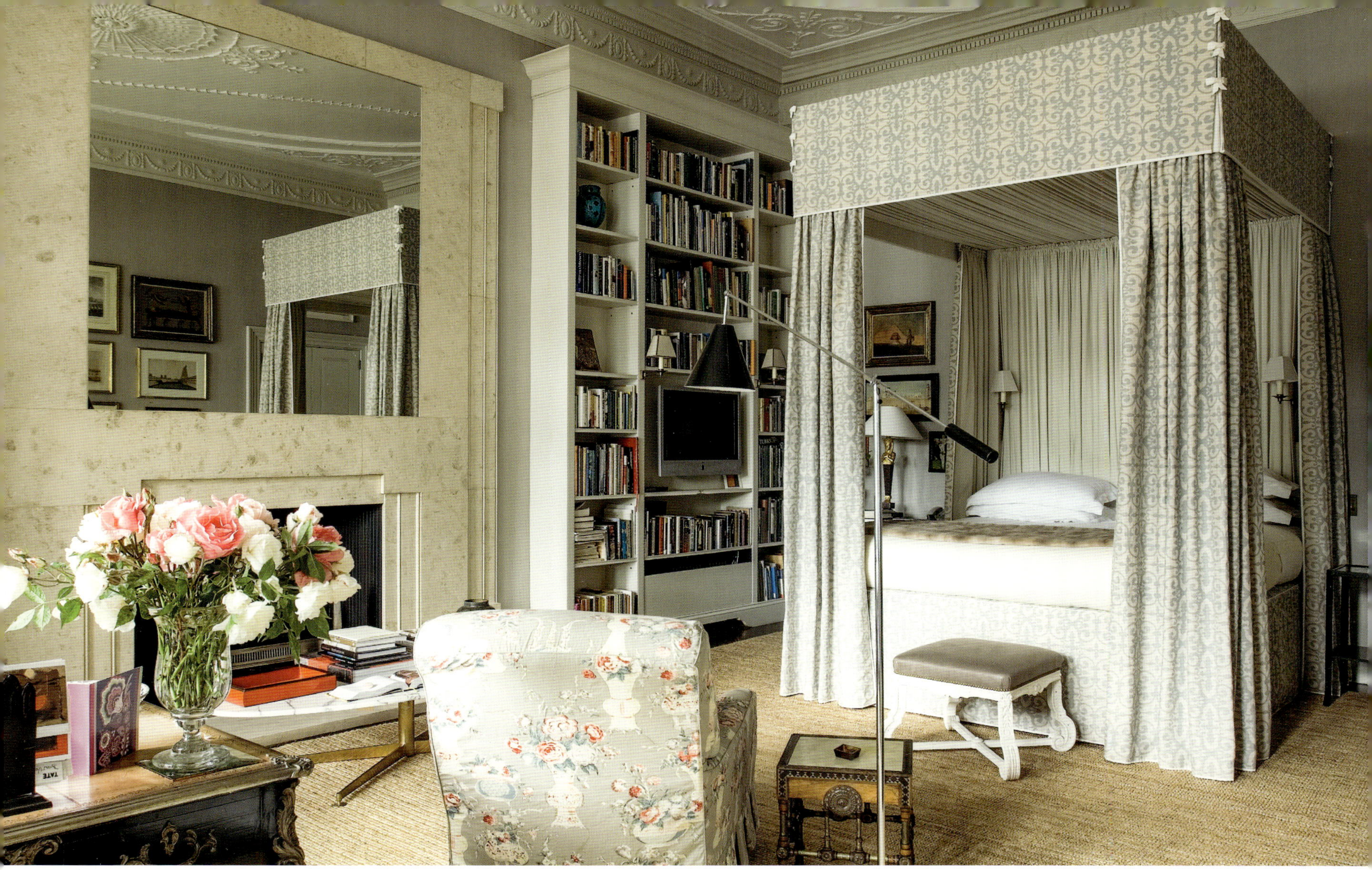

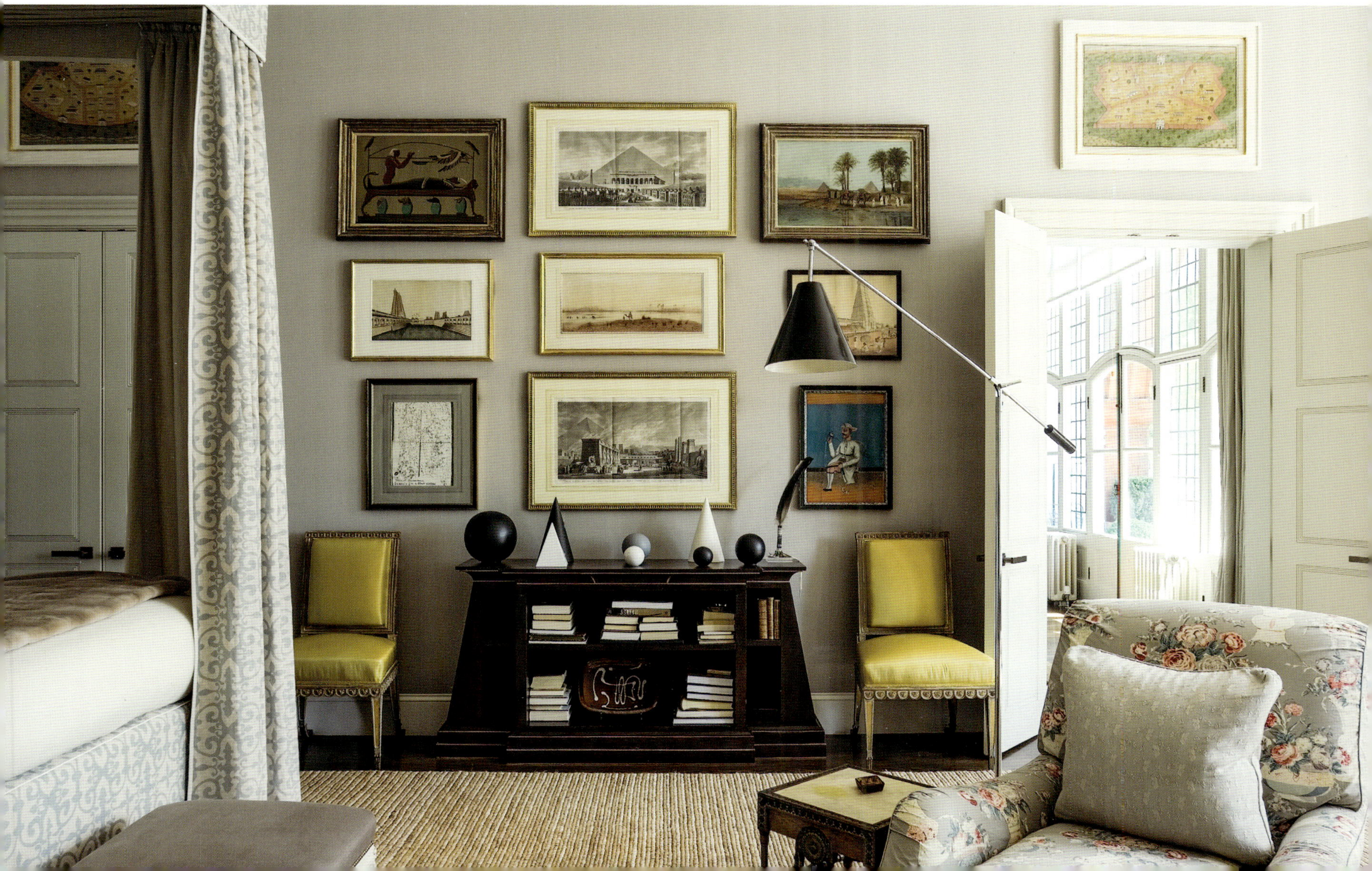

Because the flat is situated on the piano nobile floor of this Grade II listed building, it is possible to enjoy views of the river, even when seated. In the window stands Veere's writing desk, in a Louis XVI style, but made by Jansen in the 1950s. The bedroom feels soothing, with pale grey-blue linen on the walls, and an armchair covered in Jardinieres cotton from Robert Kime. In the master bathroom, mirrored doors create a glamorous Art Deco mood, to tie in with the listed 1930s fireplace in the bedroom. In the second guest bedroom, a 1950s floor lamp and an armchair designed by T H Robsjohn-Gibbings are tucked into one corner.

Die Lage der Wohnung in der Beletage dieses denkmalgeschützten Hauses eröffnet selbst im Sitzen herrliche Ausblicke auf den Fluss. Vor dem Fenster steht Grenneys Schreibtisch im Louis-seize-Stil, eine Anfertigung von Maison Jansen aus den 1950er Jahren. Im Schlafzimmer verströmen die Wandbespannung aus hellem graublauem Leinen und ein Sessel mit dem floralen Baumwollbezug Jardinieres von Robert Kime eine wohltuende Ruhe. Der von den Spiegeltüren im Bad verbreitete Art-déco-Glamour knüpft perfekt an den denkmalgeschützten 1930er-Jahre-Kamin im Schlafzimmer an. In einer Ecke des zweiten Gästeschlafzimmers drängen sich eine Stehlampe aus den 1950er Jahren und ein Armsessel von T. H. Robsjohn-Gibbings.

L'appartement étant situé à l'étage noble de ce bâtiment classé, on peut admirer la Tamise même assis. De style Louis XVI, le secrétaire de Veere Grenney disposé face au jour a en fait été créé par Jansen dans les années 1950. La chambre est apaisante, avec ses murs de lin d'un léger gris bleuté et son fauteuil habillé d'un coton « Jardinières » de Robert Kime. Dans la salle de bain de maître, des glaces sur les portes créent une ambiance glamour Art Déco en harmonie avec la cheminée années 1930 classée de la chambre de maître. Enfin, dans un coin de la seconde chambre d'amis, on peut admirer un lampadaire années 1950 et un fauteuil signé T.H. Robsjohn-Gibbings.

Tailored Elegance

At his architectural and interior design practice, John Minshaw specialises in creating "pared back classical interiors", combining antiques with a twenty-first century mood. His own Grade II listed home, a Georgian house spanning six floors, is the ultimate example of this aesthetic. As part of a two-year renovation project, he stripped back the eighteenth century architecture to its bare bones and reconfigured what had been separate floors of medical consulting rooms into a whole house. The result is an elegant, expansive interior finished with a deft touch. The spatial planning is designed to create a seamless live-work balance, so while the lower ground floor has become John's designated office zone, the ground floor houses the kitchen, dining room and library, with an imposing drawing room on the first floor. Although the colour scheme is restrained, with walls throughout painted in Farrow & Ball's Strong White, the accent walls, in subtle shades of charcoal, navy or chestnut, cleverly define key spaces, including the hall and landings. Surfaces are a sophisticated mix of timber and stone, from an ebonised oak floor in the drawing room to walnut in the kitchen. John likes to customise pieces, melding past and present. In the hall, the chandelier is a heavily modified nineteenth century antique, while in the drawing room, a scaled up copy of an eighteenth century settee, upholstered in silk, balances the four metre high ceilings. Antiques are confidently mixed, for example, 1960s mirrors are with a Vienna Secession table in the master bedroom, and a French Belle Epoque sculpture in the drawing room contrasts with an eighteenth century chair. For John, less is more. Such decorative restraint fully focuses attention on the breathtaking bones of this grand and beautiful property. Ultimately it is the architecture that sings out. "The house dictated the brief," he concludes.

Der Architekt und Inneneinrichter John Minshaw hat sich mit seinem Büro auf „reduzierte klassische Interieurs" spezialisiert, für die er Antiquitäten mit der Atmosphäre des 21. Jahrhunderts kombiniert. Sein eigenes Zuhause, ein denkmalgeschütztes georgianisches Haus mit sechs Etagen, könnte diese Ästhetik nicht besser zum Ausdruck bringen. Während der zweijährigen Sanierungsphase ließ Minshaw das Haus bis auf sein Skelett aus dem 18. Jahrhundert entkernen und die einzelnen Stockwerke, die zuvor als Arztpraxen gedient hatten, zu einem großen Wohnhaus zusammenlegen. Das Ergebnis ist ein eleganter, geräumiger und mit geschickter Hand gestalteter Innenbereich, dessen Raumaufteilung eine reibungslose Trennung von Beruf und Privatleben gewährleistet. So ist das Souterrain Johns ausgewiesener Bürobereich, während im Hochparterre die Küche, das Esszimmer und die Bibliothek untergebracht sind und ein beeindruckendes Wohnzimmer den ersten Stock beherrscht. Im Rahmen des zurückhaltenden Farbkonzepts – alle Wände wurden mit dem klaren Weißton Strong White von Farrow & Ball gestrichen – definieren einzelne Wände in unaufdringlichen Schattierungen von Kohle, Marine oder Kastanie geschickt solche Schlüsselbereiche wie den Flur und die Treppenabsätze. Die Oberflächen, ein ausgeklügelter Mix aus Holz und Stein, reichen von geschwärzter Eiche für den Wohnzimmerboden bis zu Nussbaum in der Küche. In einzelnen, individuell gestalteten Stücken lässt Minshaw Vergangenheit und Gegenwart verschmelzen. Der Deckenleuchter im Eingangsbereich ist eine stark veränderte Antiquität aus dem 19. Jahrhundert, im Wohnzimmer schafft der vergrößerte und mit Seide bezogene Nachbau einer Polsterbank aus dem 18. Jahrhundert einen Ausgleich zu den vier Meter hohen Decken. Unbeschwert und voller Selbstvertrauen kombiniert der Hausherr seine Antiquitäten, hängt im Hauptschlafzimmer Spiegel aus den 1960er Jahren neben einen Tisch der Wiener Secession und pariert eine französische Belle-Époque-Skulptur im Wohnzimmer mit einem Sessel aus dem 18. Jahrhundert. Für ihn ist weniger mehr. Diese Zurückhaltung bei der Dekoration lenkt die gesamte Aufmerksamkeit auf die atemberaubende Bausubstanz dieses großartigen und wunderschönen Anwesens, in dem die Architektur letztlich die Hauptrolle spielt. „Das Haus gab den Auftrag vor", fasst Minshaw zusammen.

Le cabinet d'architecture et de décoration de John Minshaw est spécialisé dans la création « d'espaces classiques réduits à l'essentiel » mariant antiquités et atmosphère XXIᵉ siècle. Son propre domicile, une maison géorgienne classée, distribuée sur six niveaux, est la parfaite illustration de cette esthétique. Les travaux de restauration, qui ont duré deux ans, ont consisté à mettre à nu le squelette de l'architecture du XVIIIᵉ et à réaménager les niveaux indépendants autrefois occupés par des cabinets de consultation médicale en une maison d'un seul tenant. Il en a résulté un espace intérieur élégant et généreux, avec une grande maîtrise dans la finition et un équilibre fluide entre les pièces de vie et celles de travail : le sous-sol a été affecté à l'agence de John Minshaw, tandis que le rez-de-chaussée abrite la cuisine, la salle à manger et la bibliothèque, et le premier étage un vaste salon. La tonalité générale sobre imprimée par le blanc neutre Strong White de Farrow & Ball, est relevée çà et là par de subtiles notes de charbon, de marine ou de brun, délimitant habilement des espaces clés, notamment le hall d'entrée et les paliers. Les revêtements sont constitués d'un mélange très étudié de bois et de pierre, du plancher en chêne noirci du salon au noyer de la cuisine. John Minshaw adore personnaliser des objets, en fusionnant passé et présent. Dans le hall d'entrée, c'est une antiquité du XIXᵉ qui est à la base du lustre, tandis que dans le salon, une réplique plus grande que nature d'un fauteuil XVIIIᵉ, tapissé de soie, atténue les quatre mètres de hauteur sous plafond. John Minshaw n'hésite pas à juxtaposer dans la chambre de maître des miroirs années 1960 et une table de la Sécession viennoise, et à flanquer une sculpture Belle Époque française d'une chaise XVIIIᵉ dans le salon. Pour l'architecte, moins c'est plus : ce dépouillement met en valeur le squelette époustouflant de cette magnifique demeure, faisant exulter l'architecture. « La maison nous a dicté le travail », conclut-il.

John has an acute eye for combining architectural styles, and in the hall and on the stairs, modern and Georgian architectural detailing blend seamlessly. The original stone steps had been encased in a timber frame, but now boast a new steel handrail on the lower ground floor, with the existing handrail, fully restored, on the upper floors. The wide spaces are deliberately and sparsely furnished to give full attention to each decorative piece. In John's office one of his own pen drawings, depicting a temple in Egypt, adds a focal point, teamed with a Regency convex mirror and a nineteenth century Bergere chair. To accentuate the natural daylight in the hall, a French 1930s mirror dominates one wall.

Minshaw hat ein feines Auge für die Kombination von Architekturstilen. Im Flur und im Treppenhaus fügen sich moderne und georgianische Details nahtlos ineinander. Der Stein der Originalstufen, zwischenzeitlich mit Holz verkleidet, prahlt jetzt im Souterrain mit einem neuen Stahlgeländer, während in den oberen Etagen das ursprüngliche Geländer restauriert wurde. Die großzügigen Räume sind spärlich und mit Bedacht möbliert, damit jedes der dekorativen Stücke voll zur Geltung kommt. In Minshaws Büro wird eine seiner eigenen Federzeichnungen, die Darstellung eines ägyptischen Tempels, zum Blickfang, ergänzt durch einen Regency-Wölbspiegel und einen Bergère-Sessel aus dem 19. Jahrhundert. Im Eingangsbereich des Hauses spielt ein fast wandgroßer französischer Spiegel aus den 1930er Jahren mit dem Tageslicht.

John Minshaw a un sens aigu des mélanges de styles : dans le hall d'entrée et dans les escaliers, des détails architecturaux modernes et georgiens se fondent sans transition. Les escaliers de pierre, dépouillés de leur limon, s'enorgueillissent d'une main courante neuve en acier au sous-sol, alors qu'aux niveaux supérieurs, on a restauré la main courante d'origine. Les pièces spacieuses ont été meublées avec parcimonie pour focaliser l'attention sur chaque élément décoratif. Dans le bureau de John Minshaw, l'œil est attiré par un de ses dessins au crayon, représentant un temple égyptien, ainsi que par des miroirs convexes Régence et une bergère XIXᵉ. Dans le hall d'entrée, un miroir années 1930 provenant de France magnifie l'éclairage naturel.

In the vast drawing room, with its trio of floor-to-ceiling windows, furniture has been scaled up to balance the proportions. There is also a skilful mix of silhouettes and periods, including a bespoke ottoman by John Minshaw Designs, a Moroccan ivory table, and a new mirror, set into a nineteenth century gilt frame. In the library, bespoke bookcases painted a sophisticated off-black are filled with John's personal collection of design books. On the ground floor, kitchen units are in a mixture of walnut and black Absoluto granite, and beyond in the dining room there is a John Minshaw Designs table in polished Makassar ebony. In the bedroom crisp textures, including linen curtains, a chenille headboard and walls in glazed cotton fabric, create a tranquil mood.

Im gewaltigen Wohnzimmer mit seinen drei raumhohen Fenstern sorgen extra große Möbel für ausgeglichene Proportionen. Den gekonnten Mix aus Silhouetten und Stilepochen prägen unter anderem ein maßgefertigter Polsterhocker von John Minshaw Designs, ein Elfenbeintisch aus Marokko und ein neuer Spiegel in einem Goldrahmen aus dem 19. Jahrhundert. In der Bibliothek füllt Minshaws persönliche Sammlung von Designbüchern die in elegant gebrochenem Schwarz lackierten Einbauregale. Für die Küchenzeilen im Erdgeschoss wurde Walnussholz mit Granitarbeitsflächen

in Nero Assoluto kombiniert, und im angrenzenden Esszimmer dominiert ein Tisch aus poliertem Makassar-Ebenholz von John Minshaw Designs. Im Schlafzimmer schaffen frische Textilien wie Leinenvorhänge, ein Betthaupt mit Chenille-Bezug und Wandbespannungen aus satinierter Baumwolle eine beruhigende Grundstimmung.

Dans le vaste salon éclairé par trois baies vitrées sur toute la hauteur de la pièce, le mobilier créé à l'échelle maintient l'équilibre des proportions. Dans cet habile mélange de silhouettes et d'époques, on remarquera une ottomane réalisée sur mesure par John Minshaw Designs, un guéridon marocain en ivoire et un miroir neuf dans un encadrement doré datant du XIXᵉ. Dans la bibliothèque, des étagères sur mesure peintes dans un noir chaud raffiné croulent sous la collection personnelle de livres de design de John Minshaw. Au rez-de-chaussée, les blocs cuisine marient noyer et granit noir Absoluto, tandis qu'une table en ébène de Macassar poli signée John Minshaw Designs est la pièce maîtresse de la salle à manger. Les textiles structurés de la chambre, notamment les rideaux en lin, la tête de lit en chenille et le coton satiné aux murs créent une ambiance paisible.

Breaking the Rules

John Stefanidis is an international designer and has decorated many grand houses all over the world. He brings a cosmopolitan aesthetic to each property and has an instinctive knowledge of how houses come alive. It should be no surprise, then, that his London house clearly demonstrates the fruits of over four decades of design experience. He had previously lived in two larger houses, but was unfazed by a smaller property. The result is a beautifully executed interior, vibrant, tailored, and bold. John is a bibliophile, and the house has been designed around his vast collection of books. They are everywhere, squirreled into a "secret" library, ranged across one wall in a sitting room, and lined floor-to-ceiling in a second library. These are rooms to be enjoyed: on a summery day, he'll set up a table for lunch in the garden-facing library. Those familiar with the Stefanidis signature style will understand that, despite the size restrictions in this house, John has made no concessions to his love of decorative drama. Colour is used with painterly precision. So while parakeet green lacquered doors dominate one corridor, the hall and stair carpet is in glowing red, black and beige, and the secret library has scarlet silk moiré lined walls. He knows, too, that comfort is paramount. Sofas are deep, cushions plentiful, and tables are placed in all the right corners. He has allowed the house to 'breathe': ground floor rooms have French doors that open onto the courtyard, and, in summer, there is a dining room housed in its own separate pavilion, with another set of French doors to the stunning garden. The eclectic mix of pattern, colour and texture breaks all the rules. But John Stefanidis has that elusive knack of making surprising combinations fall into place. In his talented hands, it's effortless style.

John Stefanidis ist ein international tätiger Designer, der viele prächtige Häuser rund um den Globus eingerichtet hat. Die weltoffene Ästhetik immer im Gepäck, verrät ihm sein Instinkt, wie er Häuser zum Leben erwecken kann. Daher sollte es nicht überraschen, dass sein Londoner Wohnhaus deutlich die Früchte von 40 Jahren Designerfahrung zeigt. Stefanidis wohnte zuvor in größeren Objekten, ließ sich aber von der kleineren Immobilie nicht schrecken. Er schuf ein harmonisch ausgeführtes Interieur – lebendig, maßgeschneidert und klar. Als Buchliebhaber entwarf er die Einrichtung um seine riesige Büchersammlung herum. Bücher sind überall – gehortet in einer „geheimen" Bibliothek, verteilt über eine ganze Wohnzimmerwand und deckenhoch aufgereiht in einer zweiten Bibliothek. Diese Räume sind zum Genießen da: An warmen Sommertagen kann es passieren, dass Stefanidis den Mittagstisch in der Bibliothek mit Gartenblick serviert. Wer seinen typischen Stil kennt, wird feststellen, dass er trotz der räumlichen Beschränkungen des Hauses seiner Liebe zum dekorativen Schauspiel kompromisslos gefolgt ist. Mit malerischer Präzision setzt Stefanidis Farbe ein. Während also sittichgrüne Lacktüren einen Korridor dominieren und ein Teppich in Glutrot, Schwarz und Beige den Eingangsbereich und die Treppe schmückt, sind die Wände der Geheimbibliothek mit scharlachrotem Seidenmoiré bespannt. Der Designer weiß auch, dass Bequemlichkeit Priorität hat, und zeigt dies mit tiefen Sofas, unzähligen Kissen und Tischen in allen wichtigen Ecken. Er lässt das Haus „atmen": Von den Räumen im Erdgeschoss führen Fenstertüren in den Innenhof, und im separaten Gartenhäuschen mit weiteren Fenstertüren zum umwerfend schönen Garten befindet sich das Esszimmer. Die vielseitige Mischung aus Mustern, Farben und Texturen durchbricht alle Regeln. Doch John Stefanidis hat die unglaubliche Gabe, überraschende Kombinationen wie selbstverständlich aussehen zu lassen. Mit leichter Hand kreiert er einen unangestrengten Stil.

Designer de renom international, John Stefanidis a décoré maintes belles demeures de par le monde. Appliquant à chacune un esthétisme cosmopolite, il sait d'instinct comment elles prennent vie. Rien d'étonnant donc à ce que son domicile londonien reflète sans équivoque plus de 40 ans d'expérience de la décoration. Bien qu'ayant vécu dans deux maisons plus grandes, il n'a pas été rebuté par cette petite habitation. Il en a fait un intérieur d'excellente facture, plein de vie, personnalisé et audacieux. L'artiste étant bibliophile, toute la maison est organisée autour de ses nombreux livres. On les trouve partout, stockés dans la bibliothèque « secrète », alignés le long d'un mur du petit salon ou empilés du sol au plafond dans l'autre bibliothèque. Ces pièces sont là pour le plaisir : lors de journées estivales, il installe une table pour déjeuner dans la bibliothèque face au jardin. Ceux qui connaissent son style si particulier comprendront que, malgré les limitations spatiales de cette maison, il n'a nullement dérogé à son penchant pour une décoration théâtrale. La couleur est maniée avec la précision d'un peintre. Si les portes laquées vert perroquet dominent le couloir, l'entrée et le chemin d'escalier affichent du rouge, du noir et du beige, et les murs de la bibliothèque secrète arborent des rideaux de soie écarlate moirée. Mais il sait aussi combien le confort est essentiel. Les sofas sont profonds, les coussins nombreux et les tables partout où elles sont nécessaires. Il a permis à la maison de « respirer » : le rez-de-chaussée est doté de portes-fenêtres donnant sur la cour, et la salle à manger d'été aménagée dans le pavillon séparé possède son jeu de portes-fenêtres sur le ravissant jardin. Le mariage éclectique de motifs, couleurs et textures défie toutes les règles. Mais John possède ce don unique de faire en sorte que les associations surprenantes trouvent leur équilibre. Entre ses mains talentueuses, cela devient du style avec une aisance déconcertante.

In the library, *French doors lead onto a courtyard where there are tubs of palms and acanthus and, along its length, bamboo. With characteristic Stefanidis gusto, a chair upholstered in a tailored stripe is mixed with leopard-print cotton. The first floor drawing room is decorated in honey tones, with a velvet sofa, striped velvet and brocade cushions, brass Cloud table, designed by John Stefanidis, as well as a facetted oak drum table. On the landing there is a mirror - a "secret" door when shut - that leads into an intimate library, its walls covered in hand-woven Florentine silk moiré. In the ground floor sitting room, antique china plates and Picasso ceramics are displayed. The stairs and first floor are carpeted in a John Stefanidis 'wood grain' design.*

Aus der Bibliothek *führen Fenstertüren in den Innenhof, der mit Kübelpalmen und Akanthus begrünt ist und über die gesamte Länge von einer Bambushecke begrenzt wird. In typischer Stefanidis-Manier steht ein Sessel mit speziell angefertigtem Streifen neben baumwollbezogenen Stühlen mit Leopardenprint. Das Wohnzimmer im ersten Stock ist in Honigtönen eingerichtet – mit einem Samtsofa, gestreiften Samt- und Brokatkissen, einem von Stefanidis entworfenen Wolkentisch aus Messing und einem facettierten Trommeltisch aus Eichenholz. Auf dem Treppenabsatz befindet*

sich ein Spiegel, der als „Geheimtür" in eine intime Bibliothek führt. Ihre Wände sind mit handgewobenem Florentiner Seidenmoiré bekleidet. Im Wohnzimmer im Erdgeschoss präsentiert der Hausherr Keramiken von Picasso und antike Porzellanteller. Das John-Stefanidis-Design des im Treppenhaus und im ersten Stock verlegten Teppichbodens ist einer Holzmaserung nachempfunden.

Les portes-fenêtres de la bibliothèque *ouvrent sur une cour tout du long bordée de bambous et agrémentée de palmiers et d'acanthes en bacs. Dans le style caractéristique de l'artiste, une chaise à rayures sur mesure jouxte un imprimé léopard en coton. Dominé par des tons miel, le salon du premier est décoré d'un sofa en velours, de coussins de velours rayé et de brocart, d'une table Cloud en laiton signée Stefanidis, ainsi que d'une table bouillotte facettée en chêne. Sur le palier, un miroir – porte « secrète » une fois fermé – conduit à une bibliothèque intimiste, aux murs couverts de florence, une soie moirée tissée à la main. Dans le petit salon du premier sont exposées de la vaisselle chinoise ancienne et des céramiques de Picasso. La moquette à motif « grain du bois » des escaliers et du premier étage est de John Stefanidis.*

The entrance hall *retains its original pine board panelling, which has been teamed with a plywood floor, stained black. John's skilful design for the house has incorporated plentiful storage: in a corridor, Chinese parakeet green lacquered doors slide across to reveal deep cupboards. The watercolours are by Teddy Millington-Drake. The dining room is housed in a separate pavilion off the courtyard, and is linked to the house via the kitchen. It is used all year round for lunch and dinner. The rooms share a casual, easy mood. The dining table has a top of Purbeck stone, sitting atop a pebbled cement base, and the painted bamboo chairs have cushion squabs in cherry coloured cotton. The garden is astonishing, planted with box, bay, hydrangeas, roses, camellias and evergreen jasmine.*

Die ursprünglichen Kieferndielen *im Entree blieben erhalten und wurden um schwarz gebeiztes Sperrholz ergänzt. Mit geschickter Planung schuf Stefanidis viel Stauraum: In einem Flur verstecken sich tiefe Schränke hinter chinasittichgrünen Lackschiebetüren. Die Aquarelle sind Werke von Teddy Millington-Drake. Das Esszimmer ist in einem separaten Gartenhaus neben dem Innenhof untergebracht und über die Küche mit dem Haus verbunden. Es wird für Mittag- und Abendessen rund ums Jahr genutzt und nimmt die lockere, ungezwungene Atmosphäre der anderen Räume auf. Für den Esstisch wurde eine Platte aus Purbeck-Stein auf einen mit Kieseln belegten Zementfuß gesetzt, und auf den lackierten Bambusstühlen liegen kirschrote Baumwollsitzkissen. Der erstaunliche Garten ist mit Buchsbaum, Lorbeer, Hortensien, Rosen, Kamelien und immergrünem Jasmin bepflanzt.*

Les lambris de pin d'origine *du hall d'entrée ont été associés à un plancher contreplaqué teinté noir. Habile concepteur, John Stefanidis a prévu divers rangements : dans le couloir, les portes coulissantes laquées vert perroquet dévoilent de profonds placards face aux aquarelles de Teddy Millington-Drake. Située dans le pavillon séparé de l'autre côté de la cour, la salle à manger est reliée à la maison par la cuisine. A longueur d'année, on y prend le déjeuner et le dîner. Dans toutes les pièces règne une ambiance décontractée. La table à manger est constituée d'un plateau en pierre de Purbeck reposant sur un tambour en ciment incrusté de galets, et les chaises en bambou peint sont couvertes de galettes en coton couleur cerise. L'étonnant jardin est planté de buis, de laurier, d'hortensias, de roses, de camélias et de faux jasmin.*

The top floor is a bedroom suite. John Stefanidis has used his antique pieces of Indonesian batik for this decorative scheme. A batik pattern has been used to cover the walls, for blinds and on chairs, its stripes set on the diagonal. The fireplace, with its aqua and blue tiles, has a stainless steel register grate. There's an inspired mix of furniture periods and styles, from a Garouste & Bonetti metal cupboard in one alcove, to an English 1930s chest of drawers, sitting beneath an eighteenth century Italian mirror. The Le Corbusier chair, one of a pair, is in chrome with a canvas seat and leather armrests. The Indian landscapes are by Teddy Millington-Drake.

Im oberen Stockwerk liegt eine Schlafzimmersuite, für deren Dekoration John Stefanidis seine antiken indonesischen Batiken zugrunde legte. Ein einheitliches Batikmuster mit diagonalen Streifen ziert die Wände, Vorhänge und Polsterstoffe. Der Kamin mit Edelstahleinsatz ist mit aquamarinfarbenen und blauen Fliesen eingefasst. Der inspirierte Mix aus Möbelstilen unterschiedlicher

Perioden reicht von einem Metallschrank von Garouste & Bonetti in einer Zimmernische bis zu einer englischen Schubladenkommode aus den 1930er Jahren, über der ein italienischer Spiegel aus dem 18. Jahrhundert hängt. Der verchromte Corbusier-Sessel, einer von zweien, hat einen Baumwollbezug und Lederarmlehnen. Die indischen Landschaften stammen von Teddy Millington-Drake.

Le dernier niveau abrite des chambres à coucher. John Stefanidis a utilisé pour les décorer ses anciennes pièces de batik indonésien. Un motif à rayures en diagonale a servi à orner murs, stores et fauteuils. La cheminée à carreaux verts et bleus est équipée d'une grille de registre en acier inoxydable. Pour le mobilier, l'artiste a mélangé avec inspiration périodes et styles, du placard métallique Garouste & Bonetti dans son alcôve à la commode anglaise des années 1930 sous son miroir italien XVIIIᵉ. Le siège en tubulure de chrome, dont Le Corbusier a créé deux exemplaires, dispose d'une assise de toile et d'accoudoirs en cuir. Les paysages d'Inde sont de Teddy Millington-Drake.

An Evening Retreat

There is a hint of Alice in Wonderland about this compact apartment, because its single corridor is lined with mirrored, panelled doors, offering tantalising glimpses into the cosy rooms beyond. In reality, the mirrored doors are *trompe l'oeil* devices. This basement flat is north facing, so its designer owner, Monika Apponyi of MM Design, has used the reflections to enhance the narrow space and maximise light flow. Monika's apartment is a *pied a terre* in the true sense, as she divides her time between Austria, London and the USA. She has imbued each room with her signature style, using warm colours, from deep cream to ochre, and cocooning textiles. "The chief considerations were for an outside space and a good-size drawing room," Monika says. She has divided the living space accordingly, and now the visitor is naturally drawn to the rear, where a generously proportioned drawing room has French doors onto a courtyard garden. Surfaces throughout are experimental, as Monika has designed the space just to please herself. The bathroom has an unusual polished Italian plaster marble finish, and bedroom walls are painted a lively blood orange. The kitchen cabinets are lacquered Peugeot Green, spray-painted in a car body workshop. Walls are clustered with paintings and furniture is scaled up and comfortable, so this is a space tailor-made for relaxation. Monika has used continental and English antiques with confidence: above her bed, for example, hangs a gloriously intricate three-fold eighteenth century Dutch screen. The "bare bones" of the flat are high spec, with custom-made bookshelves in the drawing room, and floor-to-ceiling cupboards in the tiny kitchen to keep paraphernalia at bay. Above all, this is the ultimate evening retreat. With an Argentinian fur throw over the bed, a deep corner sofa and silk-shaded side lights, what could be more inviting?

Ein wenig erinnert diese kompakte Wohnung an Alice im Wunderland, denn ihr einziger Flur ist eine Ansammlung von verspiegelten Holztüren, durch die der schnelle Blick auf verlockend gemütliche Räume fällt. In Wirklichkeit sollen die Spiegeltüren Größe und Helligkeit vortäuschen. Weil es sich hier um eine nach Norden gelegene Souterrainwohnung handelt, hat ihre Besitzerin, Monika Apponyi von MM Design, die vielen Spiegelungen genutzt, um den engen Raum optisch aufzuwerten und die Lichtausbeute zu maximieren. Apponyis Londoner Zuhause ist eine Zweitwohnung im besten Sinne, da die Designerin zwischen Österreich, London und den USA hin und her pendelt. Mit warmen Farben und wohnlich-einhüllenden Textilien ist jeder Raum von ihrem typischen Stil erfüllt. „Das Wichtigste waren ein Außenbereich und ein großes Wohnzimmer", erklärt Apponyi und hat die Wohnung so aufgeteilt, dass Besucher automatisch in den rückwärtigen Bereich geleitet werden, wo ein großzügiges Wohnzimmer liegt, das sich über Fenstertüren zum Innenhofgarten öffnet. Weil die Wohnung ausschließlich ihr selbst gefallen musste, hat die Hausherrin rundum mit Oberflächen experimentiert. Im Bad kam ein seltener, polierter italienischer Marmorputz zum Einsatz, die Schlafzimmerwände sind in lebhaftem Blutorange gestrichen, und die peugeotgrünen Küchenschränke wurden in einer Karosseriewerkstatt spritzlackiert. Die Wände hängen voller Bilder, die Möbel sind groß und bequem – wie geschaffen für eine maßgeschneiderte Wohlfühloase. Selbstbewusst kombinierte Apponyi englische Antiquitäten mit solchen vom Kontinent: Über ihrem Bett zum Beispiel hängt ein prachtvoll verzierter, dreiteiliger niederländischer Paravent aus dem 18. Jahrhundert. Bei den maßgefertigten Bücherregalen im Wohnzimmer und den deckenhohen Schränken, die in der winzigen Küche die Utensilien in Schach halten, handelt es sich um exklusive Einbauten. Vor allem aber ist diese Wohnung der ultimative abendliche Rückzugsort. Was könnte einladender sein als ein argentinischer Fellüberwurf auf dem Bett, ein tiefes Ecksofa und gemütliche Beistellleuchten mit Seidenschirmen?

Il y a une référence à *Alice au pays des merveilles* dans cet appartement compact avec ce couloir bordé de portes habillées de miroirs qui laissent habilement entrevoir de confortables pièces. En réalité, ces portes sont des trompe-l'œil : cet appartement étant situé au sous-sol et exposé au nord, sa propriétaire, l'architecte d'intérieur Monika Apponyi, de MM Design, a tiré parti de leur pouvoir réfléchissant pour maximiser espace et luminosité. Il s'agit d'un pied-à-terre au sens propre du terme, car Monika Apponyi partage son temps entre l'Autriche, Londres et les États-Unis. Chaque pièce porte la marque de son style caractéristique, qui repose sur des tons chauds, allant du crème à l'ocre, et sur des textiles douillets. « L'essentiel de la réflexion a porté sur l'espace extérieur et sur le salon, qui devait avoir une superficie honnête », dit Monika Apponyi. Aussi l'espace de vie est-il distribué de telle manière que le visiteur est naturellement attiré vers le fond, vers un salon aux vastes proportions qui communique avec une cour intérieure par des portes-fenêtres. Ayant conçu cet intérieur pour son propre usage, la décoratrice a osé les surfaces expérimentales d'un bout à l'autre. La salle de bain a bénéficié d'un étonnant fini marbre en plâtre italien poli, tandis que les murs de la chambre sont peints en orange sanguine vif. La laque vert Peugeot des éléments de cuisine a été appliquée au pistolet chez un carrossier. Les murs couverts de tableaux et le confortable mobilier sur mesure font de cet intérieur un endroit propice à la détente. Monika Apponyi a marié avec bonheur antiquités britanniques et d'autres pays européens, comme la tapisserie hollandaise du XVIIIe richement ouvragée, accrochée au-dessus de la tête de lit. Le « squelette » de l'appartement n'est pas si nu, avec des rayonnages dans le salon, et dans la cuisine, des placards sur toute la hauteur pour faire disparaître le fouillis. Mais ces lieux sont avant tout un refuge nocturne par excellence. Qu'y a-t-il de plus attirant qu'une couverture argentine en fourrure sur le lit, un profond sofa d'angle et des appliques à abat-jour en soie ?

The flat originally had a very narrow hall, so structural work was needed to create a better internal layout, opening up the space between the drawing room and the master bedroom. The corridor walls have been treated with panels of warm-toned Italian plaster finish, alternating polished and rough surfaces. The mirror-panel doors have been spot-lit, to maximise reflections and to add a sense of drama. In the drawing room, there are soft cream walls and a carefully arranged display of black and white photographs, including photographs taken by Monika's daughter, Geraldine, and vintage interiors. The welcoming corner sofa is upholstered in a heavy cotton stripe and the coffee table is from the Artaba furniture collection by MM Design, in a "linen" finish.

Die Wohnung hatte ursprünglich einen sehr schmalen Flur. Daher waren bauliche Veränderungen nötig, um den Binnengrundriss zu optimieren und den Raum zwischen Wohn- und Schlafzimmer zu öffnen. Die abwechselnd matte und polierte Wandverkleidung im Flur besteht aus einem warmtonigen italienischen Dekorputz. Die Spotlights über den holzgerahmten Spiegeltüren sorgen für ein Maximum an Lichtreflexen und erzeugen ein Gefühl von Dramatik. Im Wohnzimmer treffen Vintage-Möbel auf zarte cremefarbene Wände und sorgfältig arrangierte Schwarz-Weiß-Fotografien, unter anderem aufgenommen von Apponyis Tochter Geraldine. Das einladende Ecksofa ist mit kräftig gestreifter Baumwolle gepolstert, der Couchtisch mit „Leinen-Finish" ist ein Stück aus der MM-Design-Möbelkollektion Artaba.

L'entrée de l'appartement étant très exigüe, il a fallu améliorer la distribution en créant une large ouverture entre le salon et la chambre de maître. Les murs du couloir sont habillés de panneaux recouverts d'un enduit dans des tons chauds, avec une alternance de surfaces lisses et rugueuses. Les portes recouvertes de glace sont éclairées par des spots afin de magnifier la lumière réfléchie et de mettre l'espace en scène. Dans le salon, les murs crème sont couverts de photographies en noir et blanc disposées de manière étudiée, certaines prises par Geraldine Apponyi, la fille de la décoratrice, et d'autres représentant des intérieurs anciens. L'accueillant sofa d'angle est recouvert d'un épais coton à rayures, tandis que la table basse provenant de la ligne de mobilier Artaba créée par MM Design a bénéficié d'une finition « lin ».

In the spare bedroom, situated at the front of the flat, ochre painted walls, a headboard upholstered in silk and linen curtains from the Venetian company Donatus, all enhance a sense of quiet luxury. In the drawing room, a dining table and chairs take advantage of the garden views. The curtains are in silk. The master bedroom opens directly off the drawing room, via panelled, mirrored doors. Although the bathroom and kitchen are small, glossy finishes maximise light. In the bathroom, the vanity unit has glamorous mirror panels and in the kitchen, stainless steel appliances are a foil to the dark-green lacquer-fronted kitchen cupboards.

Das Gästeschlafzimmer liegt im vorderen Teil der Wohnung. Seine ockerfarbenen Wände, das Betthaupt mit Seidenpolsterung und die Leinenvorhänge des venezianischen Herstellers Donatus vermitteln ein Gefühl von dezentem Luxus. Eine von Seidengardinen umspielte Essecke im Wohnzimmer profitiert vom Blick in den Garten. Hinter einer verspiegelten Flügeltür schließt sich

das Hauptschlafzimmer an. In Küche und Bad maximieren glänzende Oberflächen die Lichtausbeute: Im Badezimmer sorgt hierfür ein verspiegelter Waschtisch, in der Küche glänzen die Edelstahlgeräte mit den dunkelgrün lackierten Küchenschränken um die Wette.

Dans la chambre d'amis, côté rue, les murs ocre, la tête de lit capitonnée de soie et les rideaux en lin de la manufacture vénitienne Donatus rehaussent le luxe discret. Dans le salon, la décoratrice a disposé une table et des chaises de manière à profiter de la vue sur le jardin. Les rideaux sont en soie. La chambre de maître communique avec le salon par des portes à battants recouverts de glaces. Dans la salle de bain et la cuisine, de dimensions réduites, les finis brillants accroissent la luminosité. Dans la salle de bain, le meuble sous vasque est habillé de glaces glamour, tandis que dans la cuisine, les équipements en acier inoxydables mettent en valeur les éléments laqués vert foncé.

Midnight Glamour

Few have the luxury of a bespoke bar/club, but in this private house, the basement has been transformed into a jewel-like evening retreat. Tara Bernerd, once she had been commissioned to do the project, rolled out a moody and bold interior. The basement floor, which also houses a gym, guest sitting room, a second kitchen and staff bedrooms, lacks natural light so is the ideal location for night entertaining. The layout has been designed to promote easy conversation and comfort. While capacious black velvet L-shaped sofas hug the walls, low-slung leather B & B Italia chairs provide flexible seating. The space has a DJ booth and colour-change lighting, shifting from cobalt to emerald to hot pink, so it sparkles with the genuine essence of a club. In a room that relies on drama and the contrast of dark and light, motifs must be eye-catching. Cushions are emblazoned with skull and crossbone emblems, and there is a feature wall with a stylised leaf design in gold and black Bisazza mosaics. Tara likens this striking effect to a woman in a black dress, accessorised with glittery earrings. Textures mix matt and shiny. The bar and low coffee tables are finished with the subtle glint of a bronze-based mixed metal, created by a specialist company, and are twinned with original 1920s Perspex side tables. Creating an inky background canvas, walls are covered in black seagrass wallpaper and there are ebony floorboards. The adjoining rooms are designed with a similar aesthetic. The gym combines a custom-made white lacquer storage unit, featuring butter soft tan leather cushions, with utility black rubber exercise mats. And in the guest suite, there is a deep sofa featuring signature skull motifs. Tara wanted to create a basement space that is both seductive and very cool. Mission accomplished.

Nur wenige leisten sich den Luxus eines individuell eingerichteten Bar- oder Klubraums, doch in diesem Privathaus wurde der Keller in eine juwelengleiche Freizeitlocation verwandelt. Nachdem sie den Zuschlag erhalten hatte, entwickelte Tara Bernerd dieses kühne und stimmungsvolle Interieur. Weil ins Kellergeschoss, in dem auch ein Fitnessraum, ein Gästewohnzimmer, eine zweite Küche und Schlafräume für das Personal untergebracht sind, nur wenig Tageslicht fällt, ist es prädestiniert für gesellige Abende und Nächte. Sein Grundriss sollte zu Wohlbefinden und lockerem Smalltalk beitragen. Während ausladende Ecksofas sich rundum an die Wände schmiegen, lassen sich loungige Ledersessel von B & B Italia flexibel im Raum verteilen. Mit DJ-Pult und farbiger Wechselbeleuchtung, von Kobaltblau über Smaragdgrün bis Pink, funkelt der Barraum wie ein echter Nachtklub. An einem Ort, der von dramatischen Effekten und Hell-Dunkel-Kontrasten lebt, müssen die Motive prägnant sein. Darum wurden die Kissen mit Totenkopfsymbolen und eine zentrale Wand mit einem stilisierten Blattmuster aus schwarz-goldenem Bisazza-Mosaik verziert. Die verblüffende Wirkung dieses Glasmosaiks vergleicht Bernerd mit einer Frau, die zum schwarzen Kleid glitzernde Ohrringe trägt. Bei den Oberflächen wechseln matt und glänzend einander ab. Der dezente Schimmer einer Metalllegierung auf Bronzebasis, hergestellt von einer Spezialfirma, überzieht den Tresen und die niedrigen Couchtische, die Bernerd mit original Plexiglas-Beistelltischen aus den 1920er Jahren kombiniert hat. Die mit schwarzer Seegrastapete verkleideten Wände bilden zum Fußboden aus Ebenholzdielen eine tiefdunkle, leinwandartige Kulisse. Die angrenzenden Räume passen sich der Ästhetik an. Im Fitnessraum liegen einem auf Maß gefertigten Weißlack-Staumöbel mit butterweichen hellbraunen Ledersitzkissen handelsübliche schwarze Übungsmatten zu Füßen. Und das Sofa im Gästebereich strotzt vor Kissen mit typischen Totenkopfmotiven. Bernerd schwebte eine Kellerflucht vor, die extrem cool und verführerisch zugleich sein sollte. Auftrag ausgeführt.

Posséder un bar ou un club chez soi est un luxe rare. Dans cette maison d'habitation, c'est au sous-sol que Tara Bernerd a créé pour se retirer le soir un magnifique endroit empreint d'une atmosphère particulière et plein d'audace. Le sous-sol, qui abrite par ailleurs une salle de gym, un salon pour les invités, une seconde cuisine et les chambres du personnel, est en lumière artificielle et donc l'endroit idéal pour organiser des soirées. Son agencement confortable invite à la conversation : tandis que les immenses canapés en L recouverts de velours noir épousent les murs, les chaises surbaissées en cuir B & B Italia peuvent être placées au gré des besoins. Équipé d'une table de mixage et d'un éclairage changeant du cobalt au rose fluo en passant par l'émeraude, cet espace jouit de l'éclat d'un authentique club privé. Dans une pièce où priment mise en scène et contraste entre le clair et l'obscur, les motifs doivent accrocher le regard. Ainsi, les coussins arborent des têtes de mort et des tibias croisés, et un pan de mur orné de feuilles stylisées en carreaux de mosaïque Bisazza noirs et or produit un effet saisissant, que Tara Bernerd compare à celui d'une robe noire accessoirisée par des boucles d'oreilles scintillantes. Textures mates et brillantes cohabitent. Le comptoir et les tables basses, dont le revêtement métallique, réalisé par une société spécialisée, possède l'éclat subtil du bronze, sont associés à des dessertes 1920 d'époque en plexiglas. Formant un écrin d'un noir profond, les murs sont tapissés de papier peint noir à base d'algues et le sol est habillé de parquet en ébène. L'aménagement des pièces adjacentes est dans le droit fil de cette esthétique. Dans la salle de gym, le bloc siège laqué blanc garni de moelleux coussins brun clair se marie aux tapis de fitness fonctionnels en caoutchouc noir. Et dans le salon réservé aux invités, un profond canapé arbore les motifs à tête de mort, véritable marque de fabrique de Tara Bernerd. Celle-ci voulait créer un sous-sol à la fois séduisant et décontracté. Mission accomplie.

In the bar area, low ceilings and ambience-inducing lighting create a bold, glowing interior. The bespoke coffee tables, designed by Tara Bernerd, boast an unusual hammered metal finish, and the bar stools are upholstered in smoked grey velvet. The twin seating areas, which can accommodate up to 40 guests, are placed immediately opposite the curved bar, and either side of a stunning glass mosaic feature panel. In the private gym, the bespoke seating unit has concealed storage for gym equipment and a mirrored wall provides a flash of glamour. In the guest suite, which benefits from shady natural light, the colour palette shifts from night-time black to softer aubergine, and has become a favourite retreat for the clients.

Im Barraum erzeugen niedrige Decken und die gedämpfte Beleuchtung eine prägnante, stimmungsvolle Atmosphäre. Die exklusiv gefertigten Couchtische von Tara Bernerd glänzen mit einer ausgefallenen, gehämmerten Metalloberfläche, die Barhocker sind mit rauchgrauem Samt bezogen. Die identischen Sitzecken auf beiden Seiten des überwältigenden Wandmosaiks direkt gegenüber der umlaufenden Bar bieten Platz für bis zu 40 Personen. Die maßgefertigte Sitzbank im privaten Fitnessraum, wo eine Spiegelwand einen Hauch von Glamour verbreitet, bietet versteckten Stauraum für die Trainingsgeräte. In der Gästesuite, die ein wenig vom Tageslicht profitiert, changieren die Farben zwischen Nachtschwarz und weicherem Aubergine. Hierher ziehen sich Bernerds Auftraggeber am liebsten zurück.

Les plafonds bas et l'éclairage d'ambiance donnent allure et éclat à l'espace bar. Les tables basses conçues sur mesure par Tara Bernerd s'enorgueillissent d'une finition métal martelé originale, et les tabourets de bar sont revêtus de velours gris fumée. Jusqu'à 40 personnes peuvent prendre place sur les sièges épousant de manière symétrique les galbes du comptoir, auquel fait face un superbe panneau mural en mosaïque de verre. Dans la salle de gym privée, le bloc siège personnalisé sert aussi à dissimuler les accessoires de fitness, tandis qu'un mur en miroir donne une note glamour. Dans le salon réservé aux invités, qui bénéficie d'un éclairage naturel tamisé, la palette de coloris s'étend du bleu nuit à l'aubergine clair, pour le plus grand plaisir des visiteurs.

A Sure Style

One only has to cross the threshold of this generously proportioned, Grade II listed home, to sense the owners' love of elegance and self-assured style. Each room is infused with its own personality, yet there's also a common thread of subtle glamour combined with an infectious party spirit. Who couldn't be entranced by a drawing room with a working glitter ball? This immaculate interior has been designed by Geraldine Apponyi and Monika Apponyi at MM Design and is the result of a close collaboration between client and designers. The mood is young, elegant and cosy. The eclectic fusion of unusual texture and colour has, in part, been inspired by specific details, seen by the owners in bars and hotels. MM Design has interpreted such elements with elan. Now there are leather-clad walls in the cloakroom, the sparkle of hand-painted wallpaper in the dining room, and a bespoke purple-painted dressing room. The sitting room takes a chic private members' club as its theme. Yet this is also a family home, so furnishings are practical. A bespoke corner sofa is perfectly proportioned for TV-viewing and upholstered in grey wool, and the dining room, despite its crystal pendant light, doubles as a casual breakfast room. Care has been devoted to the way the living spaces flow. The library, which leads directly off the drawing room, has been sparsely furnished, as it is a frequent venue for drinks parties. Yet even a party house needs tranquil rooms, so the mood alters upstairs. The master bedroom has neutral linens and calming grey walls, and curtains with a luxurious border of silk velvet. And the bathroom has walls in a special sand and plaster finish, inlaid with hand-cut metal mosaic pieces to give a subtle glint. Ultimately, that is the secret to this warm, enveloping home. Its beauty lies in the detail.

Man muss nur einen Fuß über die Schwelle dieses großzügig ausgelegten, denkmalgeschützten Hauses setzen, um die Liebe seiner Besitzer zur Eleganz zu spüren. Jeder Raum hat seine eigene Persönlichkeit, doch gleichzeitig durchzieht eine Kombination aus dezentem Glamour und ansteckender Partystimmung das gesamte Haus. Wer ließe sich nicht von einer rotierenden Diskokugel im Wohnzimmer verzaubern? Das makellose Interieur wurde von Geraldine und Monika Apponyi von MM Design entworfen und entstand in enger Zusammenarbeit mit den Auftraggebern. Die Atmosphäre ist jung, elegant und gemütlich. Der eklektische Mix aus ungewöhnlichen Farben und Texturen geht zum Teil auf die Besitzer zurück, die eine Vielfalt anregender Details, die sie auf Reisen entdeckt hatten, hier verwirklicht sehen wollten. MM Design hat diese Elemente schwungvoll interpretiert – mit Lederpolstern an den Toilettenwänden, dem Glanz handgemalter Tapeten im Esszimmer und einem maßgeschneiderten Ankleidezimmer in Lila. Für das Wohnzimmer könnte ein mondäner Privatklub Pate gestanden haben. Doch weil hier eine Familie wohnt, ist die Einrichtung in erster Linie praktisch. Ein maßgefertigtes Ecksofa mit grauem Wollbezug hat perfekte Fernsehmaße, und das Esszimmer dient trotz seines festlichen Kristallleuchters auch als zwangloser Frühstücksraum. Ein besonderes Augenmerk galt dem Ineinanderfließen der Wohnbereiche. Die Bibliothek, die direkt aus dem Wohnzimmer herausführt, ist als Schauplatz von Stehpartys nur spärlich möbliert. Doch da selbst ein Partyhaus ruhige Räume braucht, ändert sich die Stimmung im ersten Stock. Im Schlafzimmer finden sich neutrale Leinenstoffe, graue Wände und Vorhänge mit einer üppigen Seidensamtborte. In den Gips-Sand-Putz im Bad sind handgeschnittene Metallmosaike eingelegt, die den Wänden einen sanften Schimmer verleihen. Das ist letztendlich das Geheimnis dieses warmen, wohnlichen Zuhauses: Seine Schönheit liegt im Detail.

Dès le seuil de cette vaste demeure classée, on perçoit l'amour de l'élégance des propriétaires. Si les pièces ont chacune une personnalité propre, un glamour subtil associé à un goût de la fête contagieux les unit. Qui ne serait pas ravi par un salon équipé d'une boule à facettes qui tourne sur elle-même ? Cet intérieur irréprochable, signé Geraldine et Monika Apponyi de MM Design, est le fruit de l'étroite collaboration entre les clients et les décoratrices. Il y règne une atmosphère jeune, élégante et chaleureuse. Le mariage éclectique de textures et de coloris inhabituels a été en partie impulsé par les clients, désireux d'introduire une panoplie de détails inspirés de leurs voyages. Transposant ces idées avec enthousiasme, MM Design a opté pour des murs capitonnés de cuir dans les toilettes, pour l'éclat d'un papier peint à la main dans la salle à manger et pour une peinture violette dans le dressing personnalisé. Bien que puisant son inspiration dans les clubs privés chic, le salon est meublé de manière pratique car la maison abrite une famille. Ainsi, un sofa d'angle sur mesure tapissé de laine grise invite à regarder la télévision, et la salle à manger, malgré sa suspension en cristal, fait aussi office de pièce décontractée pour le « breakfast ». Il a été apporté un soin particulier à la fluidité des espaces. Située dans l'enfilade du salon, la bibliothèque est meublée avec parcimonie car elle accueille des cocktails. Une famille de fêtards ayant malgré tout besoin de pièces au calme, c'est une atmosphère différente qui règne à l'étage. La chambre de maître est dotée de tissus d'ameublement de couleur neutre et de murs gris ainsi que de rideaux ornés d'un luxueux liseré en velours de soie. Les murs de la salle de bain doivent leur subtil éclat à l'enduit au sable et au plâtre incrusté de pièces de mosaïques métalliques découpées à la main. Le secret de ce logis chaleureux et envoûtant réside précisément dans ces détails, car ce sont eux qui font sa beauté.

In the drawing room, the glitter ball is turned by a motor, but without the movement looks like a contemporary chandelier. It was important to keep the look fresh and young, yet still in keeping with the classical architecture. So the designers have created an inspired mix of furniture, teaming a custom-made corner sofa with 1940s armchairs, in aluminium and leather, which were originally made for use in a Zeppelin. MM Design's own Artaba range zebra Ottoman adds a funky touch. In the library, with its bold charcoal painted shelves and scarlet rug, furnishings are simple, as the room is often used for entertaining. In the dining room a pendant light with solid glass droplets looks chic, but the birdcage adds humour. The conservatory plays a big part in everyday family life.

Die Spiegelkugel im Wohnzimmer wird von einem Motor angetrieben und wirkt bei Stillstand wie ein moderner Kronleuchter. Um den jungen und frischen Look des Hauses mit der klassischen Architektur in Einklang zu bringen, schufen die Designerinnen einen genialen Möbelmix. Ein speziell angefertigtes Ecksofa kombinierten sie mit 1940er-Jahre-Armsesseln aus Aluminium und Leder, die ursprünglich für einen Zeppelin konstruiert worden waren. Der Zebrahocker aus der MM-Design-Möbelkollektion Artaba sorgt für den originellen Touch. Die Bibliothek mit ihren schweren schwarz lackierten Regalen und dem scharlachroten Teppich ist einfach möbliert, weil sie oft als Partyraum genutzt wird. Im Esszimmer treffen der Chic einer Pendelleuchte mit massiven Glastropfen und das Spielerische eines Vogelkäfigs aufeinander. Der Wintergarten nimmt im Familienalltag einen zentralen Platz ein.

Dans le salon, un moteur fait tourner la boule à facettes qui, à l'arrêt, ressemble à un lustre contemporain. Comme il est important de cultiver une apparence de fraîcheur et de jeunesse, tout en restant en harmonie avec l'architecture classique, les décoratrices ont mélangé avec bonheur les styles, associant un sofa d'angle sur mesure avec des fauteuils années 1940 en aluminium et en cuir produits à l'origine pour équiper les dirigeables. Le pouf zèbre, provenant de la propre ligne de mobilier Artaba de MM Design, met du piment. Dotée de rayonnages charbon très présents et d'un tapis écarlate, la bibliothèque est meublée simplement car on y reçoit souvent. Dans la salle à manger, le lustre chic à pendeloques en verre plein cohabite avec une cage à oiseau introduisant une touche d'humour. Le jardin d'hiver joue un rôle important dans le quotidien de la famille.

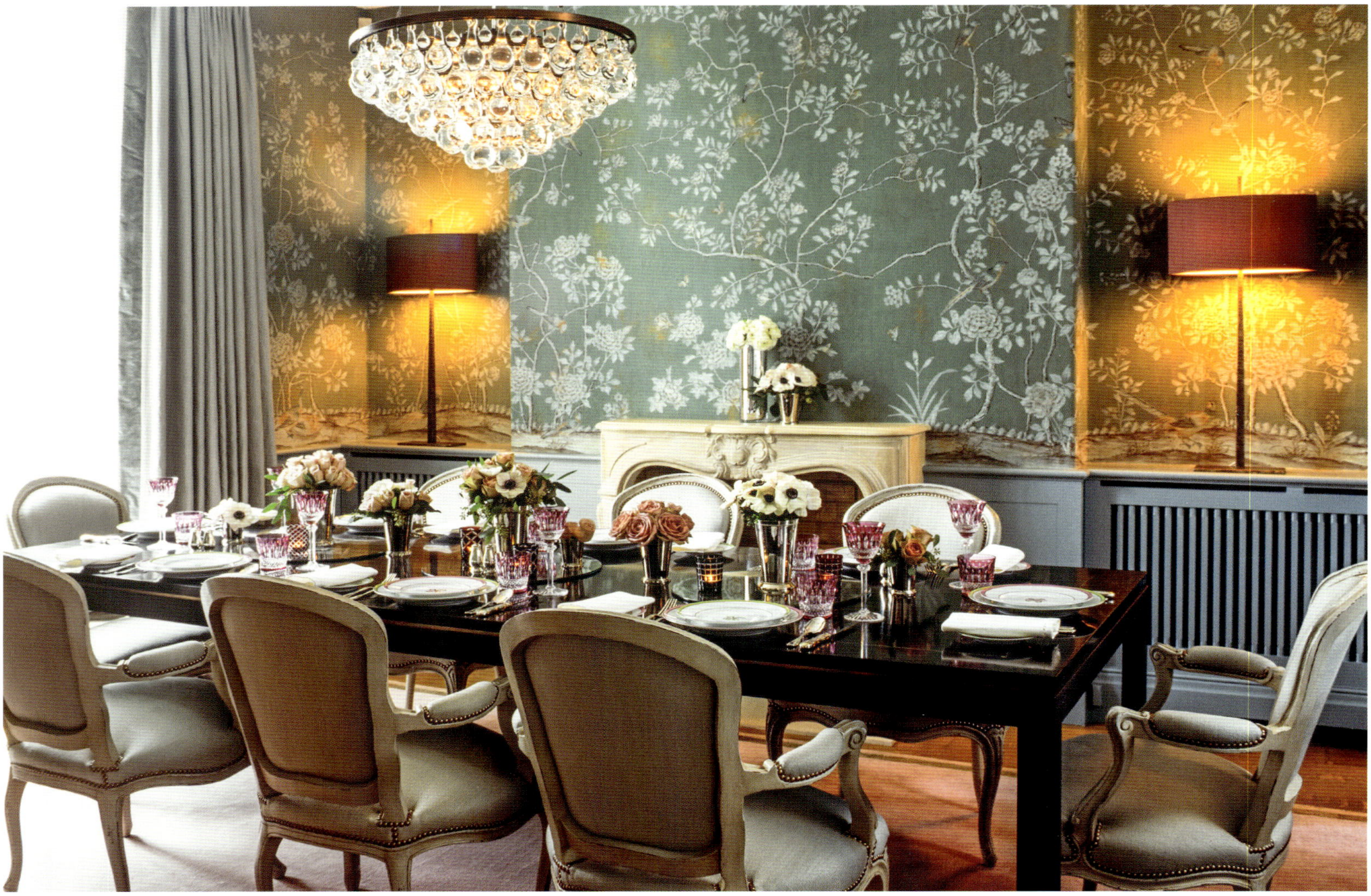

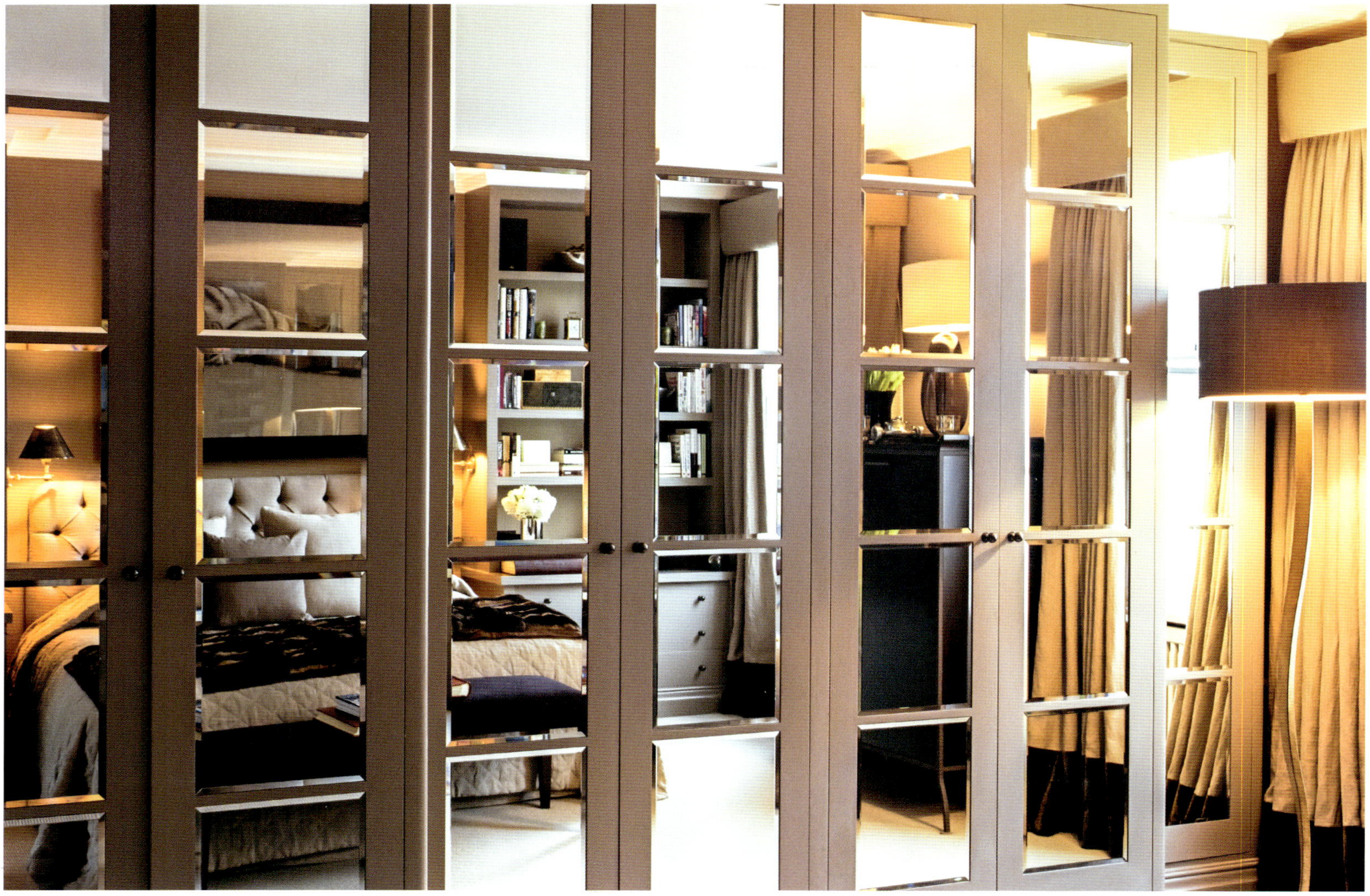

A leather-panelled lift, seen by the client in a New York club, was the inspiration for the cloakroom. The vanity unit top is made from Cohiba marble. In the top floor dressing room, open shelves flank the walls and are painted in purple, the owner's favourite colour. It is a glamorous haven, deliberately designed with a fun, young vibe. By contrast, the mood in the bathroom is soothing and calm. The original bath has been removed and in its place is a large walk-in shower. Each room in this house has an individual mood: in the guest room, fresh Indian cottons in crisp indigo and white create a cool, easy atmosphere.

Ein mit Leder ausgekleideter Lift, den die Kunden in New York gesehen hatten, lieferte die Inspiration für die Toilettenwände. Die Waschtischauflage wurde aus kubanischem Marmor gefertigt. Im Ankleidezimmer im Obergeschoss flankieren offene Regale in einem freundlichen, femininen Violett die Wände. Die glamouröse Oase wurde gezielt mit jungen Vibes gestaltet, die Spaß machen sollen. Im Gegensatz dazu ist die Atmosphäre im Bad besänftigend ruhig. Das Originalbadezimmer wurde entfernt und durch eine große begehbare Dusche ersetzt. Jeder Raum dieses Hauses hat seine eigene Stimmung: Im Gästezimmer sorgen frische indische Baumwollstoffe in kräftigem Indigoblau und Weiß für Kühle und Leichtigkeit.

C'est un ascenseur capitonné de cuir, vu par le client dans un club new-yorkais, qui a été la source d'inspiration pour les toilettes. Le plateau du meuble sous vasque est en marbre Marron Cohiba. Chaque pièce possède une atmosphère propre. Dans le dressing, qui est situé au dernier étage, les murs sont habillés de rayonnages peints en violet, la couleur préférée de la propriétaire. C'est là un refuge glamour, conçu dans un esprit jeune et festif. À l'inverse, il règne dans la salle de bain une atmosphère calme et apaisante. La baignoire d'origine a été remplacée par une spacieuse douche à l'italienne. Et dans la chambre d'amis, les cotonnades indiennes dans des tons frais d'indigo et de blanc créent une ambiance décontractée.

Quiet Luxury

With its bird's eye views of London and light-filled living spaces, this duplex designed by Michael Reeves is an oasis in the city. When its owners hired Michael, they had twin requests. They wanted a neutral interior to offset a burgeoning art collection and a furniture layout to emphasise space and light. The flat, spanning the top of a Regency terraced townhouse, required little structural work beyond reconfiguring the staircase, and new bathroom and kitchen layouts. Now, it is bathed with light from triple aspect windows, and decorated in uplifting whites, oatmeal and dove greys. The crisp background in all rooms allows the art to stand out, yet each piece has been arranged with well-judged discretion. A Miró painting hangs quietly above the bed, and to one side of the staircase in casual splendour is a Botero bronze sculpture. The spectacular long living space has been divided into discrete seating areas, whilst allowing the room to work as a whole. At one end, chic, boxy furniture from Michael Reeves' collection is drawn around a marble chimneybreast, and at the other, there's a dining area and a casual arrangement of tub armchairs. Quiet luxury is the watchword here. Tactile upholstery fabrics include mohair, velvet and leather, yet metallic furniture adds contrast. The dining table is in wrought iron, and in the hall stands an original Giacometti floor lamp. As befits a couple whose time is divided between London, Moscow, and New York, this is a *pied a terre* furnished from around the world. In the sitting area there's a funky side table with high gloss lacquered finish, purchased in Dallas, and the Art Deco style nickel silver sconces were custom-made in Istanbul. The scope may be international, but the result is an intimate city bolthole, with relaxation at its core.

Mit seinem fantastischen Ausblick über die Dächer von London und lichtdurchfluteten Wohnräumen ist dieses Duplex-Penthouse von Michael Reeves eine Oase in der Großstadt. Reeves Auftraggeber hatten zwei Wünsche: ein neutrales Interieur, das ihre wachsende Kunstsammlung zur Geltung bringt, und eine Möblierung, die Licht und Weitläufigkeit betont. Abgesehen von einer neu gestalteten Treppe und der Überplanung von Küche und Bad waren in der Dachwohnung eines Stadtreihenhauses aus dem frühen 19. Jahrhundert keine Veränderungen an der Bausubstanz notwendig. Heute fällt von drei Seiten Licht in das Objekt, das in freundlichen Weißtönen, Hellbeige und Schattierungen von Taubengrau eingerichtet ist. Die klaren Strukturen in allen Räumen lassen der Kunst den Vortritt – wobei jedes Stück einer wohldurchdachten Ordnung folgt. Ein Miró-Gemälde hängt still über dem Bett, neben der Treppe verströmt eine Bronzeplastik von Botero ihren zwanglosen Glanz. Im lang gestreckten Wohnbereich wurden verschiedene Sitzgruppen aufgestellt, ohne dem Raum die atemberaubende Gesamtwirkung zu nehmen. An einem Ende scharen sich moderne, kastige Sitzmöbel aus der Michael-Reeves-Kollektion vor einem mit Marmor verkleideten Kaminelement, am anderen finden sich die Essecke und ein Paar locker arrangierter Rundsessel. Dezenter Luxus lautet die Devise. Haptisch fühlbare Polsterstoffe wie Mohair, Samt und Leder kontrastieren mit Metallmöbeln wie dem schmiedeeisernen Esstisch oder einer original Giacometti-Stehlampe im Flur. Wie es einem Paar ansteht, das sein Leben zwischen London, Moskau und New York aufteilt, ist diese Zweitwohnung mit Möbeln aus aller Welt eingerichtet. Ein ausgefallener Beistelltisch mit Hochglanzlackierung in der Sitzecke wurde in Dallas gekauft, die Wandleuchter aus Nickelsilber im Art-déco-Stil sind Sonderanfertigungen aus Istanbul. Bei aller Internationalität ist hier ein intimer City-Schlupfwinkel entstanden, der vor allem Entspannung bietet.

Avec sa vue plongeante sur les toits de Londres et ses pièces inondées de lumière, ce duplex est une oasis urbaine occupant tout le dernier étage en terrasse d'un hôtel particulier Régence. Quand ses propriétaires firent appel aux services de Michael Reeves, ils lui soumirent deux exigences indissociables l'une de l'autre : un intérieur neutre qui mette en valeur une collection d'art naissante et un plan qui magnifie l'espace et la lumière. Les travaux de restructuration se sont limités au réaménagement de la cage d'escalier, de la salle de bain et de la cuisine. Le résultat : un appartement baigné de lumière grâce à sa triple exposition et dominé par des tons vivifiants de blanc, de beige et de gris. Les œuvres d'art, toutes disposées avec sensibilité, se détachent sur la toile de fond nette de chacune des pièces. Un tableau de Miró veille sans bruit au dessus du lit, tandis qu'un bronze de Botero est niché dans le renfoncement de la cage d'escalier resplendissante de simplicité. D'une longueur spectaculaire, le séjour a été divisé en plusieurs coins conversation discrets, qui n'empêchent pas la pièce de fonctionner comme un tout. À une extrémité, d'élégants meubles cubiques signés Michael Reeves font cercle autour d'un manteau de cheminée en marbre, et à l'autre, des fauteuils en tubulure métallique sont disposés çà et là dans le coin dîner. Le luxe discret est le maître mot. Au milieu des sièges tapissés de matières agréables au toucher, comme le mohair, le velours et le cuir, du mobilier métallique ajoute du contraste. La table de salle à manger est en fer forgé, et un authentique lampadaire Giacometti orne l'entrée. Comme il sied à un couple qui partage son temps entre Londres, Moscou et New York, le mobilier de ce pied-à-terre vient du monde entier : dans le coin salon, la desserte branchée au fini laqué ultra-brillant a été achetée à Dallas, et les appliques Art déco en maillechort faites sur mesure à Istanbul. Malgré ce cosmopolitisme, ce refuge citadin invite à la détente.

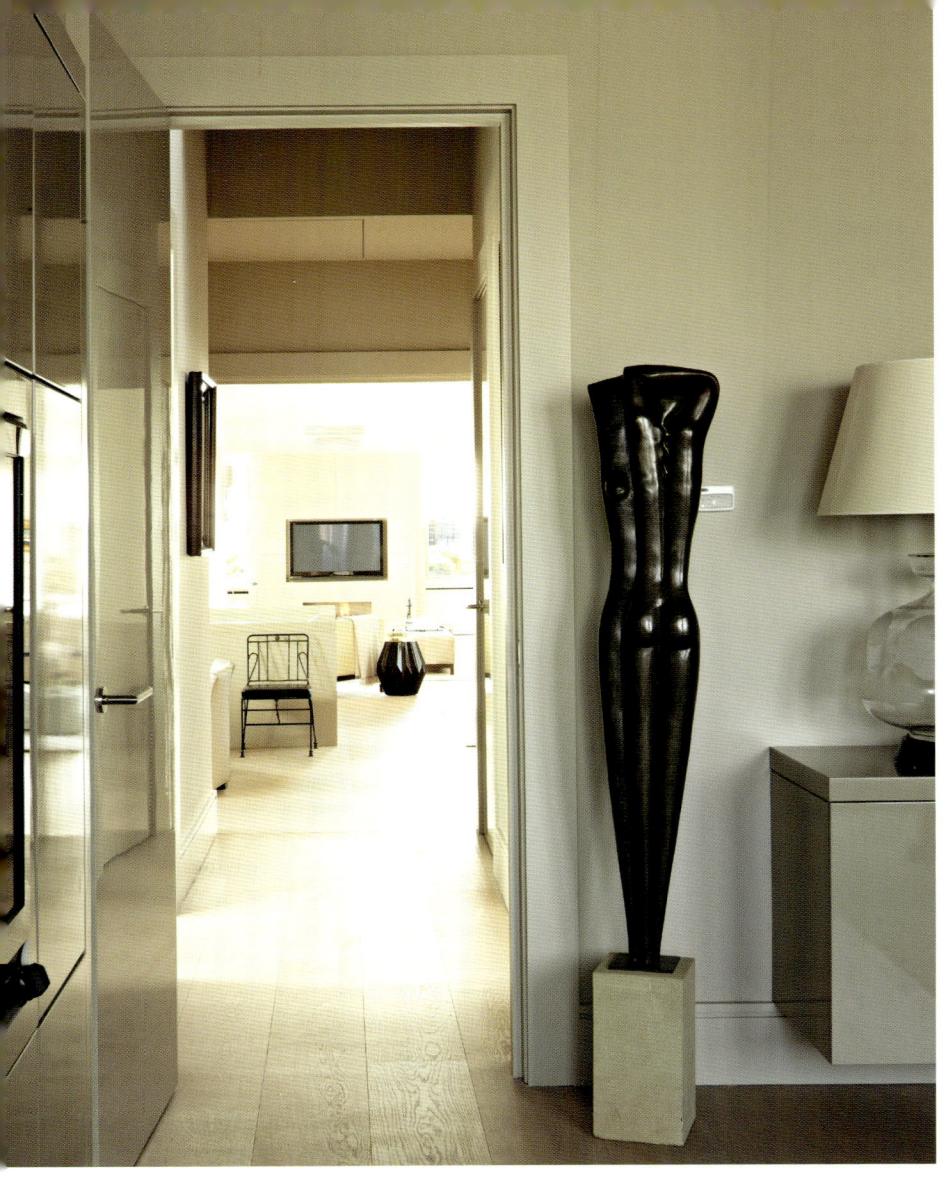

Pale, neutral tones *prevail in the sitting area, allowing the eye to focus on the carefully placed artworks. The upholstered furniture, all designed by Michael Reeves, features his signature elegant contours but with a boxy, modern twist. The sofa is in wool flannel from Michael's own collection, the Ottoman is suede, and the twin chairs are covered in luxurious mohair velvet. Michael also designed the high gloss lacquer side table. Carefully chosen sculptures dominate corners and vistas, from a bronze sculpture of a mythological animal perched on a window ledge, to the lithe sculpture standing by the master bedroom door. In a small separate library, built-in bookcases provide ample storage.*

In der Sitzecke *überwiegen helle, neutrale Farben, die den Blick auf die mit Bedacht platzierten Kunstwerke lenken. Die ausnahmslos von Michael Reeves entworfenen Polstermöbel kombinieren seine typischen, eleganten Linien mit einem kastigen, modernen Twist. Das Sofa ist mit einem Wollflanell aus Reeves' eigener Kollektion bezogen, der Polsterhocker mit Wildleder und das Sesselpaar mit luxuriösem Mohairsamt. Das Design des hochglanzlackierten Beistelltischs stammt ebenfalls von Reeves. Sorgsam ausgewählte Skulpturen dominieren Winkel und Durchblicke, vom Sagenwesen in Bronze auf einer Fensterbank bis zur schlank aufragenden Plastik neben der Schlafzimmertür. In einer kleinen separaten Bibliothek bieten Einbauregale viel Stauraum.*

Les tons neutres et pâles *du séjour permettent au regard de se concentrer sur les œuvres soigneusement disposées. Les sièges tapissés, conçus par Michael Reeves, présentent les élégants contours caractéristiques de son style avec cependant un soupçon de modernité tenant à leur forme cubique. Le sofa est recouvert d'une flanelle de laine Michael Reeves, le pouf de suédine et la paire de fauteuils d'un luxueux velours de mohair. Le designer a également créé la desserte au fini laqué ultra-brillant. Des renfoncements et des perspectives sont investis par des sculptures choisies avec soin, comme le bronze représentant un animal mythologique, juché sur un appui de fenêtre, ou la gracile sculpture à l'entrée de la chambre de maître. Dans une pièce distincte, une bibliothèque intégrée permet de stocker de nombreux livres.*

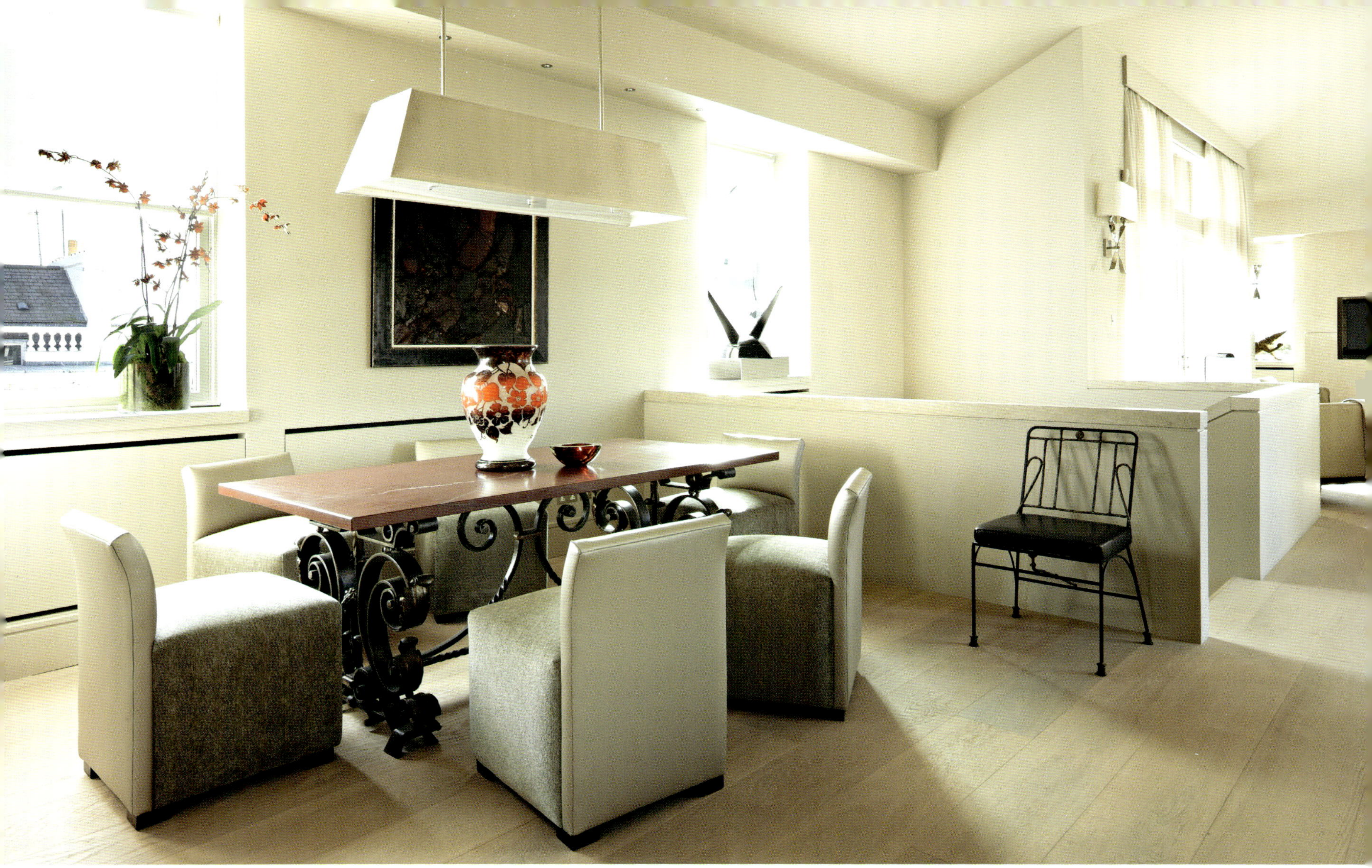
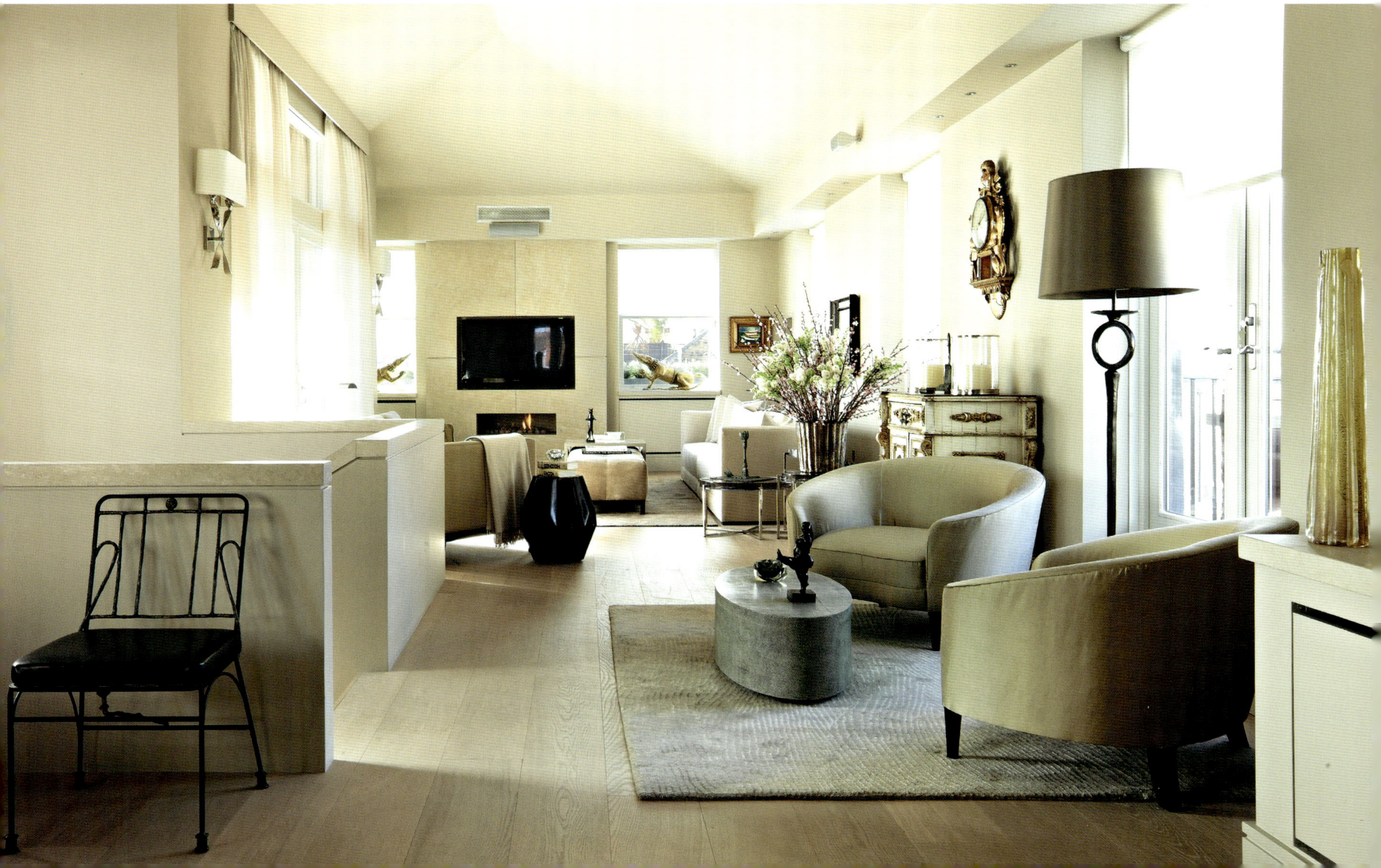

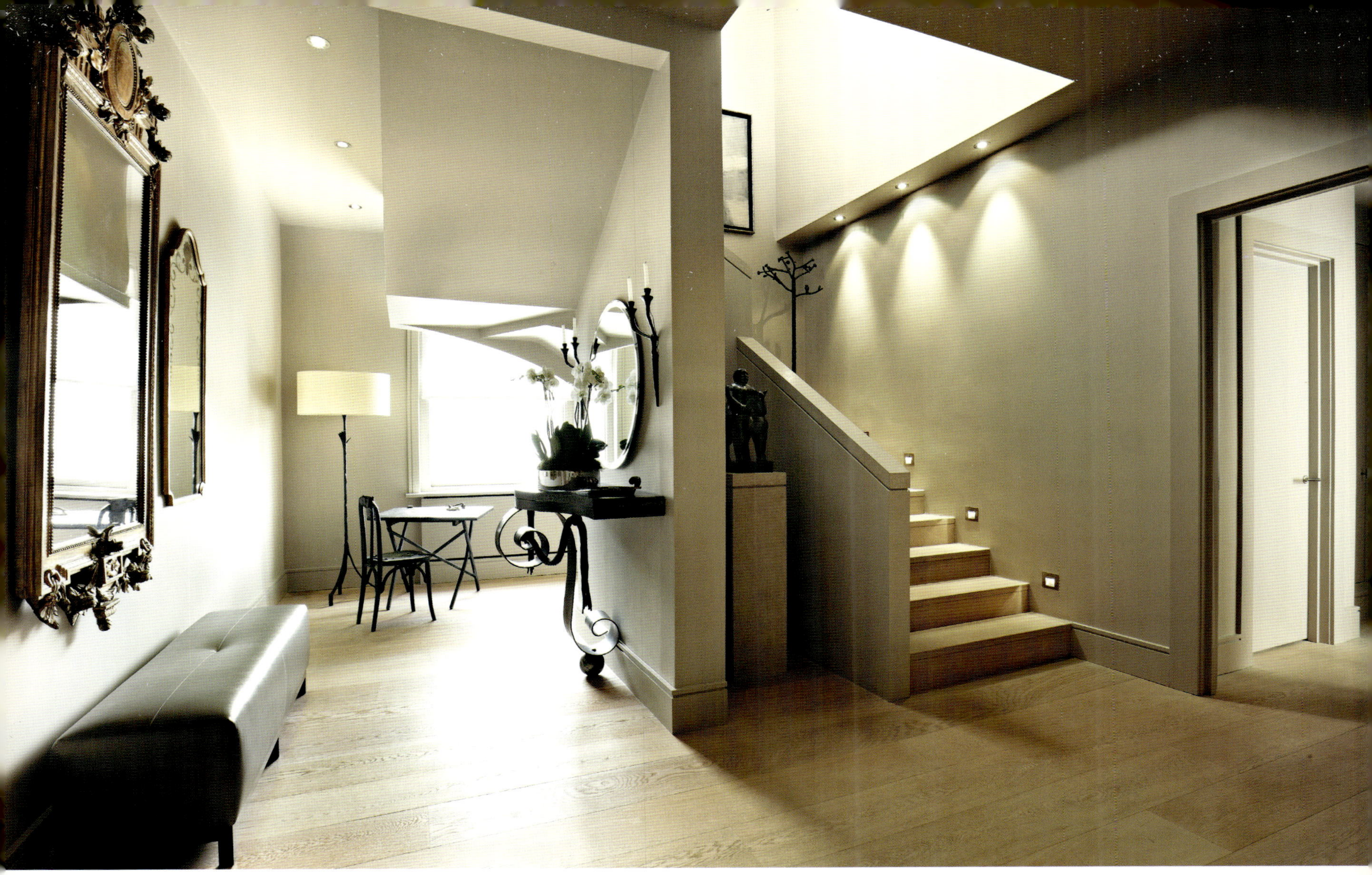

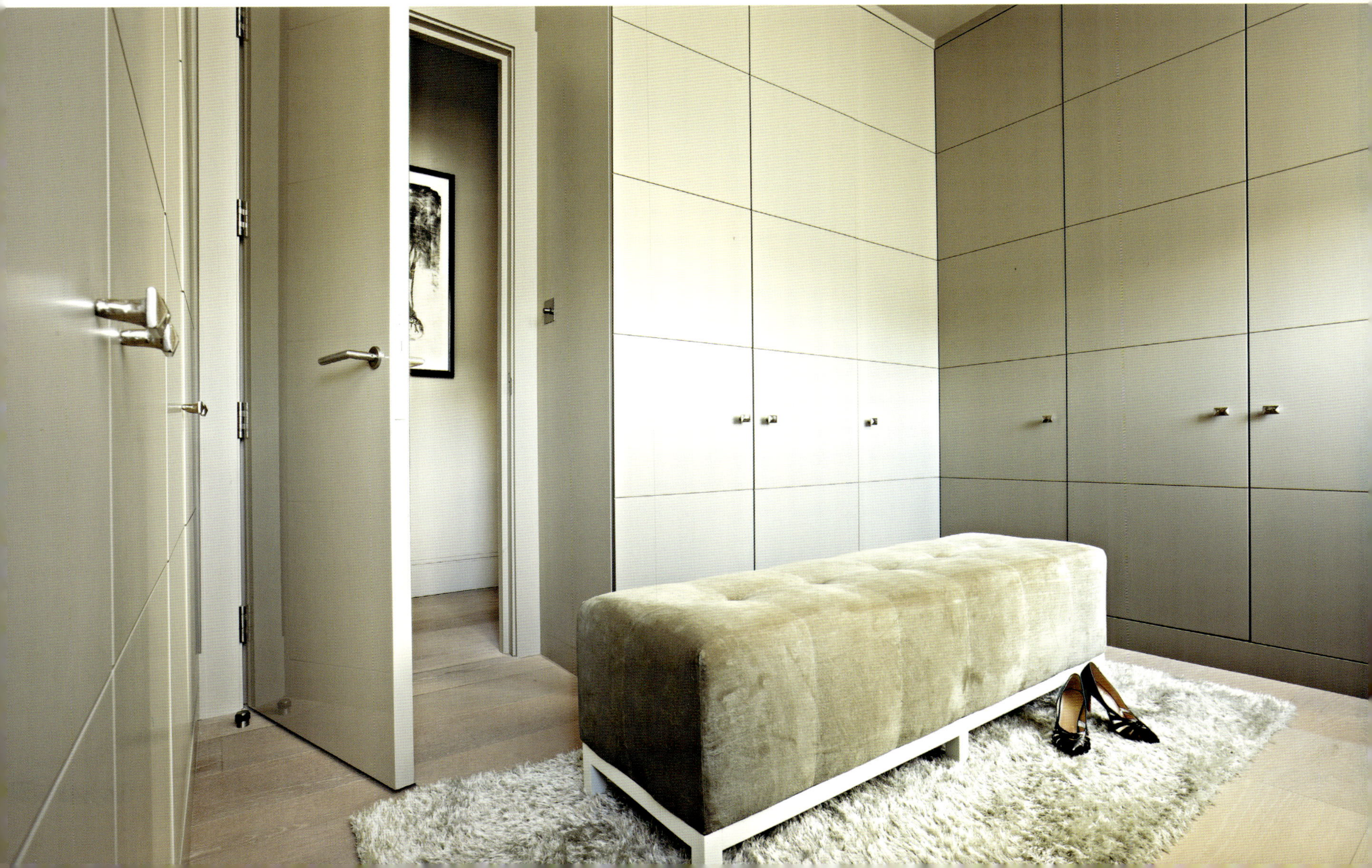

With the newly configured staircase, and wide bleached oak floorboards and biscuit-toned walls throughout, the two floors work as a cohesive whole. Each corner has its own individual mix of textures. Set around the marble-topped dining table, for example, are Michael Reeves design chairs, upholstered with a combination of faux leather for the backs and linen tweed seats. In the dressing room, lacquered wall-to-wall cupboards have been combined with a textured velvet bench. The neutral scheme extends to the kitchen, with units in pickled straight grain oak. The vintage bar chairs have been reupholstered in a metallic vinyl. In the hall, 1930s vintage French mirrors are paired with an eighteenth century Italian treasure to add sparkle and intricacy.

Mit der neuen Treppe als Bindeglied, den breiten, gebleichten Eichendielen und rundherum blassbraunen Wänden wirken die beiden Stockwerke wie ein einheitliches Ganzes. Jeder Winkel hat seinen eigenen Oberflächenmix. Um den Esstisch zum Beispiel stehen Designerstühle von Michael Reeves, gepolstert mit einer Mischung aus Kunstleder für die Lehnen und Leinentweed für die Sitzflächen. Im Ankleidezimmer wurden umlaufende Lackschränke mit einer strukturierten Samtbank kombiniert. Das neutrale Konzept macht auch vor der Küche mit ihren gerade gemaserten und gebeizten Eichenfronten nicht halt. Die Vintage-Barhocker wurden in metallisch grauem Vinyl neu gepolstert. Im Flur ergänzt ein kostbarer italienischer Spiegel aus dem 18. Jahrhundert seine französischen Pendants aus den 1930er Jahren und sorgt so für Glanz und Komplexität.

La nouvelle cage d'escalier ainsi que les larges lattes de parquet en chêne blanchi et les murs brun clair assurent la cohésion entre les deux niveaux. Les différents espaces sont caractérisés par des mélanges de textures personnalisés. Ainsi, les chaises signées Michael Reeves, qui sont disposées autour de la table à manger à plateau en marbre, ont-elles un revêtement bi-matière : simili cuir pour les dossiers, et tweed de lin pour les assises. Dans le dressing, des placards laqués occupant tous les pans de mur ont été associés à un banc recouvert de velours structuré. Les coloris neutres se retrouvent dans la cuisine, où les éléments sont en chêne à fil droit décapé. Les chaises de bar rétro ont été retapissées en vinyle métallisé. Dans le hall d'entrée, des miroirs années 1930 français flanquent une merveille italienne datant du XVIIIe, ajoutant éclat et sophistication à l'ensemble.

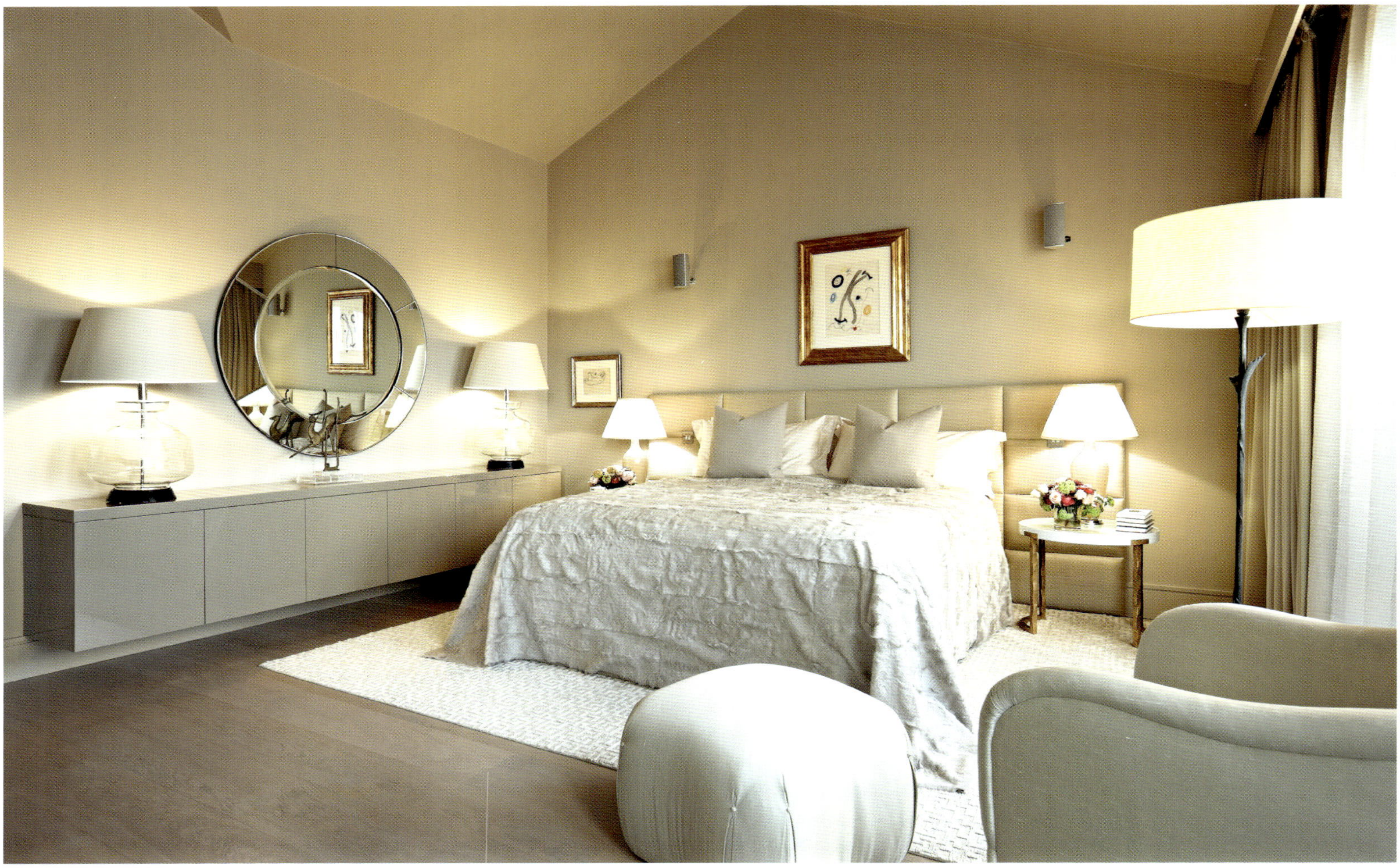

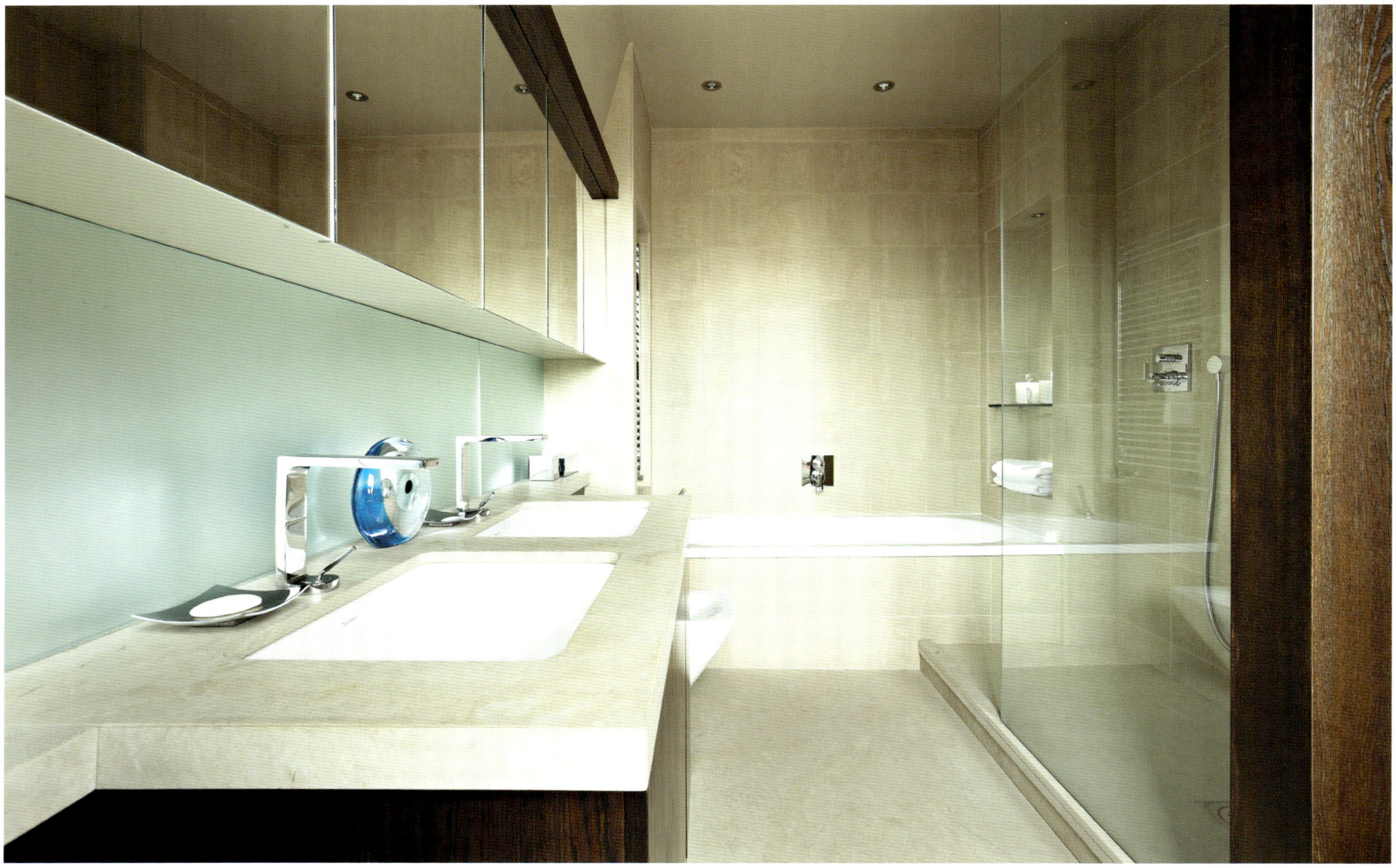

To echo the boxy visual themes in the main living space, the master bedroom features a slim, wall-mounted storage unit and upholstered headboard. In here, deep grey tones have been mixed with the wide plank bleached oak floor, but the silk and wool rug adds a soft touch. The master bathroom features double basins set into a marble surround. Up on the roof terrace, with its views of London, the tiny area has been clad in weatherproof timber and finished with a pair of zinc fountains. The textural contrasts continue up here, with an unusual mix of modern plastic chairs, ceramic stools, and vintage 1930s zinc lanterns.

Das Schlafzimmer wiederholt die kastige Optik des Wohnraummobiliars mit einem schmalen, wandhängenden Sideboard und einem gepolsterten Betthaupt. Den kräftigen Grautönen und breiten, gebleichten Eichendielen setzt der Teppich aus Seide und Wolle einen sanften Touch entgegen. Im Bad überzeugt ein marmorner Waschtisch mit Doppelwaschbecken. Die kleine Dachterrasse mit Blick über London wurde mit wetterbeständigem Holz getäfelt und mit zwei Zinkbrunnen veredelt. Selbst hier gehen die Oberflächenkontraste weiter – mit einem ungewöhnlichen Mix aus modernen Kunststoffstühlen, Keramikhockern und alten Zinklaternen aus den 1930er Jahren.

Dans la chambre de maître, les partitions du meuble de rangement mural peu profond et de la tête de lit capitonnée font écho au motif cubique de l'espace de vie principal. Dans cette pièce dominée par des tons de gris profond associés à un parquet en chêne blanchi à large lattes, le tapis en laine et soie ajoute une touche de douceur. La salle de bain attenante s'enorgueillit d'une double vasque encastrée dans un plan en marbre. La terrasse sur le toit, avec sa vue plongeante sur Londres, est un minuscule espace habillé de bois imperméabilisé et agrémenté de deux fontaines en zinc. Le contraste de structures a été poussé jusque dans ce recoin avec un mélange original de chaises en plastique modernes, de tabourets en céramique et de lanternes en zinc années 1930.

A Traveller's Touch

Like a carefully assembled outfit of clothes, the décor of a house is an expression of an owner's passions. And this beautifully collated nineteenth century home is a perfect example. Designer Monika Apponyi of MM Design had worked with her client before, so understood her needs. As a keen traveller, the owner wanted a living space where she could display treasures collected from around the world. She also likes to entertain so needed a space for dinner parties. Now, floor-to-ceiling open shelves in the drawing room provide a showcase for intriguing figurines and *objets*, while an expansive linen sofa and a pair of fauteuils, companionably pulled around a lacquered trunk, create relaxed seating. Tucked to one end of the drawing room is a dining room. With its ox-blood colour walls and an antique leather-panelled screen, newly resized to fit the wall, it presents a cosy nook for candlelit dinners. It takes a clever designer to devise a unified visual theme that allows the exoticism of each treasure to shine through. In this house, a tightly managed colour palette, majoring on ochre, deep red, and sage green, and tactile surfaces, from polished plaster to wood panelling, create a strong mood. Visual surprises abound: the cloakroom, for example, has a WC that has been dressed as a tribal throne. Despite its perfectly balanced proportions, this house was compact and Monika Apponyi's skill has been to maximise each precious centimetre. Her boldness has paid off. One bedroom has twin four-poster beds to make the space seem bigger, and on the first floor landing, a glass wall allows a vista to a terrace, creating the illusion of light and space. The owner of this gloriously detailed house may love to travel, but coming home is also a perpetual delight.

Genau wie eine sorgfältig zusammengestellte Garderobe ist auch die Ausstattung eines Hauses Ausdruck der Leidenschaften seines Besitzers. Dieses wunderschön arrangierte Wohnhaus aus dem 19. Jahrhundert ist dafür ein perfektes Beispiel. Die Designerin Monika Apponyi von MM Design hatte schon früher mit ihrer Kundin gearbeitet und kannte so deren Bedürfnisse. Als begeisterte Reisende wünschte sich die Hausbesitzerin einen Wohnraum, in dem sie ihre gesammelten Schätze aus aller Welt präsentieren konnte. Und weil sie gerne Gäste um sich hat, benötigte sie auch einen Raum für Dinnerpartys. Heute dienen raumhohe, offene Regale im Wohnzimmer als Schaukasten für allerlei faszinierende Figurinen und Kunstgegenstände. Direkt davor entstand aus einem ausladenden Leinensofa und einem Paar Lehnsesseln, die locker um eine Lacktruhe gruppiert sind, eine zwanglose Sitzgruppe. Zu einer Seite des Wohnzimmers schließt sich ein Esszimmer an. Mit seinen ochsenblutroten Wänden und einem antiken Wandschirm aus Leder, der erst der Wandgröße angepasst werden musste, eignet sich das gemütliche Eckchen perfekt für Abendessen bei Kerzenschein. Damit die Exotik jedes einzelnen Kleinods zur Geltung kommen konnte, bedurfte es einer klugen Designerin, die ein einheitliches visuelles Thema formulierte. In diesem Haus schaffen eine streng eingehaltene Farbpalette aus Ocker, Dunkelrot und Salbeigrün sowie markante Oberflächen vom Feinputz bis zur Holzvertäfelung eine feste Grundstimmung. Daneben gibt es Überraschendes: Das Toilettenbecken zum Beispiel ist wie der Thron eines Stammesfürsten herausgeputzt. Trotz der absolut ausgewogenen Proportionen hatte Apponyi es mit einem gedrungenen Haus zu tun, dem sie gekonnt jeden Quadratzentimeter wertvoller Fläche abtrotzte. Ihre Unerschrockenheit hat sich gelohnt. In einem Schlafzimmer stehen die Himmelbetten einzeln, damit es größer wirkt. Auf dem Flur im ersten Stock gewährt eine Glaswand den Ausblick auf eine Terrasse und täuscht so Licht und Weite vor. Die Besitzerin dieses herrlich detailreichen Hauses mag gerne reisen, doch auch nach Hause zu kommen, ist jedes Mal aufs Neue ein Vergnügen.

À l'instar d'une tenue vestimentaire soigneusement composée, la décoration d'une maison reflète les passions de ses occupants. Cette demeure du XIXe siècle parfaitement agencée en est la parfaite illustration. La décoratrice Monika Apponyi de MM Design connaissait les besoins de sa cliente pour avoir déjà travaillé avec elle. Celle-ci souhaitait un espace de vie dans lequel elle puisse exposer des trésors glanés au cours de ses nombreux voyages dans le monde entier, mais aussi recevoir à dîner. C'est ainsi que, dans le salon, des rayonnages sur toute la hauteur de la pièce font office de vitrines ouvertes accueillant des figurines et autres « objets » remarquables, tandis qu'un sofa d'angle et une paire de fauteuils disposés autour d'un coffre en bois vernis forment un coin conversation convivial. Dans la salle à manger située dans l'enfilade du salon, les murs couleur sang de bœuf et le paravent ancien en panneaux de cuir, retaillé récemment aux dimensions du pan de mur, créent une atmosphère chaleureuse, idéale pour les dîners aux chandelles. Il faut une grande maîtrise de l'architecture intérieure pour concevoir un thème visuel unifié qui mette en valeur l'exotisme de chacun des trésors exposés. Aussi cette maison a-t-elle une forte personnalité, qui tient à la palette de couleurs très maîtrisée, dans laquelle dominent les tons ocre, le rouge profond et le vert sauge, et à la variété des touchers, de l'enduit poli au lambris de bois. Le visiteur va de surprise en surprise : dans les toilettes, par exemple, la cuvette des WC est dissimulée dans un coffrage qui évoque un trône tribal. Malgré l'équilibre de ses proportions, la maison avait une superficie réduite. Aussi le talent de Monika Apponyi a-t-il consisté à optimiser le moindre centimètre. Son audace a été payante. Avec ses deux lits jumeaux à baldaquin, une des chambres semble plus spacieuse qu'elle ne l'est en réalité, et sur le palier du premier étage, un mur vitré avec vue sur une terrasse crée l'illusion de lumière et d'espace. La propriétaire de cette maison admirablement conçue jusque dans les moindres détails a beau adorer les voyages, elle a toujours plaisir à retrouver son chez-soi.

The décor skilfully combines English classicism with ornate, global treasures. While the hall is illuminated with Baroque wall lanterns, originally from the poles of Venetian gondolas, a first-floor terrace is filled with Oriental plants. In the drawing room, the shelves have been designed to create a focal point as visitors enter the room. While soft cream-painted and panelled shelves form a blank canvas to show off paintings, precious treasures and books, deep jewel tones have been used on the corner sofa to create an intimate, warm space. Against the dramatic backdrop of deep red walls and leather panelling, the dining chairs have been dressed in loose covers in neutral linen.

Die Dekoration verknüpft die kunstvollen Schätze aus aller Welt geschickt mit dem englischen Klassizismus. Barocke Wandlaternen, die ursprünglich von venezianischen Gondeln stammen, erhellen den Eingangsbereich, orientalische Pflanzen bevölkern eine Terrasse im ersten Stock. Die Regalwände im Wohnzimmer sollen eintretenden Besuchern als Blickfang dienen. Während die rückseitig vertäfelten, eierschalenfarbenen Regale den Gemälden, kostbaren Kleinoden und Büchern eine neutrale Bühne bieten, wurden für das Ecksofa dunkle Edelsteintöne verwendet, um einen warmen, intimen Raum zu schaffen. Vor der dramatischen Kulisse aus ledernem Wandschirm und tiefroten Wänden überraschen die Esszimmerstühle mit neutralen Leinenhussen.

La décoration marie admirablement classicisme anglais et trésors ouvragés du monde entier. Tandis que le hall est éclairé par des appliques réalisées à partir de lanternes baroques vénitiennes, une terrasse au premier étage croule sous des plantes exotiques. Dans le salon, les étagères ont été conçues pour attirer le regard du visiteur franchissant le seuil de la pièce. Peints en coquille d'œuf, les rayonnages et les lambris forment une toile de fond vierge sur laquelle se détachent tableaux, objets précieux et livres, tandis qu'il émane chaleur et intimité des tons rubis du sofa d'angle. Dans leurs amples housses en lin nature, les chaises de la salle à manger se détachent sur les spectaculaires murs rouge profond et panneaux recouverts de cuir.

To play up the eclectic, beautiful artefacts, Monika Apponyi has selected a range of fabrics, from a chic multi-coloured striped silk in the drawing room to casual gingham for the breakfast room banquette. Each one of the bedrooms and bathrooms has a contrasting theme. One spare bedroom, with twin four-poster beds, is in soothing duck egg blue, while the master bedroom is Venetian in mood, featuring Fortuny-cotton dressed walls. The designer has used light and dark to vary the decorative tone from room to room. A heavily textured bamboo wallpaper looks masculine and exotic in the cloakroom and creates the perfect backdrop to the African tribal treasures, while the pale polished plaster walls in the master bathroom exude luxury. Water cascades from a generous spout, sourced from an Italian garden centre.

Mit einer Reihe verschiedener Stoffe, von der elegant gestreiften mehrfarbigen Seide im Wohnzimmer bis zum legeren Gingham für die Sitzbank im Frühstücksraum, ist es Monika Apponyi gelungen, die bunte Ansammlung von schönen Artefakten hervorzuheben. Alle Schlafzimmer und Bäder haben ein eigenes Thema. Ein ungenutzter Schlafraum mit zwei Himmelbetten wurde in Enteneiblau gestaltet, das Hauptschlafzimmer, dessen Wände mit Fortuny-Baumwolle bekleidet sind, erinnert an Venedig. Mit Hell-Dunkel-Kontrasten variierte die Designerin die dekorative

Note von Raum zu Raum. Eine kräftige Strukturtapete mit Bambusoptik in der Toilette wirkt nicht nur maskulin und exotisch, sondern bildet auch den perfekten Hintergrund für die im Raum versammelten afrikanischen Schätze. Die hellen, geschliffenen Feinputzwände im Bad dagegen verströmen einen Hauch von Luxus. Der großzügige Speier stammt aus einem italienischen Gartencenter.

Pour magnifier les splendides artéfacts éclectiques, Monika Apponyi a joué sur une palette de tissus allant de l'élégante soie à rayures multicolores dans le salon au vichy rustique de la banquette dans la pièce affectée au « breakfast ». Les chambres et les salles de bain ont chacune un style différent : une chambre d'amis, équipée de lits jumeaux à baldaquin, est dans un bleu-gris œuf de cane reposant pour l'œil, tandis que la chambre de maître est d'inspiration vénitienne, avec des murs tendus de coton Fortuny. La décoratrice a joué sur l'opposition entre clair et obscur pour imprimer à chaque pièce une ambiance particulière. Dans les toilettes, un papier peint fortement structuré en bambou introduit une note masculine et exotique, tout en créant le cadre idéal pour de l'art premier africain, tandis que les murs à enduit lisse et pâle exsudent le luxe. L'eau coule en cascade par un bec de fontaine provenant d'une jardinerie italienne.

Salon Chic

Christophe Gollut has always championed timeless, thoughtful interior design and at his beautifully executed first floor apartment, he practises what he preaches. "I remodelled everything 22 years ago and have not changed it since," he says. Here are the bones for the perfect gentleman's abode: tall ceilings, original cornices and expansive proportions. A visitor will immediately guess at Christophe's passion for nineteenth century antiques, English and continental. He also has a knack for combining a mood of easy elegance with the formality of a European salon. In the drawing room, artist's paint effects have been used to create a subdued backdrop for the antiques: crackled paintwork the colour of eggshell for the woodwork, a lightly sponged aqua on walls. Textiles have been consciously layered to create the mood of an interior evolved over time, a look that has become Christophe's trademark. In keeping with this aesthetic, there is a mix of family heirlooms and antiques. The dining chairs, still covered in their original 1880 velour de Genes upholstery, belonged to his grandparents and by contrast, the Turkish antique rug in the dining room was bought from Christie's. Yet there are simple decorative touches: on the bedroom floor is scented rush matting from Suffolk, walls are lined to resemble a campaign room and there are plain silk curtains. Christophe enjoys manipulating ambience. With its muted colours and ruched Italian silk blinds, the drawing room is sunny, yet the deep reds and mahogany shades in the dining room provide a swift mood gear change. Every home has its "wow" factor, and in Christophe's, it is the 1747 portrait of the Irish girl. "It is made special by the red shoes," comments Christophe with a gimlet eye for detail. And the details throughout this apartment make the whole space sing.

Christophe Gollut war schon immer ein Meister der durchdachten, zeitlosen Raumgestaltung. In seiner eigenen, im ersten Stock gelegenen Londoner Wohnung hat er seine Prinzipien auf fantastische Weise umgesetzt. „Vor 22 Jahren habe ich alles komplett umgestaltet und seitdem nicht mehr verändert", erklärt er. Der Rahmen ist perfekt für den Wohnsitz eines Gentlemans: hohe Decken, alter Stuck und große Räume. Sofort sticht jedem Besucher Golluts Leidenschaft für englische und kontinentaleuropäische Antiquitäten aus dem 19. Jahrhundert ins Auge – und auch sein Talent, unbeschwerte Eleganz mit der Förmlichkeit eines europäischen Salons zu kombinieren. Im Wohnzimmer haben künstlerische Farbeffekte – eierschalenfarbener Reißlack für die Hölzer, dezente Schwammtechnik in grünlichem Aquamarin an den Wänden – einen zurückhaltenden Hintergrund für die Antiquitäten geschaffen. Lagen von Stoffen sollen bewusst den Eindruck eines mit der Zeit gewachsenen Interieurs erwecken – ein Look, der zu Golluts Markenzeichen geworden ist. Zu dieser Ästhetik passen die vielen verschiedenen Familienerbstücke und Antiquitäten. Die Esszimmerstühle mit den original Velours-de-Gênes-Bezügen von 1880 gehörten Golluts Großeltern, der antike türkische Teppich im Wohnzimmer dagegen stammt von Christie's. Daneben fallen die einfachen dekorativen Akzente auf: ein Bastteppich aus Suffolk, gepolsterte Wände wie in einem Wahlkampfbüro und schlichte Seidenvorhänge im Schlafzimmer. Gollut liebt die atmosphärischen Gegensätze. Während das Wohnzimmer mit seinen gedeckten Farben und den gerüschten italienischen Seidenrollos von der Sonne verwöhnt wird, sorgen die dunklen Rot- und Mahagonitöne im angrenzenden Esszimmer für einen abrupten Stimmungswechsel. Den „Wow"-Faktor, der in keinem Zuhause fehlen darf, bildet bei Gollut das Porträt eines irischen Mädchens von 1747. „Seine Besonderheit sind die roten Schuhe", sagt der Hausherr mit dem scharfen Blick für Details. Und es sind die Details in der gesamten Wohnung, die diese Räume zum Schwingen bringen.

Christophe Gollut s'est toujours fait le chantre d'une décoration d'intérieur intemporelle et élaborée, un principe mis en pratique dans ce magnifique appartement situé au premier étage. « J'ai tout remodelé il y a 22 ans et je n'ai rien changé depuis », précise-t-il. Et l'on y trouve les éléments clés de la demeure du parfait gentleman : hauts plafonds, corniches d'origine et vastes proportions. Les visiteurs noteront immédiatement sa passion pour les antiquités XVIIIe d'Angleterre et du reste de l'Europe. Mais il possède également un don pour combiner une élégance décontractée au formalisme d'un séjour à l'européenne. Dans le salon, l'artiste s'est servi d'effets de teintes comme d'un écrin discret pour les antiquités : peintures craquelées, couleur coquille d'œuf pour les boiseries et vert d'eau appliqué délicatement à l'éponge aux murs. Les textiles ont été délibérément superposés pour suggérer un intérieur ayant évolué au fil du temps, un look qui est devenu la marque de fabrique de Christophe Gollut. Dans le droit fil de cette esthétique, on trouve un mélange de souvenirs de famille et d'antiquités. Dans la salle à manger, les chaises encore revêtues de leur velours de Gênes 1880 d'origine et qui avaient appartenu à ses grands-parents s'opposent au tapis turc ancien acheté chez Christie's. On trouve aussi des touches décoratives simples : dans la chambre, des tapis en joncs odorants du Suffolk, des murs habillés d'imprimés campagnards et des rideaux de soie pure. Christophe Gollut aime jouer avec l'ambiance : on passe sans transition du salon clair avec ses couleurs sourdes et ses stores italiens de soie froncés aux rouges profonds et aux nuances d'acajou de la salle à manger. Chaque intérieur a son « détail qui frappe », et dans celui de Christophe Gollut, c'est le portrait de 1747 d'une jeune fille irlandaise. « Ce qui le rend si particulier, ce sont les chaussures rouges » commente Christophe Gollut avec son regard exercé pour le détail. Et ce sont les détails clairsemés dans l'appartement qui font chanter tout l'espace.

A glimpse into the drawing room reveals a Breche Louis XVI fireplace, which was installed by Christophe to suit the prevailing architecture. The mahogany dining table is Empire French with a grey marble top, and the walls are lined with fabric. Although the mood is deliberately intimate in the dining room, a pelmet, originally from an old club in St James's, filters the daylight. Precious finds cluster on console tables, including an unusual globe lamp, dated 1900, and a selection of terracotta finish plaster or marble pots, Grand Tour souvenirs. There is a deliberate mix of fine textiles in the drawing room, including a Fortuny fabric on the Duchesse Brisee Louis XVI chair in the window.

Im Wohnzimmer fällt der erste Blick auf den Louis-seize-Kamin aus Brèche-Marmor, den Gollut passend zur vorherrschenden Architektur einbauen ließ. Der Mahagoni-Esstisch mit grauer Marmorplatte stammt aus dem französischen Empire, die Wände sind mit Textiltapeten bespannt. Trotz der ohnehin schon gewollt intimen Atmosphäre im Esszimmer filtert eine Schabracke, die ursprünglich in einem alten Klub im Londoner Stadtteil St. James's hing, noch zusätzlich das Tageslicht. Kostbare Fundstücke drängen sich auf Konsolentischen, darunter eine ungewöhnliche Globuslampe von 1900 und eine Sammlung von Gips- und Marmorgefäßen mit Terrakotta-Finish, Souvenirs von der Grand Tour. Zu der bewusst gewählten Mixtur von edlen Stoffen im Wohnzimmer gehört auch ein Fortuny-Stoff, mit dem die gebrochene Louis-seize-Chaiselongue am Fenster bezogen ist.

Un regard dans le salon révèle une cheminée Louis XVI en marbre brèche installée par l'artiste pour respecter l'architecture dominante. La table d'acajou style Empire de la salle à manger porte un plateau en marbre gris et les murs sont tendus de tissu. L'ambiance est délibérément feutrée dans la salle à manger, une cantonnière issue d'un vieux club de St James's filtrant la lumière du jour. Les consoles croulent sous les objets précieux, notamment une lampe globe singulière, datant de 1900, et un assortiment de récipients en plâtre ou en marbre finition terre cuite, souvenirs de Grand Tour. Le salon abrite un mélange délibéré de textiles précieux, notamment le Fortuny de la duchesse brisée Louis XVI face à la fenêtre.

Each exquisite item in the drawing room has been artfully arranged to give it maximum attention. On a console, Christophe has combined a bust by a Renaissance artist, Francesco de Laurana, and one of a pair of Regency terracotta pots, mounted as lamps. In the bedroom, Biedermeier furniture sets a masculine, elegant tone. The Art Deco wardrobe is in maple and ebony, as is the desk, and the Swiss walnut bed, with black painted details, is placed centrally to dominate the space. In the bathroom, the original stained glass window is complemented by faux marble, painted by an artist to resemble a pattern of Siena and Portoro. In keeping with Christophe's love of the timeless, and the antique, all the bathroom fittings are reclaimed.

Das kunstvolle Arrangement der Kostbarkeiten im Wohnzimmer garantiert jeder einzelnen von ihnen ungeteilte Aufmerksamkeit. Auf einer Konsole hat Gollut eine Büste aus der Hand des Renaissancekünstlers Francesco de Laurana mit zwei Regency-Vasenleuchten aus Terrakotta kombiniert. Im Schlafzimmer setzt das Biedermeier-Mobiliar eine elegante männliche Note. Der Art-déco-Kleiderschrank wurde wie der Sekretär aus Ahorn und Ebenholz gefertigt, das mit schwarzen Farbdetails abgesetzte Schweizer Walnussbett so zentral platziert, dass es den Raum dominiert. Im Bad imitiert falscher Marmor, von Künstlerhand gemalt, ein Muster aus Siena- und Portoro-Marmor und ergänzt so die erhaltenen Buntglasfenster. Golluts Vorliebe für Zeitloses und Antikes entsprechend, stammen sämtliche Badezimmerarmaturen aus Originalbeständen.

Chaque article précieux du salon a été artistiquement disposé pour qu'il recueille le maximum d'attention. Sur une console, Christophe Gollut a réuni un buste de Francesco Laurana, artiste de la Renaissance, et l'un des deux récipients en terre cuite Regency transformés en lampes. Dans la chambre, un mobilier Biedermeier donne un ton masculin élégant. L'armoire Art Déco est en érable et en ébène, comme le bureau, et le lit suisse en noyer, avec ses ornements noirs peints, est placé au centre pour dominer l'espace. Dans la salle de bain, la verrière d'origine est rehaussée par du faux marbre imitant les marbres de Sienne et de Portoro. Conformément à l'amour de Christophe Gollut pour l'intemporel et l'ancien, tous les éléments de la salle de bain sont de récupération.

A Happy Compromise

A remarkable lightness of touch defines this pretty London townhouse, owned by antiques dealers, Marc and Heather Weaver. The nineteenth century property has been their family home for over 20 years, and is filled with "pieces that we love". Marc and his brother, Kevin, run *Guinevere Antiques* in Chelsea, which was originally set up by their mother, Genevieve Weaver, in 1963. Today, the shop remains a mecca for those in search of eclectic, decorative antiques. Marc's home is similarly filled with unusual pieces, often brought back from travels abroad: the early twentieth century portrait of a fencer, for example, was a chance buy in Belgium. In the drawing room, the simplicity of off-white walls and waxed oil parquet floor belies careful thought. After the house was remodelled in 2000, Marc recalls how he and Heather lived with just a pair of armchairs for two months, whilst deciding how to decorate. The décor had to blend with the muted tones of Marc's selection of carved ivory heads, and Heather's collection of Val Saint Lambert Belgian crystal. The result is a happy compromise. With the boldness of experience, Marc and Heather have mixed up furniture styles with flair. The dining room is dominated with a 1960s glass and steel dining table by American furniture designer and artist Paul Evans, while in the drawing room, an Anglo Indian chaise longue, originally caned, has been re-covered in chic pony skin. In the kitchen, the couple got a specialist to build units to order. As inspiration, they chose to copy a 1940s American metal desk: the kitchen units are in aged lacquered steel with brass handles. "It's not complicated or clever, but it works," says Marc. Just like the rest of the house, the design melds inspiration from the past with today's need for easy, practical living.

Eine bemerkenswerte Leichtigkeit macht den Charme dieses hübschen Londoner Stadthauses aus dem 19. Jahrhundert aus. Es wird seit über 20 Jahren von den Antiquitätenhändlern Marc und Heather Weaver bewohnt und steckt voller „Stücke, die wir lieben". Marc Weaver und sein Bruder Kevin betreiben das Antiquitätengeschäft *Guinevere Antiques* in Chelsea, das 1963 von ihrer Mutter, Genevieve Weaver, gegründet wurde und sich zu einem Mekka für Liebhaber verschiedenster dekorativer Antiquitäten entwickelt hat. Wie das Geschäft ist Marc Weavers Zuhause angefüllt mit ungewöhnlichen, häufig auf Reisen erworbenen Stücken. Das Porträt eines Fechters aus dem frühen 20. Jahrhundert beispielsweise ist ein Zufallskauf aus Belgien. Im Wohnzimmer täuschen die schlichten, gebrochen weißen Wände und der geölte und gewachste Parkettfußboden über eine sorgfältige Planung hinweg. Nach dem Umbau des Hauses im Jahr 2000, erinnert sich Marc Weaver, haben Helen und er zwei Monate lang nur mit einem Paar Sesseln gewohnt, während sie über die Ausstattung nachdachten. Das Dekor sollte sich mit den gedeckten Tönen von Marcs Kollektion von Elfenbeinköpfen und mit Heathers Kristallsammlung aus der belgischen Kristallerie Val Saint Lambert verbinden. Das Ergebnis ist ein überaus geglückter Kompromiss. Mit dem Mut der Erfahrung und viel Fingerspitzengefühl kombinierten die Weavers unterschiedliche Möbelstile. Das Esszimmer wird von einem 1960er-Jahre-Esstisch des amerikanischen Möbeldesigners und Künstlers Paul Evans aus Glas und Stahl beherrscht, im Wohnzimmer wurde das Originalgeflecht der anglo-indischen Chaiselongue durch exklusives Ponyfell ersetzt. Für die Kücheneinbauten beschäftigte das Paar einen Spezialisten, der nach dem Vorbild eines amerikanischen Metalltischs aus den 1940er Jahren Fronten aus gealtertem und lackiertem Stahl mit Messinggriffen anfertigte. „Das ist nicht kompliziert oder smart, aber es funktioniert", sagt Marc Weaver. So wie der Rest des Hauses verbindet das Küchendesign Inspirationen aus der Vergangenheit mit dem heutigen Wunsch nach bequemen, praktischen Wohnlösungen.

Propriété du couple d'antiquaires Marc et Heather Weaver, cette jolie maison de ville est empreinte d'une grande délicatesse. Cette demeure du XIXᵉ, foyer du couple depuis plus de 20 ans, abonde en « objets qu'ils aiment ». Marc a repris en outre avec son frère Kevin *Guinevere Antiques*. Créé à Chelsea en 1963 par leur mère Genevieve Weaver, ce magasin est encore une caverne d'Ali Baba pour ceux qui recherchent des antiquités éclectiques et décoratives. La maison de Marc est elle aussi remplie d'objets originaux, souvent ramenés de ses voyages à l'étranger : le portrait d'un escrimeur du début du XXᵉ, par exemple, est un achat fait par hasard en Belgique. Dans le salon, la simplicité des murs blanc cassé et du parquet huilé montrent que le couple a mûrement réfléchi à l'harmonie des couleurs. Marc se souvient comment, après la rénovation de la maison en 2000, lui et Heather ont vécu deux mois avec seulement quelques fauteuils, le temps de décider de la future décoration. Le décor devait se marier avec les teintes neutres des têtes en ivoire sculpté de Marc et, pour Heather, de sa collection d'articles provenant des cristalleries belges du Val Saint-Lambert. Le résultat est un heureux compromis. Avec l'audace que donne l'expérience, Marc et Heather ont combiné les styles de mobilier avec goût. La pièce maîtresse de la salle à manger est une table en verre et acier des années 1960 réalisée par le créateur de mobilier et artiste américain Paul Evans. Dans le salon, une méridienne anglo-indienne, cannée à l'origine, a été tendue d'un élégant cuir de poney. Pour les éléments de la cuisine, le couple a passé commande à un cuisiniste et s'est inspiré d'un bureau métallique américain des années 1940 : les éléments sont donc en acier laqué vieilli avec des poignées en laiton. « Ce n'est ni compliqué ni astucieux, mais cela fonctionne », précise Marc. Comme pour le reste de la maison, le design mêle l'inspiration du passé et les impératifs de simplicité et de commodité imposés par la vie moderne.

In the drawing room, antique French shutters have been resized to fit the windows. A vellum-covered trunk, with reconditioned brass fittings, sits in front of a pair of English early nineteenth century curule chairs. On the floor is a Tibetan "tiger" rug from the 1930s. Heather's collection of Val Saint Lambert crystal from the 1940s and 1950s creates a splash of colour in both alcoves. This is a home where beauty conceals the everyday: a Baroque-style late seventeenth century chest, carved and painted, holds outdoor gear and dog leads. Marc says that while most children are given toys for Christmas, his antiques dealer mother gave him carved ivory heads. In the drawing room, his now prized collection sits on a marble-topped console of European origin, bought in Maine, USA.

Im Wohnzimmer wurden die alten französischen Fensterläden den Maßen der Fenster angepasst. Vor einem Paar kurulischer Stühle aus England, frühes 19. Jahrhundert, steht eine Truhe mit Pergamentbezug und aufgearbeiteten Messingbeschlägen. Der tibetanische „Tiger-Teppich" stammt aus den 1930er Jahren. Heather Weavers 1940er- und 1950er-Jahre-Kristallsammlung von Val Saint Lambert sorgt in zwei Regalnischen für Farbtupfer. Alltägliches verschwindet in diesem

Zuhause hinter schönen Fassaden: In einer barocken Kommode aus dem späten 17. Jahrhundert sind Wetterkleidung und Hundeleinen verstaut. Marc Weaver berichtet, er habe von seiner mit Antiquitäten handelnden Mutter zu Weihnachten nicht wie andere Kinder Spielzeug bekommen, sondern geschnitzte Elfenbeinköpfe. Die von ihm inzwischen sehr geschätzte Sammlung steht im Wohnzimmer auf einer in Maine gekauften Konsole europäischer Herkunft mit Marmorplatte.

Dans le salon, d'anciens volets d'intérieur à persiennes ont été redimensionnés à la taille des fenêtres. Une malle tendue de vélin, à fermetures en laiton restaurées, fait face à deux fauteuils anglais de style Empire début XIXᵉ. Sur le sol est étendu un tapis « tigre » tibétain des années 1930. Les renforcements semblent éclaboussés de couleurs par la collection de cristallerie du Val Saint-Lambert des années 1940 et 1950. Dans cette demeure, la beauté dissimule le quotidien : un coffre fin XVIIᵉ de style baroque, sculpté et peint, renferme des équipements de plein air et des laisses pour chien. Marc dit que si l'on offre à presque tous les enfants des jouets à Noël, son antiquaire de mère lui offrait des têtes en ivoire sculpté. Sa collection désormais très prisée est exposée dans le salon, sur une console à plateau de marbre venue d'Europe et achetée dans le Maine, aux États-Unis.

The new open plan kitchen / dining room *was created when the house was remodelled, as the original kitchen and dining room to the rear had felt cramped. Now, sunlight filters through two skylights close to the dining table and above the island unit, and a slate floor in variegated greys is teamed with warm, yellow-toned walls. The owners have employed a mix of reflective surfaces to enhance light flow and create a dash of glamour. A mirrored 1930s chest of drawers has been combined with a 1940s drinks cabinet, and the Paul Evans table is in glass and steel. The 1960s black leather chairs came from Marc's childhood home.*

Der neue Essbereich mit offener Küche *wurde im Zuge der Umgestaltung des Hauses geschaffen, weil die alten, nach hinten gelegenen Räume sich beengt angefühlt hatten. Heute fällt Sonnenlicht durch zwei Oberlichter in der Nähe des Esstischs und über der Kücheninsel in den Raum, und der Schieferplattenboden in unterschiedlichen Grautönen passt gut zu den warmen, gelblich gestrichenen Wänden. Ein Mix aus reflektierenden Oberflächen macht die Räume heller und sorgt*

für eine Spur von Glamour. Eine verspiegelte Schubladenkommode aus den 1930er Jahren wurde mit einem Barschrank aus den 1940er Jahren kombiniert, und der Esstisch von Paul Evans glänzt in Glas und Stahl. Die schwarzen 1960er-Jahre-Lederfreischwinger standen schon in Marc Weavers Elternhaus.

La nouvelle cuisine / salle à manger *a été créée lors de la rénovation, les pièces d'origine situées à l'arrière étant apparues trop exiguës. Désormais, la lumière entre par les lucarnes situées près de la table à manger et à l'aplomb de l'îlot de cuisine. Un sol en ardoise mêlant diverses nuances de gris est associé à des murs aux chaleureuses teintes jaunes. Les propriétaires ont utilisé une combinaison de surfaces réfléchissantes pour améliorer la circulation de la lumière et créer une pointe glamour. À la commode en miroir des années 1930 répond un bar des années 1940. La table en verre et en acier est signée Paul Evans. Enfin, les chaises en cuir noir des années 1960 proviennent de la maison d'enfance de Marc.*

In the master bathroom, *Marc and Heather have enjoyed playing with texture. They have flouted convention to create an unusual decorative effect, laying wood on the floor and tiling the walls with large format slate tiles. Above the vanity unit hangs a 1930s French Venetian style mirror. The master bedroom is dominated by an imposing Anglo Indian four-poster bed and a campaign chest of drawers, both pieces bought whilst the couple were on a trip to India. The Italian painting is eighteenth century. In the kitchen, aged lacquered steel units with brass handles and an island unit worktop in timber create robust surfaces. Marc has had a pair of antique cast iron window frames mirrored: fixed against one wall, they make the tiny terraced garden seem bigger.*

In ihrem Badezimmer *entwickelten Marc und Heather Weaver Spaß am Spiel mit den Oberflächen. Anders als üblich erzielten sie mit einem Fußboden aus Holz und großformatigen Schieferfliesen an den Wänden eine ausgefallene dekorative Wirkung. Über dem Waschtisch hängt ein französischer 1930er-Jahre-Spiegel im venezianischen Stil. Im Schlafzimmer dominieren ein stattliches anglo-indisches Himmelbett und eine Feldkommode. Beide Möbelstücke haben die Weavers von einer Indienreise mitgebracht. Das italienische Ölgemälde datiert aus dem 18.*

Jahrhundert. In der Küche bilden Fronten aus gealtertem und lackiertem Stahl mit Messinggriffen und eine Holzarbeitsplatte auf der Kücheninsel robuste Oberflächen. In zwei antike gusseiserne Sprossenrahmen hat Marc Weaver Spiegel einsetzen lassen. An die Außenwand montiert, lassen sie den winzigen Garten mit Terrasse größer wirken.

Dans la salle de bain de maître, *Marc et Heather ont aimé jouer avec les textures. Bafouant les conventions pour créer un effet décoratif original, ils ont utilisé du bois sur le sol et des plaques en ardoise grand format aux murs. Au-dessus du meuble sous vasque, le miroir français de style vénitien date des années 1930. Dans la chambre de maître, l'espace est marqué par un imposant lit à colonnes anglo-indien et une commode rustique, tous deux achetés par le couple lors d'un voyage en Inde. Le tableau est une peinture italienne du XVIIIe. Dans la cuisine, les éléments en acier laqué vieilli à poignées en laiton et le dessus en bois de l'îlot créent de solides surfaces. Marc a fait monter des miroirs sur de vieux cadres de fenêtre en fer forgé : fixés au mur, ils donnent l'illusion de profondeur dans le petit jardin dallé.*

Art of Living

The owners of this early twentieth century apartment commissioned Rabih Hage to transform it into a refined, sophisticated home. The clients wanted impeccable, comfortable entertaining spaces, yet also needed a practical, multi-functional living zone. As an acclaimed architect and interior designer, Rabih has forged a reputation for creating chic interiors: spaces that are visually arresting, yet devised with a deeply intelligent approach to design. In this apartment, merging the aesthetic sensitivity of his clients with functionality, Rabih has opened up the reception room and dining room to create a single entertaining zone, one area reserved as a library corner. The layout maximises the space, yet also provides tempting vistas. The original grand panelling and mouldings have been retained, and a palette of flax, cream and chocolate adds a modern vibe. Rabih combines the simple with the complex, so while furniture silhouettes are elongated and linear, furnishings are an indulgent combination of silks, linen, velvet and cotton, pepped up with the occasional textural surprise. The bespoke dining chairs are an intriguing contrast of leather and natural raffia fabric. In every space Rabih includes contemporary art hand-picked to reflect his client's personality. Thus, in the public entertaining rooms, walls bristle with eye-popping modern pieces. Above the drawing room sofa hangs a painting by Aki Kuroda, while François Bard's dog painting dominates the dining zone. Ambience matters in a lateral living space, so much of the lighting here has been custom-designed by Rabih, including wall lights in steel with an antique bronze finish. Tactile surfaces prevail. Curtains are silk, while underfoot there is a polished parquet floor, overlaid with handwoven wool and silk rugs in bespoke designs. With such attention to detail, it is no wonder that Rabih hails this apartment a "special project". It is also a hymn to harmonious living.

Die Eigentümer dieser Wohnung aus dem frühen 20. Jahrhundert erteilten Rabih Hage den Auftrag, die Räume in ein niveauvolles und kultiviertes Zuhause zu verwandeln. Die Kunden wünschten sich einerseits makellose, behagliche Gesellschaftsräume, andererseits einen praktischen, multifunktionalen Wohnbereich. Als gefeierter Architekt und Inneneinrichter hat sich Hage mit mondänen Interieurs einen Namen gemacht – Entwürfen, die das Auge fesseln und dabei einen hochintelligenten Designansatz verfolgen. In dieser Wohnung verband er das ästhetische Feingefühl seiner Auftraggeber mit Funktionalität. Empfangs- und Esszimmer bilden einen offenen Bewirtungsbereich, in dem eine Ecke für die Bibliothek reserviert ist. Der Grundriss ermöglicht eine optimale Nutzung des vorhandenen Raums und eröffnet verlockende Sichtachsen. Die deckenhohen Originalpaneele und Stuckarbeiten wurden erhalten und mit einer Palette aus Flachs, Creme und Schokoladenbraun vorsichtig modernisiert. Hage kombiniert das Schlichte mit dem Aufwendigen. So sind die Möbelsilhouetten lang und geradlinig, die verwendeten Raumtextilien dagegen eine ausschweifende Komposition aus Seide, Leinen, Samt und Baumwolle mit gelegentlich eingestreuten Überraschungsmomenten. Die spezialangefertigten Esszimmerstühle faszinieren mit einem Kontrast aus Naturbastgewebe und Leder. Als Ausdruck der Persönlichkeit seiner Auftraggeber dekorierte Hage jeden Raum mit handverlesener zeitgenössischer Kunst. Im öffentlichen Bereich etwa strotzen die Wände vor modernen Hinguckern. Über dem Wohnzimmersofa hängt ein Gemälde von Aki Kuroda, im Essbereich regiert ein Hundebild von François Bard. Weil gerade in Etagenwohnungen Atmosphäre wichtig ist, stammt auch das Lichtdesign größtenteils von Hage – einschließlich der stählernen Wandlampen mit Antikbronze-Finish. Markante Oberflächen überwiegen. Die Vorhänge sind aus Seide, handgewebte Woll- und Seidenteppiche mit eigens entworfenen Dessins dämpfen den Schritt auf dem polierten Parkett. Bei so viel Liebe zum Detail verwundert es nicht, dass Hage die Wohnung als ein „besonderes Projekt" hervorhebt. Sie ist eine Hymne auf harmonisches Wohnen.

Les propriétaires de cet appartement du début du XXᵉ siècle ont chargé Rabih Hage d'en faire un logis raffiné, qui associe des espaces de réception épurés et confortables à un lieu de vie multifonctionnel. Architecte d'intérieur renommé, Rabi Hage a établi sa réputation sur des aménagements chic, qui accrochent le regard, mais dénotent une approche d'une grande intelligence. Dans cet appartement fonctionnel et conforme au sens esthétique des clients, il a éliminé la cloison entre le salon et la salle à manger afin de créer un espace de vie unique, avec un coin bibliothèque. Le plan tire le meilleur parti possible de l'espace, tout en dégageant des perspectives séduisantes. L'architecte a conservé les grandioses lambris et moulures d'origine et créé une ambiance moderne avec une palette de tons lin, crème et chocolat. Adepte des contrastes, Rabih Hage a privilégié un mobilier aux lignes effilées et n'a pas hésité à marier des tissus d'ameublement aussi variés que la soie, le lin, le velours et le coton, créant çà et là des effets de texture saisissants. Ainsi, les chaises de salle à manger ont été commandées pour certaines avec un habillage cuir et pour d'autres avec un revêtement en toile de raphia. Dans chaque espace, les œuvres d'art choisies reflètent la personnalité du client. Ainsi, dans les espaces de vie publics, les murs sont investis par des pièces modernes qui captent l'attention : une nature morte d'Aki Kuroda surmonte le canapé du salon, tandis qu'un tableau de François Bard représentant un chien donne le ton dans le coin repas. Pour les besoins spécifiques de l'ambiance dans un espace de vie organisé sur un seul niveau, Rabih Hage a conçu la plupart des luminaires, notamment les appliques murales en acier agrémentées d'une finition bronze à l'ancienne. Le sens tactile est à l'honneur dans les surfaces, avec des rideaux en soie et des tapis en laine et soie sur mesure tissés main qui émaillent le parquet ciré. Ce souci du détail fait de ces lieux un « projet particulier », pour reprendre l'expression de Rabih Hage. C'est aussi un hymne à l'harmonie dans l'habitat.

The walls in the drawing room and dining zone are finished in a subtle flax paint effect to seamlessly link the spaces. Using his skills as an art curator, Rabih has combined a cheeky mixture of modern art, from the wobbly charm of limited edition blown PVC light sculptures by Paul Cocksedge, to the green glass vases by Tord Boontje and Emma Woffenden. Yet glamour also features: as well as a sophisticated dining table, designed by Rabih, there is a specially commissioned Baccarat chandelier. To give a modern twist to the tranquil drawing room, Rabih has included visual surprises. On a plinth stands a multi-coloured glass sculpture by Nathalie Pasqua, while in the hall, a bespoke wool and silk rug features a circular motif.

Dank des dezenten flachsfarbenen Finishs der Wände gehen Wohnzimmer und Essbereich nahtlos ineinander über. Seine Fähigkeiten als Kunstkurator nutzte Hage, um eine raffinierte Mischung aus modernen Kunstwerken zusammenzustellen, vom wackeligen Charme einer limitierten Edition geblasener PVC-Lichtskulpturen von Paul Cocksedge bis zu den grünen Glasvasen von Tord Boontje und Emma Woffenden. Den nötigen Glamour steuern ein eleganter, von Hage selbst entworfener Esstisch und die Sonderanfertigung eines Baccarat-Kronleuchters bei. Dem ruhigen Wohnraum hat Hage mit optischen Überraschungen eine moderne Wendung gegeben. Auf einem hohen Sockel strahlt eine bunte Glasskulptur von Nathalie Pasqua, und im Flur sorgt ein maßgefertigter Teppich aus Wolle und Seide mit einem grafischen Kreismotiv für Aufsehen.

La teinte lin subtile des cloisons du salon et du coin repas fait discrètement le lien entre ces espaces. Mettant à profit son savoir-faire de conservateur, Rabih Hage a composé un cocktail détonnant d'art moderne, alliant de voluptueuses sculptures lumineuses en PVC expansé en édition limitée de Paul Cocksedge à des vases en verre vert créés par Tord Boontje et Emma Woffenden. Le glamour est présent dans le coin repas avec la table sophistiquée conçue par Rabih Hage et le lustre Baccarat, commandé spécialement pour la pièce. Pour donner une touche de modernité, Rabih Hage a disposé sur une console dans le paisible salon une sculpture en verre multicolore signée Nathalie Pasqua, et dans l'entrée, un tapis en laine et soie sur mesure à motif circulaire.

The bedrooms have been tailor-made for each family member, and major on seamless storage options. In the master bedroom, a custom-made headboard has been scaled up to balance the high ceilings. Texture is a watchword, expertly used by Rabih to add visual spice. In the cloakroom, walls are in a specialist paint finish to create a cross-woven linen effect, and the basin is set into a glossy washstand. In one nook of the drawing room, a silk-upholstered sofa sits in front of a coffee table designed by Mark Harvey, its chunky criss-crossed slats in deliberate contrast with the squiggles on the rug. With its sweetie colours and urban vibe, the Susan Shup abstract sums up the tongue-in-cheek mood in this apartment.

Die Schlafzimmer wurden nach den Ansprüchen der einzelnen Familienmitglieder eingerichtet und tun sich durch unsichtbaren Stauraum hervor. Das extra hohe, maßgearbeitete Betthaupt im Elternschlafzimmer soll die hohen Decken ausgleichen. Texturen lautet das Schlagwort, mit dem Hage den Räumen virtuos ihre optische Würze verleiht. Die Spezialfarbe in der Toilette sieht aus wie ein Leinengewebe in Leinwandbindung, und das Waschbecken ist in einen Hochglanzwaschtisch eingelassen. In einem Wohnzimmerwinkel steht vor einem Sofa mit Seidenpolster ein Couchtisch von Mark Harvey, dessen stabile Zick-Zack-Holzleisten einen gezielten Kontrast zu den Schlangenlinien des Teppichs bilden. Mit seinen Bonbonfarben und urbanen Schwingungen bringt das abstrakte Gemälde von Susan Shup das augenzwinkernde Flair dieser Wohnung auf den Punkt.

Dans les chambres répondant aux besoins spécifiques des membres de la famille, l'architecte a misé sur des rangements intégrés. Dans la chambre de maître, la haute tête de lit atténue la hauteur sous plafond. Le mot d'ordre est la texture, sur laquelle l'architecte joue pour attiser le regard. Dans le cabinet de toilette, le grain de la peinture des murs imite la toile, et la vasque est encastrée dans une table de toilette au fini brillant. Dans un coin du salon, un sofa recouvert de soie fait face à une table basse conçue par Mark Harvey et dont les lignes géométriques tranchent avec les arabesques du tapis. Avec ses couleurs acidulées et sa note citadine, l'œuvre abstraite de Susan Shup résume parfaitement l'ambiance badine qui règne dans cet appartement.

Geraldine and Monika, Photo: © Georgia Oetker, courtesy of MM Design

Geraldine Apponyi, Editor

With her intriguing mix of Austrian, Hungarian, Italian and German blood, it is no surprise that Geraldine Apponyi has a natural ease with the European arts. From an early age, she was highly motivated to pursue a career in the arts, and, prior to university, worked as an assistant in set and costume design at the prestigious Almeida Theatre and National Theatre in London. Geraldine studied a Fine Arts degree at Corcoran College of Art and Design, Washington DC, and emerged with flying colours. But the lure of interior design proved too great, and Geraldine launched herself into the exacting world of commercial design. She joined Adamstein and Demetriou, a leading architecture and design firm, and became the sole designer on a hotel project as well as bar, club and restaurant commissions. Here, she learned the art of working to a deadline and managing budgets, and she prides herself on seamless project-management. In 2007, keen to return to residential work, Geraldine joined her mother, Monika Apponyi, as a Partner at Monika's award-winning design practice, MM Design. Geraldine has emerged as one of London's most exciting young interior designers, with a unique talent for drama and colour. In particular, she focuses on a warm, defined atmosphere, as well as a practical, tailor-made interior. MM Design's trademark has always been an enticing combination of luxurious detailing and rich colour, a razor-sharp eye for detail and an understanding of how best to maximise space. Geraldine and Monika's many projects have included luxury houses in Umbria, a chalet, a new-build large farmhouse in Austria, and elegant flats and houses in London. Even when relaxing, Geraldine constantly gathers fresh inspiration on visits to galleries and museums, whilst window-shopping or when visiting antique shops. With her background in theatrical design she enjoys many cultural pursuits, and music, especially opera, is a passion. For the fortunate client embarking on a new project with Geraldine, one thing is assured. The journey will be exciting, refreshing and tailor-made to please.

Geraldine Apponyis Vorfahren kamen aus Österreich, Ungarn, Italien und Deutschland. Darum wundert es nicht, dass sie sich in den europäischen Künsten zu Hause fühlt. Schon in jungen Jahren wollte sie unbedingt Künstlerin werden, und noch vor ihrem Studium sammelte sie erste Erfahrungen als Bühnen- und Kostümbildassistentin an zwei renommierten Londoner Theatern, dem Almeida Theatre und dem Royal National Theatre. Ihr Kunststudium am Corcoran College of Art and Design in Washington absolvierte sie mit Bravour. Doch die Verlockungen der Innenarchitektur erwiesen sich als übermächtig, und so stürzte sich Apponyi in die anspruchsvolle Welt der Gestaltung kommerzieller Objekte. Bei Adamstein and Demetriou, einem führenden Architektur- und Designbüro, übertrug man ihr die alleinige Verantwortung für ein Hotelprojekt sowie für Bar-, Club- und Restaurantaufträge. Hier lernte sie die Kunst, Fristen einzuhalten und Budgets zu verwalten, und ist bis heute stolz auf ihr geräuschloses Projektmanagement. Als sie 2007 den Wunsch verspürte, wieder mehr im Wohnsektor zu arbeiten, schloss sie sich MM Design, dem Designbüro ihrer Mutter Monika Apponyi, als Partnerin an und entpuppte sich als eine der spannendsten jungen Innenarchitektinnen Londons mit einem einzigartigen Talent für Dramatik und Farbe. Sie konzentriert sich besonders auf eine warme, klar definierte Atmosphäre und auf praktische, maßgeschneiderte Interieurs. Markenzeichen von MM Design sind die verführerische Kombination von luxuriöser Detailausführung mit satten Farben, ein messerscharfes Auge für Kleinigkeiten und ein Gefühl für die maximale Ausnutzung des jeweils vorhandenen Raums. Zu den vielen umgesetzten Projekten von Mutter und Tochter zählen Luxusvillen in Umbrien, ein Chalet, ein großes, neu erstelltes Bauernhaus in Österreich und elegante Wohnungen und Häuser in London. Selbst in ihrer Freizeit, ob in Galerien und Museen, beim Schaufensterbummel oder in Antiquitätenläden, ist Geraldine Apponyi ständig auf der Suche nach neuen Inspirationen. Als ehemalige Theaterdesignerin hat sie ein Faible für alles Kulturelle und eine Leidenschaft für Musik entwickelt, insbesondere für die Oper. Für die glücklichen Kunden, die mit ihr ein neues Projekt angehen, steht eines fest: Die Reise wird aufregend, erfrischend und erfreulich individuell sein.

Avec ce curieux mélange de sangs autrichien, hongrois, italien et allemand qui coule dans ses veines, Geraldine Apponyi ne peut qu'avoir des affinités avec les arts européens. Très tôt, elle ressent une forte motivation pour une carrière artistique et, avant même d'entrer à l'université, elle travaille comme assistante des créateurs de décors et de costumes dans deux prestigieux théâtres londoniens, l'Almeida Theatre et le National Theatre. Elle étudie à Washington DC les beaux-arts au Corcoran College of Art and Design, dont elle ressort avec les honneurs. Cependant, l'attrait de la décoration d'intérieur est si fort que Geraldine Apponyi se lance dans cet univers astreignant. Elle entre alors chez Adamstein & Demetriou, une agence d'architecture de premier plan, et se voit confier la responsabilité d'un projet hôtelier ainsi que de commandes pour des bars, des clubs et des restaurants. Elle y apprend l'art de tenir les délais et gérer les budgets, tirant une certaine fierté de passer sans transition de la conception à la réalisation. En 2007, désireuse de retravailler pour le secteur résidentiel, elle s'associe à sa mère, Monika Apponyi, dans le cadre de l'agence MM Design, lauréate de prix de décoration. Avec son sens inégalé de la mise en scène et des couleurs, Geraldine Apponyi s'affirme comme une étoile montante de l'architecture d'intérieur londonienne. Elle privilégie plus particulièrement l'ambiance, qui doit être chaleureuse et personnelle, mais aussi le caractère fonctionnel, en réponse à des besoins spécifiques. Depuis toujours, MM Design est synonyme de séduisant mariage de détails raffinés et d'une riche palette de couleurs, de sens aigu du détail et de talent pour tirer le meilleur parti possible de l'espace. Parmi les nombreuses réalisations de Geraldine et Monika Apponyi figurent de luxueuses résidences en Ombrie, un chalet, une grande ferme de construction récente en Autriche ainsi que d'élégants appartements et maisons de ville à Londres. Même quand elle ne travaille pas, Geraldine Apponyi glane constamment de nouvelles idées tout en visitant des galeries d'art et des musées, en faisant du lèche-vitrine ou en chinant dans les magasins d'antiquités. Marquée par son expérience de décoratrice et de costumière de théâtre, elle est passionnée de culture, vouant une véritable passion à la musique, principalement l'opéra. Le client fortuné qui se lance dans un projet avec la jeune décoratrice est assuré d'une chose: ce sera une aventure stimulante, revigorante et qui devrait le ravir.

Monika Apponyi, Editor

For discerning individuals in search of a sumptuous, beautifully crafted home, Monika Apponyi is the designer of choice. At MM Design, Monika has been creating exquisitely detailed private homes across Europe for over 30 years, building an impressive list of devoted clients. Clients appreciate her finely tuned design vision, discretion and focus: in pursuit of the perfect interior, she leaves no stone unturned. Interior design was always Monika's goal. After graduating from the University of Vienna and getting married, she moved to London. Here, she took the opportunity to study at The Inchbald School of Design, despite her parents' grave reservations about a career in design. In 1981, she moved to Germany and established MM Design Frankfurt, then, after returning to London in 1985, set up MM Design London. Monika's signature style is unmistakeable: a blend of luxurious fabrics, warm colours, elegant antiques and contemporary detailing. She has that rare talent for creating a functional home, using subtle lighting and clever spatial planning to create the ultimate interior. For Monika, it is clients that make each project special, and many become friends, returning for repeat commissions. Now Monika's daughter, Geraldine, is a Partner at MM Design, they form a dynamic, creative team. Monika has worked on every conceivable project, from luxury hotels to commercial offices and beautiful private homes. Clients frequently entrust her with the complete remodelling of houses, and the restoration of Grade II London homes are a speciality. She has been honoured with awards, including Best Designer in 1990 and 1991, and the *House & Garden* prize for Best Room in 1991, both at the British Interior Design Exhibition. Her work has featured in worldwide publications, and she is a Fellow of the British Institute of Interior Design (BIID) and the Chartered Society of Designers (CSD). Monika divides her time between London, where she enjoys the culture, and a new-build lakeside house near Salzburg. With her dedication to clients and talent for creating immaculate homes, she remains one of today's foremost designers.

Für anspruchsvolle Auftraggeber, die sich ein schönes und opulentes Zuhause wünschen, ist Monika Apponyi die Designerin der Wahl. Unter dem Namen MM Design gestaltet sie seit mehr als 30 Jahren Privathäuser in ganz Europa mit ungeheurem Detailreichtum und hat sich eine beeindruckende Liste ergebener Kunden aufgebaut. Diese schätzen Apponyis fein abgestimmtes Designverständnis, ihre Umsicht und ihre Fokussierung: Auf der Suche nach dem perfekten Interieur dreht sie jeden Stein um. Apponyi wollte schon immer Innenarchitektin werden. Nachdem sie ihr Studium an der Universität Wien abgeschlossen und geheiratet hatte, zog sie nach London, wo sie trotz der massiven Vorbehalte ihrer Eltern gegen eine Designkarriere die Gelegenheit ergriff, an der Inchbald School of Design zu studieren. 1981 ging sie nach Deutschland und gründete MM Design Frankfurt. Nach ihrer Rückkehr an die Themse 1985 baute sie MM Design London auf. Ihr Stil ist unverkennbar: eine Mischung aus luxuriösen Textilien, warmen Farben, eleganten Antiquitäten und zeitgemäßen Details. Apponyi hat die seltene Begabung, mit unaufdringlicher Beleuchtung und kluger Raumplanung nicht nur ein funktionales Zuhause, sondern das ultimative Interieur zu kreieren. Für sie sind es die Kunden, die aus jedem Projekt etwas Besonderes machen. Viele von ihnen werden zu Freunden, die später mit neuen Aufträgen wieder zu ihr kommen. Seit Apponyis Tochter Geraldine Partnerin bei MM Design wurde, bilden die beiden Frauen ein dynamisches Kreativteam. Es gibt kein Projekt, an dem Monika Apponyi noch nicht gearbeitet hat, von Luxushotels über Büroräume bis hin zu prächtigen Privathäusern. Für viele Kunden gestaltet sie Häuser von oben bis unten neu; ihre Spezialität ist dabei die Restaurierung von denkmalgeschützten Londoner Wohnhäusern. Im Rahmen der British Interior Design Exhibition wurde Apponyi unter anderem als Best Designer 1990 und 1991 ausgezeichnet und gewann 1991 den von *House & Garden* verliehenen Preis in der Kategorie Best Room. Sie ist Mitglied des British Institute of Interior Design (BIID) und der Chartered Society of Designers (CSD). Ihre Arbeiten wurden weltweit publiziert. Apponyi teilt ihre Zeit zwischen London, wo sie die Großstadtkultur genießt, und einem neu gebauten Haus am See in der Nähe von Salzburg auf. Mit ihrem Engagement für ihre Auftraggeber und ihrem Talent, makellose Wohnhäuser zu gestalten, zählt sie zu den führenden Designern unserer Zeit.

Pour les clients exigeants en quête d'un somptueux logis d'excellente facture, c'est le nom de Monika Apponyi qui s'impose. Cette décoratrice de MM Design, qui crée depuis plus de 30 ans des intérieurs raffinés pour des particuliers d'un bout à l'autre de l'Europe, s'est constitué au fil du temps une impressionnante liste de fidèles clients. Ceux-ci apprécient son sens très fin de la décoration, son tact et son approche : pour créer le parfait intérieur, elle ne laisse aucun détail au hasard. N'ayant qu'une idée en tête, l'architecture intérieure, elle étudie à l'université de Vienne puis, pour suivre son mari, s'installe à Londres, où elle en profite pour fréquenter la Inchbald School of Design, malgré les fortes réticences de ses parents à l'idée qu'elle fasse carrière dans la décoration. Après un intermède de quatre ans en Allemagne, où elle crée MM Design Frankfurt, elle retourne en 1985 à Londres pour monter MM Design London. Reconnaissable entre mille, le style de Monika Apponyi se caractérise par un mélange de luxueux tissus, de coloris chauds, d'élégantes antiquités et de détails contemporains. Elle possède le rare don de créer des intérieurs fonctionnels d'exception reposant sur un éclairage subtil et une distribution judicieuse. Pour Monika Apponyi, ce sont les clients qui font la spécificité de chaque réalisation. D'ailleurs, ceux-ci deviennent souvent ses amis à la faveur de commandes répétées. La décoratrice forme une équipe dynamique et créative avec sa fille Geraldine, désormais associée de MM Design. Monika Apponyi travaille sur tous les types de projets imaginables, depuis des hôtels de luxe jusqu'à de splendides maisons de particuliers, en passant par des locaux commerciaux. Ses clients lui confient souvent la restructuration complète de maisons, et elle s'est fait une spécialité de la restauration de demeures londoniennes classées. Elle est lauréate de différents prix décernés dans le cadre de la British Interior Design Exhibition : en 1990 et 1991, le prix de meilleur designer (Best Designer), et en 1991 également, le prix *House & Garden*, qui récompense la plus belle pièce. Ses travaux sont présentés dans des publications internationales. Elle est membre du British Institute of Interior Design (BIID) et de la Chartered Society of Designers (CSD). Monika Apponyi partage son temps entre Londres, où elle profite de la vie culturelle, et la maison qu'elle vient de construire en bordure d'un lac, dans les environs de Salzbourg. Son sens du service et le don qu'elle a de créer des intérieurs parfaits font d'elle l'une des architectes d'intérieur les plus en vue du moment.

Judith Wilson, Photo: © Polly Wreford

Judith Wilson, Writer

Judith Wilson has always had a passion for writing, and grew up determined to turn her love of books into a career as an author and journalist. She studied English Literature at university, and completed her studies with an MA at the University of Warwick, specialising in the twentieth century novel. After coming to London, and a short spell in book publishing, she transferred into magazine journalism, and spent six years at *Homes & Gardens,* latterly as Decorating Editor. Since 1997, Judith has pursued a highly successful freelance career as a writer and stylist, and has interviewed many talented interior designers. Judith is a Contributing Editor for *House & Garden* and has written for numerous publications including *House & Garden, Homes & Gardens,* the *Telegraph Magazine, Living etc* and *The English Home.* She lectures on Styling at the KLC School of Design, and has appeared as a design expert on TV and radio. She is the author of 13 best-selling books on interior design including *Children's Spaces, The Vintage Home* and *Casual Living,* and her books have been translated into over ten languages. As a writer, Judith gets to the heart of design, seeking out the essence of a designer's style and the true spirit that defines a vibrant interior. She has styled and written about interiors across Europe and the USA, and never tires of visiting beautifully designed houses, feeling it is always a privilege to glimpse real lives, in real homes. When Judith isn't interviewing designers, she enjoys family life with her husband, Anthony, and their teenage children, Cicely and Felix. She relishes the stimulation of living in London, yet still finds time for her weekly ballet class. On high days and holidays, she loves to escape to the beaches, the sea and the big blue skies of Cornwall.

Judith Wilson hat schon immer leidenschaftlich gern geschrieben und war von jeher fest entschlossen, ihre Liebe zu Büchern eines Tages als Autorin und Journalistin beruflich zu nutzen. Sie studierte englische Literatur, spezialisierte sich auf den Roman des 20. Jahrhunderts und schloss das Studium mit einem Master an der University of Warwick ab. Nach ihrem Umzug nach London und einer kurzen Zwischenstation im Buchverlagswesen wechselte sie zum Zeitschriftenjournalismus und arbeitete sechs Jahre lang für *Homes & Gardens,* zuletzt als Redakteurin für Inneneinrichtung. Seit 1997 verfolgt Wilson mit großem Erfolg ihre freiberufliche Karriere als Journalistin und Designerin und hat in dieser Zeit zahlreiche begabte Innenarchitektinnen und -architekten interviewt. Sie schreibt regelmäßig Autorenbeiträge für *House & Garden* und hat Artikel in zahlreichen Zeitschriften veröffentlicht, darunter schon früher in *House & Garden,* aber auch in *Homes & Gardens,* dem *Telegraph Magazine,* in *Living etc* und *The English Home.* Wilson unterrichtet Gestaltung an der KLC School of Design in London, tritt als Designexpertin in Hörfunk und Fernsehen auf und hat 13 Bestseller über Innenarchitektur verfasst, darunter *Kinderzimmer, The Vintage Home* und *Wohlfühlen.* Insgesamt wurden ihre Bücher in mehr als zehn Sprachen übersetzt. Als Autorin dringt Wilson zum Kern des Designs vor und spürt das Wesentliche im Stil eines Designers auf, den wahren Geist, der ein lebendiges Interieur ausmacht. Sie hat über Inneneinrichtungen in Europa und den USA berichtet, auf beiden Kontinenten eigene Entwürfe verwirklicht und wird niemals müde, schön gestaltete Häuser zu besuchen, da sie es stets als Privileg empfindet, einen Blick auf das wahre Leben in echten Häusern werfen zu dürfen. Wenn Wilson keine Designer interviewt, genießt sie das Familienleben mit ihrem Mann Anthony und ihren jugendlichen Kindern Cicely und Felix. Sie liebt die Anregungen, die London ihr bietet, und findet dennoch Zeit für ihren wöchentlichen Ballettkurs. An Feiertagen und im Urlaub zieht sie sich am liebsten an die Strände und das Meer unter dem hohen blauen Himmel von Cornwall zurück.

Animée depuis toujours par la passion de l'écriture et l'amour des livres, Judith Wilson décide très tôt de se lancer dans la carrière d'auteure et de journaliste. Elle étudie la littérature anglaise et obtient le Master of Art en littérature anglaise, mention roman du XXᵉ siècle, délivré par l'université de Warwick. Elle s'installe à Londres où elle fait un passage éclair dans l'édition avant de devenir journaliste pour magazines. Elle travaille alors pendant six ans chez *Homes & Gardens,* où elle termine rédactrice en chef des pages décoration. Depuis 1997, elle poursuit une brillante carrière en tant qu'auteure et styliste indépendante, qui l'amène à interviewer de nombreux architectes d'intérieur talentueux. Outre son activité de rédactrice pour les magazines *House & Garden,* ainsi que *House & Garden, Homes & Gardens, Telegraph Magazine, Living etc* et *The English Home,* Judith Wilson enseigne le stylisme à la KLC School of Design et intervient à la télévision et à la radio en tant que spécialiste. Elle est aussi l'auteure de 13 livres à succès sur la maison, parmi lesquels *Décors d'enfance, La Maison vintage* et *Intérieurs faciles à vivre.* Ses livres ont été traduits dans plus de dix langues. Mettant le design à nu, l'auteure Judith Wilson recherche l'essence du style des décorateurs et l'âme qui caractérise les intérieurs. En tant que styliste, elle décore des intérieurs dans toute l'Europe et aux États-Unis et écrit sur le sujet, ne se lassant jamais de visiter des demeures merveilleusement aménagées, consciente du privilège que représente le fait de jeter un œil dans de vrais foyers, dans des maisons habitées. Quand elle n'interviewe pas des décorateurs, Judith Wilson se consacre à son mari, Anthony, et à leurs enfants adolescents, Cicely et Felix. Elle trouve aussi le temps de suivre un cours hebdomadaire de danse classique. Bien qu'appréciant de travailler à Londres, elle profite des jours fériés et des vacances pour faire des escapades au bord de la mer sous l'immense ciel bleu de Cornouailles.

Designers

Alidad

Alidad has lived in London for over 40 years and established his reputation at Sotheby's in the 1970s and 1980s. In 1985 he launched Alidad Ltd. and was quickly acknowledged for his lavishly textured and eclectically furnished rooms. His extraordinary richly layered rooms combine boldly patterned and often luxurious fabrics in colours that evoke the faded beauty of 17th and 18th century textiles and interiors. Invariably his rooms combine a mix of antique, vintage and modern designs, with colour, pattern, texture and scale confidently combined. His inimitable eye allows him to create rooms from scratch that look as though they have come together over decades. Alidad was awarded Best Interior Designer by three highly respected magazines: *World of Interiors*, *House & Garden* and *Elle Decoration*. Alidad believes, as life is so hectic and stressful, home is a vital haven in which to forget the outside world. 'I like to think my designs lift the spirit'.

Alidad lebt seit mehr als 40 Jahren in London und machte sich in den 1970er und 1980er Jahren bei Sotheby's einen Namen. 1985 gründete er Alidad Ltd. und wurde schon bald für die verschwenderische Materialvielfalt und eklektische Möblierung seiner Interieurs gerühmt. In außerordentlich vielschichtigen Räumen versammelt er kühn gemusterte und oftmals luxuriöse Stoffe in Farben, die die einstige Schönheit der Textilien und Einrichtungen des 17. und 18. Jahrhunderts heraufbeschwören. Ohne Ausnahme setzt er auf eine Mischung aus antiken, traditionellen und modernen Designs und kombiniert selbstbewusst Farben, Muster, Texturen und Maßstäbe. Mit unnachahmlichem Auge kreiert er Räume aus dem Nichts, die aussehen, als seien sie über Jahrzehnte gewachsen. Von drei hoch angesehenen englischen Zeitschriften – *World of Interiors*, *House & Garden* und *Elle Decoration* – wurde Alidad zum Best Interior Designer gekürt. Er glaubt fest daran, dass in einem hektischen und anstrengenden Alltag das Zuhause eine unverzichtbare Oase sein sollte, in der man die Außenwelt vergisst.

Installé à Londres depuis plus de 40 ans, Alidad perce chez Sotheby's dans les années 1970 et 1980 puis monte la société Alidad Ltd. en 1985. Il ne tarde alors pas à être reconnu pour ses pièces aux textures variées et au mobilier éclectique. Adepte des superpositions, il combine des tissus audacieusement ornementés et souvent luxueux, dans des tons qui évoquent la beauté fanée des textiles et des intérieurs des XVIIᵉ et XVIIIᵉ siècles. Invariablement, il marie des éléments décoratifs anciens, rétro et modernes sans hésiter à jouer sur les couleurs, les motifs, les textures et l'échelle. Doté d'un coup d'œil exceptionnel, il n'a pas son égal pour créer de A à Z des pièces qui semblent avoir mis plusieurs dizaines d'années à prendre leur forme actuelle. Alidad a été sacré Meilleur Décorateur par trois magazines de renom : *World of Interiors*, *House & Garden* et *Elle Décoration*. Pour Alidad, nos vies sont tellement trépidantes et stressantes que le chez-soi est le havre par excellence qui permet d'oublier le monde extérieur.

Collett-Zarzycki Ltd.

Collett-Zarzycki Ltd. is a 25 year-old architectural design practice which employs a team with interlocking skills as well as a huge network of outside specialists, artists and crafts people. The company tackles an extensive range of projects from conceptual ideas to implementation of architecture, interiors, furniture, gardens and landscapes and is specialised in residential architectural and interior design. Best known for its classic contemporary work, the studio has a natural tendency towards a formal design approach. The company is led by Anthony Collett and Andrzej Zarzycki. Anthony Collett was born in Zambia and studied sculpture at Cape Town University before moving to England where he gained a diploma in Interior Design at Hornsey College of Art and graduated from the Royal College of Art. Andrzej Zarzycki was born in Zambia and was educated in England. He studied at Reading College of Technology and graduated in 3-Dimensional Design from Buckingham College of Higher Education.

Das Architekturbüro Collett-Zarzycki Ltd. wurde vor 25 Jahren gegründet und verfügt neben einem multiprofessionellen Team über ein großes Netzwerk von Spezialisten, Künstlern und Handwerkern. Das umfassende Angebot, von der Konzeptidee bis zur Umsetzung, reicht von Architekturprojekten und Interieurs über Möbeldesign bis hin zum Garten- und Landschaftsbau. Das auf Wohn- und Innenarchitektur spezialisierte Büro ist am besten für seine klassisch-modernen Arbeiten bekannt und hat eine natürliche Neigung zu einem formalen Designansatz. Das Unternehmen wird von Anthony Collett und Andrzej Zarzycki geleitet. Collett wurde in Sambia geboren und studierte Bildhauerei an der Cape Town University, bevor er nach England übersiedelte. Dort erwarb er ein Diplom für Innenarchitektur am Hornsey College of Art und absolvierte ein Masterstudium am Royal College of Art. Andrzej Zarzycki wurde in Sambia geboren und ging in England zur Schule. Er studierte am Reading College of Technology und erwarb am Buckingham College of Higher Education einen Abschluss in Dreidimensionalem Design.

Cabinet de conception architecturale créé il y a maintenant de plus de 25 ans, Collett-Zarzycki Ltd. emploie en interne une équipe aux compétences complémentaires ainsi qu'un réseau externe très étendu de spécialistes, d'artistes et d'artisans. Spécialisée dans l'architecture résidentielle et l'aménagement intérieur, la société est très polyvalente : élaboration de concepts, réalisations architecturales, création de mobilier et aménagement d'intérieurs, de jardins et de paysages. Surtout connue pour le classicisme de ses réalisations contemporaines, l'agence cultive une approche formelle du design. La société est dirigée par Anthony Collett et Andrzej Zarzycki. Né en Zambie, Anthony Collett étudie la sculpture à l'université du Cap avant de partir pour l'Angleterre, où il décroche un diplôme d'architecture d'intérieur au Hornsey College of Art puis termine ses études au Royal College of Art. Également né en Zambie, Andrzej Zarzycki fait sa scolarité en Angleterre, avant d'étudier au College of Technology de Reading puis au Buckingham College of Higher Education, dont il sort avec un diplôme de conception en 3D.

David Carter

David Carter is a London based interior designer, who works principally on high end residential projects both in the UK and abroad. He has been running his interior design practice for over sixteen years, providing his expertise to an international clientele that has included Middle Eastern potentates, captains of industry and City professionals. He works for people who don't want an 'off-the-peg' design solution, but who are looking for something special, unique and bespoke. His signature style might loosely be described as 'contemporary classic', but all this really means is that he loves mixing old and new, and he is equally adept at conjuring up all the theatrical flamboyance of a Marie Antoinette-inspired boudoir as he is masterminding the muted *machismo* of a Bond-esque bachelor pad. He has been short-listed for the highly prestigious Andrew Martin International Interior Designer of the Year Award in 2001 and 2007.

David Carter, Innenarchitekt mit Sitz in London, arbeitet hauptsächlich an Wohnprojekten der Luxusklasse im In- und Ausland. Mit seinem Büro für Innenarchitektur berät er seit mehr als 16 Jahren eine internationale Klientel, zu der schon Machthaber aus dem Nahen Osten, Industriekapitäne und Angehörige der Londoner Finanzbranche gehörten. Carter arbeitet für Menschen, die keine Entwürfe von der Stange suchen, sondern die besondere, die einzigartige, die maßgeschneiderte Designlösung. Sein typischer Stil könnte lose als „moderne Klassik"

bezeichnet werden, womit letztendlich jedoch nichts anderes gemeint ist, als dass er gerne Altes mit Neuem verbindet und die theatralische Extravaganz eines von Marie Antoinette inspirierten Boudoirs ebenso gekonnt heraufbeschwört wie er den verhaltenen Machismo einer Junggesellenbude im James-Bond-Stil entwickelt. 2001 und 2007 stand Carter auf der Shortlist des äußerst prestigeträchtigen Andrew Martin International Interior Designer of the Year Award.

Architecte d'intérieur installé à Londres, David Carter travaille surtout sur des projets résidentiels haut de gamme dans de nombreux pays, notamment au Royaume-Uni. Dirigeant un cabinet d'architecture d'intérieur depuis plus de seize ans, il fait bénéficier de son expertise une clientèle internationale, parmi lesquels des potentats du Moyen-Orient, des capitaines d'industrie et des professionnels de la City. Il travaille pour une clientèle qui refuse une décoration « prêt-à-porter » et recherche un agencement particulier, unique et sur mesure. On pourrait en gros qualifier son style si particulier de « contemporain classique », une expression qui dans son cas signifie qu'il aime conjuguer l'ancien et le moderne. Ainsi, il sait aussi bien faire revivre le spectaculaire éclat d'un boudoir de style Marie-Antoinette que mettre en scène le machisme discret d'une garçonnière à la James Bond. En 2001 et 2007, il a été retenu parmi les lauréats pressentis pour l'Andrew Martin International Interior Designer of the Year, un titre prestigieux pour les architectes d'intérieur.

David Collins

David Collins was born and grew up on the coast outside Dublin, Ireland and studied architecture at Bolton Street School of Architecture. David Collins Studio was founded on this architectural training and from the outset, the Studio was organised with a holistic approach in mind, incorporating Interior Designers, Furniture Designers and Graphic Designers into its multifaceted team. The vision was simple: to create a design service whereby an initial concept is developed, detailed and successfully delivered through to the final stages. The David Collins Studio aesthetic is discernible in the attention to detail, texture and technique of the workmanship, as well as careful manipulation of lighting and sophisticated use of colour to add depth and interest to an interior, fulfilling every criterion of client and consumer alike.

David Collins wurde in einem Küstenort außerhalb der irischen Hauptstadt Dublin geboren, wuchs dort auf und studierte Architektur an der Bolton Street School of Architecture in Dublin. Seine Architektenausbildung bildete die Basis für das Kreativbüro David Collins Studio, dessen von Beginn an ganzheitlicher Ansatz Innenarchitekten, Möbeldesigner und Grafikdesigner in einem vielseitigen Team unter einem Dach vereinte. Die Vision war einfach: eine Designagentur zu kreieren,

die ein Anfangskonzept entwickelt, detailliert ausarbeitet und bis in die finale Phase der Umsetzung erfolgreich begleitet. Die Ästhetik von David Collins Studio ist erkennbar an der Detailgenauigkeit, Struktur und Technik der Ausführung, aber auch an der sorgfältigen Handhabung von Licht und dem ausgeklügelten Einsatz von Farbe, die einem Interieur Bedeutung und Tiefe verleihen sollen, um sämtliche Ansprüche des Auftraggebers wie des Endverbrauchers zu erfüllen.

Né puis élevé non loin de Dublin, sur la côte irlandaise, David Collins étudie l'architecture à la Bolton Street School of Architecture. Cette formation le conduit à créer David Collins Studio, un atelier reposant dès le départ sur une approche holistique et une équipe pluridisciplinaire de décorateurs d'intérieur, créateurs de mobilier et graphistes. L'objectif est simple : créer un service de design dans lequel un concept initial est développé, approfondi puis mené à bien par étapes successives jusqu'au stade final. L'esthétique du David Collins Studio se distingue par l'attention aux détails, aux textures et aux techniques dans l'exécution des travaux, ainsi que par le maniement adapté de l'éclairage et l'utilisation subtile des couleurs pour donner plus de profondeur et d'attrait à un intérieur, répondant ainsi aux désirs du client et du consommateur.

David Gill

David Gill is known internationally as a leading editor and dealer of art and contemporary design. In an exceptional 570 sq m gallery just south of the River Thames, he exhibits work by the best creators of their generation. He opened his first gallery in 1987, after working in modern and old master prints for Christie's. At first, he showed predominantly French pieces by early 20th century figures such as Charlotte Perriand, Jean Prouvé, J.E. Ruhlmann and Eileen Gray, before adding to his roster with celebrated names including Donald Judd and Yves Klein. In 1989, Gill began what would turn into a major list of collaborations with artists when he produced a collection of pieces with French designers Elisabeth Garouste and Mattia Bonetti. From then on David worked with some of the most important designers. Pieces from his Galleries are to be found in both private and museum collections worldwide. Gill himself has been honoured with the title 'both honours' (as 'chevalier' and 'officer' of the Order of Arts and Letters).

David Gill ist international als führender Verleger und Händler für moderne Kunst und zeitgenössisches Design bekannt. In seiner 570 Quadratmeter großen Ausnahmegalerie unmittelbar südlich der Themse zeigt er Werke der jeweils besten Vertreter ihrer Generation. Gill eröffnete seine erste Galerie 1987, nachdem er bei Christie's für moderne und alte Druckgrafik zuständig gewesen war. Zuerst zeigte er überwiegend französische Stücke des frühen 20. Jahrhunderts von Designern wie Charlotte Perriand, Jean Prouvé, J. E. Ruhlmann und Eileen Gray. Später fügte er seiner Liste berühmte Namen wie Donald Judd oder Yves Klein hinzu.

1989 produzierte Gill eine Kollektion mit den französischen Designern Elisabeth Garouste und Mattia Bonetti und legte damit den Grundstein für eine bedeutende Reihe von Künstlerkooperationen. Seit damals hat er mit den einflussreichsten Designern unserer Zeit gearbeitet. Stücke aus Gills Galerien sind weltweit in Museen und Privatsammlungen vertreten. Gill selbst wurde mit dem Ritterkreuz und dem Offizierskreuz des französischen *Ordre des Arts et des Lettres* ausgezeichnet.

David Gill est reconnu à l'échelon international comme l'un des plus grands directeurs artistiques et marchands d'œuvres d'art et de design contemporain. Dans une splendide galerie de quelque 570 m² au sud de la Tamise, il expose les œuvres des plus grands créateurs de leur génération. Après avoir travaillé dans le département des estampes de maîtres anciens et modernes chez Christie's, il ouvre sa première galerie en 1987. Au début, il présente surtout du mobilier français créé par des grandes figures du début du XXe, telles que Charlotte Perriand, Jean Prouvé, J.E. Ruhlmann et Eileen Gray. Puis il élargit cette liste à des noms célèbres, parmi lesquels Donald Judd et Yves Klein. En 1989, David Gill sort une collection d'objets en partenariat avec le duo de designers franco-suisse Elisabeth Garouste et Mattia Bonetti ; il entame ainsi la première d'une longue série de collaborations avec des artistes. Dès lors, David Gill travaille avec certains des plus grands designers. Des objets issus de ses galeries sont exposes dans des collections privées et de musées partout dans le monde. David Gill a été fait chevalier et officier dans l'Ordre des Arts et des Lettres par le gouvernement français.

Christophe Gollut

Warmth and atmosphere are the hall-marks of English decorating style, while formality and slickness characterise continental design sensibility. Rooms designed by Christophe Gollut offer a blend of the two, due to his background, being Swiss, and his studies at boarding schools and Geneva University. He moved to London, where he studied at the Inchbald School, and stayed in England until today. He favours 19th century period style, both continental and English, mixing patterns and colours with personal design flair, and making homes look like they have been there forever, even if his work was finished a few seconds before you see it. He does not understand the *charme* of 'fashion'. For him, rooms should not just decorated for a short while since he believes decoration ought to last. The timeless side of his art is the greatest compliment and he worships this.

Atmosphäre und Wärme kennzeichnen den englischen Einrichtungsstil, Förmlichkeit und Glattheit das kontinentaleuropäische Designempfinden. In den Räumen von Christophe Gollut verschmilzt beides – infolge seiner schweizerischen Herkunft, seiner Internatsbesuche und seines Studiums an der Universität Genf – zu einer einzigartigen Melange. Gollut kam nach London, um an der Inchbald School of Design zu studieren, und wurde in England heimisch. Er bevorzugt die englischen und kontinentalen Einrichtungsstile des 19. Jahrhunderts, kom-

biniert Muster und Farben mit persönlichem Designtalent und lässt Wohnungen und Häuser aussehen, als seien sie schon immer da gewesen – selbst dann, wenn er erst Sekunden vorher letzte Hand angelegt hat. Der Charme von „Moden" lässt ihn kalt. In seinen Augen sollten Räume nicht nur für kurze Zeit eingerichtet werden, sondern auf Dauer. Für den Verfechter des Zeitlosen in seiner Kunst ist dieses Prädikat das größte Lob.

Si les intérieurs britanniques sont marqués par la chaleur et la convivialité, ceux du reste de l'Europe sont dominés par le formalisme et la sophistication. Grâce à son parcours, Christophe Gollut nous propose des pièces conciliant ces deux courants. Né en Suisse, il poursuit sa scolarité en pensionnat avant d'entrer à l'université de Genève. Parti pour Londres étudier à l'Inchbald School, il s'installe définitivement en Angleterre. Privilégiant le style du XIXᵉ, d'Angleterre comme du reste de l'Europe, il conjugue motifs et couleurs avec un sens très personnel du design : les intérieurs qu'il crée semblent exister depuis toujours, même s'ils viennent d'être terminés à l'instant. La fascination qu'exerce la « mode » lui est étrangère. Il pense que l'on ne doit pas aménager des pièces pour un temps limité car la décoration est faite pour durer. Que l'on dise de son art qu'il est intemporel est pour lui le plus grand des compliments. Aussi cultive-t-il religieusement cette intemporalité.

John Minshaw

As an Architectural and Interior Design Practice, John Minshaw Designs has been designing and building private residences for over 30 years. His pared back classical interiors combine precious antiques with a 21st century mood. A former winner of Designer of the Year at the Design & Decoration Award, John was recently the focus of a book published by Frances Lincoln that covers ten projects, spanning twenty years. A graduate of Camberwell School of Art, where he was taught by Hans Coper and Lucie Rie, amongst others, he turned from ceramics to making furniture. His break into interior design came in 1988 when the house he and his wife rescued from dereliction was published and work flowed from this article.

Das Büro für Architektur und Innenarchitektur John Minshaw Designs entwirft und baut seit mehr als 30 Jahren Privathäuser. Die reduzierten klassischen Interieurs des Firmengründers verbinden kostbare Antiquitäten mit der Stimmung des 21. Jahrhunderts. Der ehemalige Designer of the Year, gekürt im Rahmen der britischen Design & Decoration Awards, stand kürzlich im Mittelpunkt einer bei Frances Lincoln erschienenen Publikation, in der zehn seiner Projekte aus 20 Jahren zusam-

mengefasst sind. Nach dem Studium an der Camberwell School of Arts and Crafts, wo er unter anderem von den Keramikkünstlern Hans Coper und Lucie Rie unterrichtet wurde, wechselte er vom Keramik- zum Möbeldesign. Sein Durchbruch als Innenarchitekt gelang ihm 1988, als ein Presseartikel über das Haus, das er und seine Frau vor dem Verfall gerettet hatten, ihm eine Reihe von Aufträgen bescherte.

Le cabinet d'architecture et de décoration John Mishaw Designs conçoit et réalise des résidences pour particuliers depuis plus de 30 ans. Ces intérieurs classiques réduits à l'essentiel marient antiquités et atmosphère XXIᵉ siècle. Sacré designer de l'année lors d'une précédente édition du Design & Decoration Award, John Minshaw a récemment fait l'objet d'un ouvrage publié aux éditions Frances Lincoln qui présente dix de ses projets réalisés en l'espace de vingt ans. Diplômé de la Camberwell School of Art, où il a pour maîtres notamment Hans Coper et Lucie Rie, il passe de la céramique à l'ébénisterie. En 1988, il perce dans le domaine de l'architecture intérieure avec la publication du travail de sauvetage d'une maison en ruine entrepris avec sa femme. Depuis, il enchaîne commande sur commande.

John Stefanidis

John Stefanidis is one of the world's leading and most sought after interior designers. His hallmark is the blend of comfort and practicality with an eclectic and sophisticated aesthetic. Born and educated in Egypt, John moved to the UK to study at Oxford University. His shift towards a career in interior design began after he bought and renovated a 16th century house on the Greek island of Patmos in the Dodecanese. In 1967, Stefanidis established his architecture and interior design practice from a studio in Chelsea, London and has for over four decades kept the highest standard of traditional and innovative design, producing unique concepts for a discerning international client portfolio. John Stefanidis Brands Limited specialises in the architectural and interior design of exclusive new build and renovated residential properties across the globe. As a medium-sized practice of interior architects and designers, John Stefanidis and his team maintain close long-term relationships with their clients.

John Stefanidis zählt zu den führenden und zu den gefragtesten Innenarchitekten der Welt. Sein Markenzeichen ist eine kultivierte, vielschichtige Ästhetik, in der Wohnlichkeit und Funktionalität zu einer Einheit verschmelzen. Geboren und aufgewachsen in Ägypten, ging Stefanidis nach England, um an der Oxford University zu studieren. Seine Wendung zur Innenarchitektur begann mit dem Kauf und der Renovierung eines Hauses aus dem 16. Jahrhundert auf der Dodekanesinsel Patmos. 1967 gründete Stefanidis sein Büro für Architektur und Innenarchitektur in einer Atelierwohnung im Londoner Stadtteil Chelsea. Für einen anspruchsvollen Kreis internationaler Auftraggeber entwickelt er einzigartige Konzepte und setzt

seit inzwischen mehr als vier Jahrzehnten höchste Maßstäbe sowohl im klassischen als auch im innovativen Design. John Stefanidis Brands Limited ist spezialisiert auf die architektonische Gestaltung und die Innenarchitektur von exklusiven, neuen und renovierten Wohnimmobilien rund um den Globus. Als mittelständisches Innenarchitektur- und Designbüro pflegen Stefanidis und sein Team enge und langjährige Beziehungen zu ihren Kunden.

John Stefanidis compte parmi les architectes d'intérieur les plus prisés au monde. Son style caractéristique allie confort et esprit pratique à un esthétisme éclectique et sophistiqué. Natif d'Égypte, où il poursuit son éducation, il émigre vers l'Angleterre pour étudier à l'université d'Oxford. Il décide de se consacrer à la décoration d'intérieur suite aux travaux de rénovation qu'il réalise sur une demeure du XVIᵉ siècle, sur l'île grecque de Patmos, dans le Dodécanèse. En 1967, il fonde son propre cabinet d'architecture et de décoration à partir d'un atelier situé dans le quartier londonien de Chelsea. Pendant plus de 40 ans, il réalise des travaux de décoration traditionnels et novateurs du plus haut niveau, créant des concepts uniques pour un portefeuille de clients internationaux exigeants. Le cabinet Brands Limited de John Stefanidis est spécialisé dans la conception architecturale et l'aménagement intérieur de luxueuses demeures résidentielles nouvellement construites ou rénovées tout autour du globe. Formant un cabinet d'architectes et de designers d'intérieur à taille humaine, John Stefanidis et son équipe entretiennent des liens étroits et durables avec leurs clients.

Michael Reeves

Michael Reeves opened his first London showroom in 1994 after living and working in New York for four years and in 1998 won the Andrew Martin International Designer of the Year Award. This led to interior design commissions for private homes and commercial projects in London, New York, Connecticut, France and Mustique BVI. The new showroom in Pimlico Road epitomises his interior design style and sells furniture, decorative items, fabrics and contemporary art. Michael is known for his ability to work in a range of styles for clients and for mixing his furniture and decorative accessories with contemporary and antique pieces. He also designs exclusive ranges of Michael Reeves furniture at Osborne & Little and rugs for The Rug Company. His neutral, chic interiors have become so popular, as they combine the pared-down look of the moment with comfort and elegance. Although clients come to Michael for that contemporary look, he excels in a range of styles and enjoys mixing together furniture and decorative accessories of his own designs with both modern and antique items.

Nachdem Michael Reeves vier Jahre lang in New York gelebt und gearbeitet hat, eröffnete er 1994 seinen ersten Showroom in London und gewann 1998 den Andrew Martin International Designer of the Year Award. Die Auszeichnung brachte dem Innenarchitekten Aufträge für Privathäuser und kommerzielle Objekte in London, New York, Connecticut, Frankreich und auf der Grenadineninsel Mustique ein. Sein neuer Showroom in der Pimlico Road steht stellvertretend für seinen Stil als Innenarchitekt und bietet Möbel, Designobjekte, Stoffe und zeitgenössische Kunst an. Reeves ist bekannt für seine Fähigkeit, seinen Stil je nach Auftrag zu variieren und die eigenen Möbel und Wohnaccessoires gekonnt mit modernen und antiken Stücken zu mischen. Außerdem entwirft er Möbelkollektionen exklusiv für den Tapetenhersteller und Designvertrieb Osborne & Little und Teppiche für The Rug Company. Seine sachlich-stilvollen Interieurs sind deshalb so populär, weil sie den reduzierten Look der Gegenwart mit Komfort und Eleganz verbinden.

Après avoir vécu et travaillé pendant quatre ans à New York, Michael Reeves ouvre son premier showroom londonien en 1994. L'obtention en 1998 de l'Andrew Martin International Designer of the Year Award, prix qui récompense le meilleur architecte d'intérieur international de l'année en cours, débouche sur des commandes de décoration d'intérieurs de particuliers et de locaux commerciaux à Londres, à New York, au Connecticut, en France et à Moustique (Caraïbes). Son nouveau showroom sur Pimlico Road, dans lequel il vend du mobilier, des articles de décoration, des tissus et de l'art contemporain, est la parfaite illustration de son style mariant des pièces contemporaines et anciennes avec du mobilier et des accessoires de décoration de ses propres collections. Il crée notamment des lignes exclusives de mobilier pour Osborne & Little et des tapis pour The Rug Company. Très apprécié de la clientèle pour ses intérieurs chic et neutres combinant confort et élégance avec le look dépouillé contemporain, Michael Reeves n'en excelle pas moins dans une large palette de styles et se plaît à mêler meubles et accessoires de décoration modernes à des antiquités.

Nicky Haslam

Nicky Haslam was born in Buckinghamshire and educated at Eton College, where he won many of the major Art prizes, before leaving to rejoin the world of adults and art. A visit to the United States in 1962 resulted in joining the staff of American *Vogue* under the inspiring editorship of Diana Vreeland. Following *Vogue*, he was made Art Director of *Show Magazine,* a forerunner of *Vanity Fair,* as the youngest art director of an editorial magazine in the country. In 1972 he returned to London and established a fully-fledged international design company NH Design. Since then he has worked all over the world. He is also a frequent columnist for the *London Evening Standard* and other newspapers and magazines, besides regularly writing reviews for such publications as *The World of Interiors, The Spectator*, and the *Financial Times*. Nicky Haslam has been a contributing editor of British *Vogue* and *Tatler* for many years.

Nicky Haslam wurde in Buckinghamshire geboren und ging in Eton zur Schule, wo er viele große Kunstpreise einheimste, bevor er sich der Kunstwelt der Erwachsenen zuwandte. Während einer Reise in die USA 1962 heuerte er bei der amerikanischen *Vogue* an, damals geleitet von der inspirierenden Diana Vreeland. Nach seinem Engagement bei *Vogue* machte *Show Magazine*, ein Vorläufer von *Vanity Fair*, ihn zum jüngsten Artdirector eines redaktionellen Magazins in Amerika. 1972 kehrte er nach London zurück und gründete NH Design, eine Vollagentur für internationales De-sign. Seitdem hat er überall auf der Welt gearbeitet. Daneben schreibt er regelmäßig Kolumnen für den *London Evening Standard* und andere Zeitungen und Zeitschriften und verfasst Rezensionen für Publikationen wie *The World of Interiors*, *The Spectator* und die *Financial Times*. Seit vielen Jahren arbeitet Haslam als Autor für die britische *Vogue* und das Lifestylemagazin *Tatler*.

Né dans le Buckinghamshire, Nicky Haslam étudie à l'Eton College, où il remporte nombre de grands prix artistiques, avant d'entrer dans le monde des adultes et de l'art. En 1962, une visite aux États-Unis lui ouvre les portes du magazine *Vogue* américain, où il travaille sous la direction stimulante de Diana Vreeland. Ensuite, il devient directeur artistique au *Show Magazine*, une publication dans la veine de *Vanity Fair* ; il est ainsi le plus jeune à ce poste dans un magazine rédactionnel aux États-Unis. En 1972, il revient à Londres et crée NH Design, une société de design international à part entière. Depuis, il travaille dans divers endroits du globe. Il intervient aussi souvent en tant qu'éditorialiste au *London Evening Standard* et dans d'autres journaux et magazines. Par ailleurs, il rédige souvent des critiques dans des publications telles que *The World of Interiors, The Spectator* et le *Financial Times*. Enfin, Nicky Haslam a collaboré de nombreuses années à la rédaction des éditions britan-niques des magazines *Vogue* et *Tatler*.

Nina Campbell

Nina Campbell is one of the world's most respected and influential interior design-ers. Her list of clients and design expertise is unparalleled. Renowned for her con-tagious wit and brilliant sense of personal style, her designs appeal to young and old alike and sit well in both contemporary and traditional interiors. Nina opened her first shop in 1970 on Pimlico Road specialising in 'unashamed luxury'. It was here that Nina launched her signature 'hearts' design on fabric and china. This was re-worked in 2009 on a range of fine bone china to celebrate the quality and heritage of the Nina Campbell brand. The Nina Campbell line continued to expand with an ensemble of bespoke furniture, launched in 2000, a collaboration with Britan-nia on a collection of range cookers featuring her fabric designs, a fashion range with Ted Baker, a rug collection in association with Stark Carpets and home ranges comprising table linen, china and glassware, home fragrance, branded gift wrap, cashmere throws and travel accessories.

Nina Campbell ist eine der angesehensten und einflussreichsten Innenarchitektin-nen der Welt. Ihre Berufserfahrung und ihre Referenzliste sind beispiellos. Die Designerin ist bekannt für ihren ansteckenden Humor und ihr brillantes Gespür für persönlichen Stil. Ihre Entwürfe treffen den Geschmack von Jung und Alt und passen sowohl zu zeitgenössischen als auch zu traditionellen Interieurs. Ihr erstes Geschäft, spezialisiert auf „ungenierten Luxus", eröffnete Campbell 1970 in der Pimlico Road. Hier entstand auch ihr unverwechselbares Herzchendesign für Stoffe und Porzellan, das 2009 für eine Kollektion aus feinem Knochenporzellan aufge-frischt wurde, um die Qualität und Tradition der Marke Nina Campbell zu feiern. Die Nina-Campbell-Produktpalette wuchs weiter: mit einer Maßmöbelkollektion im Jahr 2000 und einer Serie von Landhausherden, für die der Küchengeräte-hersteller Britannia Muster aus Campbells Stoffkollektion verwendete. Es folgten eine gemeinsame Modelinie mit Ted Baker, eine Teppichkollektion in Zusammen-arbeit mit Stark Carpets sowie eine Reihe schöner Wohnaccessoires – von Tisch-wäsche, Porzellan und Glas über Raumdüfte und Geschenkpapier bis hin zu Kasch-mirüberwürfen und Reisezubehör.

Nina Campbell compte parmi les décorateurs d'intérieur les plus en vue et les plus influents au monde. Ses références sont impressionnantes. Renommée pour sa vivacité d'esprit contagieuse et son don pour appréhender le style personnel de ses clients, elle crée pour toutes les générations des objets qui ont leur place dans des intérieurs aussi bien contemporains que classiques. C'est sur Pimlico Road que Nina Campbell ouvre en 1970 sa première boutique, spécialisée dans « le luxe sans complexe ». C'est là qu'elle lance ses emblématiques cœurs sur tissu et sur porce-laine, un motif repris sous une forme différente en 2009 sur une ligne de porce-laine fine pour célébrer la marque de qualité et de tradition Nina Campbell. Nina Campbell élargit sa gamme de produits à du mobilier sur mesure, avec notamment une collection de gazinières-tables de cuisson arborant les motifs de ses tissus en partenariat avec Britannia en 2000, ainsi que du prêt-à-porter avec Ted Baker, des tapis en collaboration avec Stark Carpets et diverses gammes d'articles pour la mai-son, notamment du linge de table, de la porcelaine et de la verrerie, des produits parfumés, du papier cadeau, des plaids en cachemire et des accessoires de voyage.

Rabih Hage

Rabih Hage is an Architect, Designer, Curator and owner of Rabih Hage Studio and Rabih Hage Gallery. Rabih creates beautiful interiors and architecture with a cutting edge and creative vision. He contributes regularly to various publications and his work has been recognised with numerous awards, including the 2011 Andrew Martin International Interior Designer of the Year Award. Since 2001, Rabih has dedicated himself to contemporary design and creative collaborations, which lead him to discover new talents and pioneering design and design-art. With a forward-thinking approach Rabih Hage curates cutting edge furniture and works by up-and-coming designers and established talents, whilst directing his creative team at his Design Studio focusing on international interior and architecture projects. In 2008 Rabih Hage created the Rough Luxe Hotel which triggered a worldwide movement in design. As an authority on collectible design, Rabih Hage also acts as an advisor to investors and collectors and established the online design think tank for information and exchange, DeTnk.com in 2007.

Der Architekt, Designer und Kurator Rabih Hage, Eigentümer der Firma Rabih Hage Studio und der Rabih Hage Gallery, entwirft schöne Architektur und exklusive Interieurs mit kreativem Weitblick und dem gewissen Etwas. Die Arbeit des Visionärs, der regelmäßig für verschiedene Publikationen schreibt, wurde vielfach ausgezeichnet, zuletzt 2011 mit dem Andrew Martin International Interior Designer of the Year Award. Seit 2001 widmet Hage sich ganz dem zeitgenössischen Design und kreativen Partnerschaften, über die er sowohl neue Talente als auch wegweisende Tendenzen in Design und Designkunst entdeckt. Mit vorausdenkendem Ansatz kuratiert er innovative Möbelstücke und Werke von Nachwuchsdesignern und erfahrenen Könnern und leitet zugleich das Kreativteam seiner Designwerkstatt, die auf internationale Innenausbau- und Architekturprojekte spezialisiert ist. 2008 schuf Hage in London das Rough Luxe Hotel und löste damit einen globalen Designtrend aus. Als Experte für das Sammeln von Design berät Hage Investoren und Sammler und gründete 2007 den Design-Thinktank DeTnk.com, eine Informations-, Ideen- und Produktbörse im Internet.

Propriétaire du Rabih Hage Studio et de la Rabih Hage Gallery, Rabih Hage est architecte, designer et conservateur d'art. Ses splendides intérieurs et réalisations architecturales d'avant-garde dénotent une vision créatrice. Contribuant régulièrement à diverses publications, il est lauréat de nombreux prix, notamment en 2011 du Andrew Martin International Interior Designer of the Year Award, distinction qui récompense le meilleur architecte d'intérieur international de l'année en cours. Depuis 2001, Rabih Hage se consacre au design contemporain et à des collaborations dans le domaine de la création, ce qui le conduit à découvrir de nouveaux talents ainsi que le design artistique d'avant-garde. Avec une grande clairvoyance, Rabih Hage conserve du mobilier et d'autres travaux à la pointe de la création qui émanent tant d'étoiles montantes que de talents établis. Dans le même temps, il dirige l'équipe de créatifs de son agence spécialisée dans les projets d'architecture et de décoration à l'international. En 2008, il achève le Rough Luxe Hotel, qui initie un mouvement international dans le domaine du design. Il conseille par ailleurs des investisseurs et des collectionneurs dans le domaine du design de collection. En 2007, il crée DeTnk.com, une plate-forme de réflexion en ligne d'information et d'échange.

Stephen Ryan

Stephen Ryan graduated with distinction from the Inchbald School of Design in London in 1980 and went on to work for leading London designers. Having apprenticed with Bill Bennette, he was headhunted after three years by Robin Guild, creator of Designers Guild and Homeworks. In 1985, headhunted once again, he became Chief Designer for the legendary decorator David Hicks. Having established himself within the national and international design community, Stephen Ryan Design & Decoration was established in 1993. Stephen Ryan has been commissioned to design houses, hotels, showrooms, offices, palaces and yachts. Whilst his work is international in style and execution, the company prides itself on not having a 'house-style' and will happily work in either contemporary or traditional genres. Much of his output has been award winning. Stephen is a full and founding member of the BIID (British Institute of Interior Design) and sits on its board of Past Presidents Club.

Stephen Ryan schloss die Inchbald School of Design in London 1980 mit Auszeichnung ab und arbeitete anschließend für führende Londoner Designer. Nach drei Jahren praktischer Ausbildung bei Bill Bennette wurde er von Robin Guild, dem Gründer des Einrichtungs- und Lifestyle-Unternehmens Designers Guild und des Showroom-Komplexes Homeworks, abgeworben. Nachdem man ihn bei Guild erneut abgeworben hatte, wurde er Chefdesigner beim legendären Inneneinrichter David Hicks. 1993 gründete der inzwischen national und international anerkannte Designer die Firma Stephen Ryan Design & Decoration. Ryans Portfolio umfasst Wohnhäuser, Hotels, Ladenlokale, Büros, Paläste und Jachten. Während seine eigene Arbeit in Stil und Ausführung international zu nennen ist, rühmt sich sein Büro, keinen „Haus-Stil" zu pflegen, sondern sowohl moderne als auch traditionelle Entwürfe anzubieten. Ryans Projekte wurden vielfach ausgezeichnet. Ryan ist Gründungs- und Vollmitglied des British Institute of Interior Design (BIID) und Vorstandsmitglied im Past Presidents Club des Instituts.

Diplômé avec mention de l'Inchbald School of Design de Londres en 1980, Stephen Ryan est aussitôt recruté par des décorateurs londoniens de premier plan. Au bout de trois d'apprentissage auprès de Bill Bennette, il est débauché par Robin Guild, fondateur des entreprises Designers Guild et Homeworks. En 1985, il est de nouveau débauché, cette fois par le légendaire décorateur David Hicks, dont il devient le designer en chef. Fort d'une réputation nationale et internationale dans le domaine de la décoration, il crée Stephen Ryan Design & Decoration en 1993. Stephen Ryan conçoit la décoration de maisons, d'hôtels, de magasins, de bureaux, de manoirs, d'hôtels particuliers et de yachts. Si ces réalisations sont plutôt internationales de par leur style et leur facture, son entreprise se targue de ne pas avoir de « style maison » et de travailler avec plaisir aussi bien dans le contemporain que dans le traditionnel. La plupart de ses travaux sont primés. Fondateur et membre titulaire du British Institute of Interior Design (BIID), Stephen Ryan est aussi l'un de ses présidents d'honneur.

Tara Bernerd & Partners

British Designer, Tara Bernerd is founder of the established interior architectural practice, Tara Bernerd & Partners. Working with an executive team of highly experienced architects and designers based out of the London Headquarters in Belgravia the focus for Bernerd is on the relevance of creative direction and interior design. Bernerd's business interests continue to grow, working increasingly on a global platform with projects in New York, London, Hong Kong, Switzerland and Spain. Key clients include the LeFraks, Thompson Group, MARC Restaurants, Blackstone, Center Parcs, Heron, Grosvenor Asia, amongst a select few and private clients who as always remain anonymous. Tara Bernerd & Partners' designs reflect intelligent space planning and layouts, with a strong use of texture and colour which typify their projects. With a more edgy approach Bernerd's work is renowned for creating warmth and atmosphere. Increasingly focusing on the Hotel and Restaurant industries the practice is committed to making a difference through design.

Die britische Designerin Tara Bernerd ist die Gründerin des etablierten Innenarchitekturbüros Tara Bernerd & Partners. Gemeinsam mit einem Team von erfahrenen Architekten und Designern lenkt sie die Geschicke des Unternehmens aus der Londoner Zentrale in Belgravia heraus und konzentriert sich dabei auf die Bedeutung von Kreativdirektion und Innenarchitektur. Ihr wachsendes Interesse an ausländischen Märkten trägt dazu bei, dass sie zunehmend international agiert – mit Projekten in New York, London, Hongkong und der Schweiz. Zu ihren Hauptkunden zählen der Baukonzern LeFrak, die Thompson Group, MARC Restaurants, Blackstone, Center Parcs, Heron, Grosvenor Asia und einige ausgewählte Privatkunden, die auf Anonymität vertrauen. Die Entwürfe von Tara Bernerd & Partners zeichnen sich durch intelligente Raumplanung, durchdachte Grundrisse und einen beherzten, für Bernerds Projekte typischen Einsatz von Texturen und Farbe aus. Ihr ausgefallener Denkansatz ist dafür bekannt, Wärme und Atmosphäre zu schaffen. Zunehmend spezialisiert auf Hotels und Restaurants, will das Team sich auch auf diesem Feld mit besonderen Designlösungen abheben.

Architecte d'intérieur britannique, Tara Bernerd est la fondatrice d'une agence bien établie sur le marché, Tara Bernerd & Partners. En partenariat avec une équipe de direction composée d'architectes et de designers très expérimentés détachés du siège londonien à Belgravia, Tara Bernerd s'emploie à suivre l'orientation donnée par ses clients en matière de créativité et d'architecture d'intérieur. En constant essor, son entreprise intervient de plus en plus à l'échelon international, notamment à New York, Londres et Hong-Kong ainsi qu'en Suisse. Elle compte parmi ses principaux clients LeFraks, Thompson Group, MARC Restaurants, Blackstone, Center Parcs, Heron, Grosvenor Asia, ainsi qu'une poignée de particuliers qui, comme toujours en pareil cas, conservent l'anonymat. Faisant la part belle aux textures et aux couleurs, les réalisations de Tara Bernerd & Partners témoignent d'une grande intelligence de l'espace et du plan. Tara Bernerd est connue pour créer chaleur et ambiance avec une approche plutôt audacieuse. L'agence se spécialise dans le secteur de l'hôtellerie et de la restauration, imprimant à chaque établissement un design qui lui permette de se démarquer.

Mark and Heather Weaver

The founder of Guinevere, French-born Genevieve Weaver, trained as a hat designer in Paris in the 1950s. She became drawn to the world of antiques when she moved to London, where she opened Guinevere Antiques in 1963, in what was then the disreputable end of the famous Kings Road, Chelsea. Today, the store is very much at the smart end of the Kings Road, and its famous windows are a wonderful invitation to step inside the warren of beautifully styled rooms. Guinevere is now run by Genevieve's sons, Kevin and Marc Weaver, and Marc's wife Heather. All three follow Genevieve's philosophy of mixing different styles and eras of furniture together – a way of thinking that is as relevant today as it was then, and a concept that is still considered revolutionary in the antiques trade. Heather is very much the force behind the textiles collections and bespoke side of the business, with her keen eye for colour, design, and importantly, knowing what customers want. There is very little that Heather can't do, from helping clients choose the best textiles for a luxurious table setting, to designing beautiful yet functional vellum trunks that people didn't know they needed. The Weavers travel around the world to source unique furniture, accessories and textiles for the home and Guinevere Antiques now consists of four adjoining shops on the Kings Road.

Die gebürtige Französin Genevieve Weaver, Gründerin des Antiquitätenhandels Guinevere Antiques, ließ sich in den 1950er Jahren in Paris zur Hutdesignerin ausbilden. Anschließend ging sie nach London, wo sie der Welt der Antiquitäten verfiel und 1963 in Chelsea, am damals noch verrufenen Ende der Kings Road, Guinevere Antiques eröffnete. Inzwischen liegt das Geschäft eindeutig am schicken Ende der Kings Road und ist berühmt für seine wunderbaren Schaufenster, die dazu einladen, dieses Labyrinth von zauberhaft gestalteten Räumen zu betreten. Guinevere wird heute von den Söhnen der Gründerin, Kevin und Marc Weaver, gemeinsam mit Marcs Frau Heather geführt. Alle drei beherzigen Genevieve Weavers Philosophie, Möbel unterschiedlicher Stilrichtungen und Epochen zu mischen – eine Denkweise, die heute genauso aktuell ist wie damals, und ein Konzept, das im Antiquitätengeschäft unverändert als revolutionär gilt. Heather Weavers scharfes Auge für Farbe und Design sowie, nicht unwichtig, ihr Wissen um die Wünsche ihrer Kunden machen sie zur treibenden Kraft hinter den Textilkollektionen und Maßanfertigungen des Unternehmens. Es gibt so gut wie nichts, was ihr nicht gelingt – ganz gleich, ob es darum geht, Kunden bei der Auswahl der besten Stoffe für eine prächtig gedeckte Tafel zu helfen oder schöne wie praktische Truhen mit Pergamentbezug zu entwerfen, von denen die Käufer zuvor nicht einmal ahnten, dass sie sie brauchen würden. Immer auf der Suche nach einzigartigen Möbelstücken, Accessoires und Wohntextilien reisen die Weavers um die ganze Welt. Ihre Verkaufsräume in der Kings Road erstrecken sich mittlerweile über vier zusammenhängende Ladenlokale.

Née en France, Genevieve Weaver suit une formation de dessinatrice de chapeaux à Paris dans les années 1950. Elle découvre l'univers des antiquités lorsqu'elle s'établit à Londres et ouvre en 1963 *Guinevere Antiques*, dans la portion alors mal famée de Kings Road, dans le quartier de Chelsea. Aujourd'hui, ce magasin se trouve dans la partie « chic » de Kings Road et ses célèbres vitrines sont une magnifique invitation à entrer dans un labyrinthe de pièces admirablement décorées. *Guinevere Antiques* est désormais dirigé par les fils de Genevieve, Kevin et Marc Weaver, ainsi que par Heather, la femme de Marc. Tous les trois adhèrent à la philosophie de Genevieve qui consiste à mélanger des meubles de styles et de périodes différentes – une façon de voir aussi pertinente aujourd'hui qu'elle l'était à cette époque, mais un concept encore considéré comme révolutionnaire dans le négoce d'antiquités. C'est surtout Heather qui est à l'origine des collections de textiles et des créations sur mesure dans l'entreprise, avec un regard affûté pour les couleurs et le design, ainsi qu'une précieuse connaissance des désirs des clients. Heather peut pratiquement tout faire pour eux : cela va du choix des meilleurs textiles pour un décor de table luxueux à la conception de malles tendues de vélin, belles mais aussi fonctionnelles, dont ses clients ne se doutaient pas qu'ils en ait eu besoin. Les Weavers parcourent le monde afin de trouver des meubles, des accessoires et des textiles uniques pour la maison et pour *Guinevere Antiques*, qui se compose désormais de quatre magasins contigus sur Kings Road.

Veere Grenney

Veere Grenney, originally from New Zealand, has been at the forefront of the international design industry for over 25 years. Starting at Mary Fox Linton he went on to become a director at Sibyl Colefax & John Fowler before launching his own company. More recently he has also designed his own fabric, wallpaper and furniture collections. For Veere, purity of design and quality of finish are paramount, but the client will also get an intriguing combination of styles – perhaps a 1950s lamp juxtaposed with an 18th century chair. Working with many clients who are art collectors allows Veere to create interior spaces where architecture and finishes complement the client's collection and allow art and design to work seamlessly with one another. He is very architectural in his approach but clients' wishes followed by comfort are first and foremost, closely trailed by beauty and a sense of humour. With a wide client list on both sides of the Atlantic, current projects include three major London houses, in the US a house in Wyoming, a townhouse in Manhattan's Upper East Side and a new house on Long Island, a large estate in Sweden and a house in the Caribbean.

Veere Grenney stammt ursprünglich aus Neuseeland und zählt seit mehr als 25 Jahren zur Spitze der internationalen Designindustrie. Nach dem Berufseinstieg bei Mary Fox Linton und einer Direktorenposition bei den Innenarchitekten Sibyl Colefax & John Fowler gründete er sein eigenes Unternehmen. Seit einiger Zeit entwirft er auch eigene Stoffe, Tapeten und Möbel. Für Grenney haben pures Design und exzellentes Finish oberste Priorität. Gleichzeitig bietet er faszinierende Stilmischungen an, etwa eine 1950er-Jahre-Lampe zu einem Stuhl aus dem 18. Jahrhundert. Weil viele seiner Kunden auch Kunstsammler sind, kann Grenney Innenräume kreieren, in denen Architektur und Ausführung die Sammlung des Kunden ergänzen und Kunst und Design sich nahtlos ineinanderfügen. Er verfolgt einen architektonischen Ansatz, bei dem jedoch die Wünsche seiner Auftraggeber und der Komfort an erster Stelle stehen, dicht gefolgt von Schönheit und einem Sinn für Humor. Mit einer langen Kundenliste auf beiden Seiten des Atlantiks arbeitet Grenney zurzeit unter anderem an drei Häusern in London, einem Haus im US-Bundesstaat Wyoming, einem Stadthaus in der Upper East Side von Manhattan, einem Neubauprojekt auf Long Island, einem großen Anwesen in Schweden und einem Haus in der Karibik.

D'origine néo-zélandaise, Veere Grenney est à l'avant-garde de l'industrie internationale du design depuis plus de 25 ans. Après des débuts chez Mary Fox Linton, il devient directeur de Sibyl Colefax & John Fowler puis il lance sa propre société. Plus récemment, il a conçu ses propres collections de tissus, de papiers-peints et de meubles. Alors que la pureté du design et la qualité de la finition sont primordiales pour lui, il propose à ses clients une impressionnante combinaison de styles – faisant par exemple cohabiter une lampe des années 1950 avec une chaise XVIIIe. Le fait de travailler avec de nombreux clients également collectionneurs d'art lui permet de créer des espaces intérieurs dans lesquels architecture et finitions complètent la collection du client et permettent à l'art et au design de se renforcer mutuellement en parfaite harmonie. Même s'il adopte une approche très orientée vers l'architecture, les vœux de confort des clients passent avant tout, suivis de près par la beauté et un certain sens de l'humour. Comptant une longue liste de clients des deux côtés de l'Atlantique, il poursuit actuellement divers projets : trois grandes demeures londoniennes, une maison dans le Wyoming, aux États-Unis, une maison de ville dans le Upper East Side de Manhattan et une maison à Long Island, ainsi que l'aménagement d'une grande propriété en Suède et une maison aux Caraïbes.

© 2012 teNeues Verlag GmbH + Co. KG, Kempen

Photographs: Front cover © Marc Rogoff/The Interior Archive; Back cover © James
Mortimer, courtesy of Collett-Zarzycki Limited; p 18-31 Marc Rogoff/The Interior
Archive; p 32-43 © Simon Upton/The Interior Archive; p 44-51 © James Mortimer,
courtesy of Collett-Zarzycki Limited; p 52-59 © courtesy of David Collins; p 60-67
© courtesy of Nicky Haslam for NH Design; p 68-75 © Simon Upton, courtesy of Alidad;
p 76-85 © Philip Vile, courtesy of Tara Bernerd and Partners; p 86-91 © James Balston,
courtesy of Stephen Ryan Design & Decoration; p 92-97 © Gavin Kingcome, courtesy
of Nina Campbell; p 98-109 © Andreas von Einsiedel; p 110-117 © Paul Redman,
courtesy of John Minshaw; p 118-129 © Fritz von der Schulenburg/The Interior Archive;
p 130-139 © Tim Beddow, courtesy of MM Design; p 140-147 © Philip Vile, courtesy of
Tara Bernerd and Partners; p 148-157 © Tim Beddow, courtesy of MM Design; p 158-171
© Andrew Twort/The Interior Archive; p 172-181 © Tim Beddow, courtesy of MM
Design; p 182-189 © Ivan Terestchenko; p 190-201 © Chris Drake/Recover; p 202-209
© Brian Benson, courtesy of Rabih Hage

Edited by Geraldine Apponyi and Monika Apponyi
Texts by Judith Wilson
Foreword by HRH Princess Michael of Kent
Proofreading by Suzanne Kirkbright
German translation by Kurt Rehkopf
French translation by Claude Checconi and Christèle Jany
Design by Jan Haux
Editorial coordination by Inga Wortmann, teNeues Verlag
Production by Alwine Krebber, teNeues Verlag
Color separation by Medien Team-Vreden

Published by teNeues Publishing Group

teNeues Verlag GmbH + Co. KG
Am Selder 37, 47906 Kempen, Germany
Phone: +49-(0)2152-916-0
Fax: +49-(0)2152-916-111
e-mail: books@teneues.de

Press department: Andrea Rehn
Phone: +49-(0)2152-916-202
e-mail: arehn@teneues.de

teNeues Digital Media GmbH
Kohlfurter Straße 41–43, 10999 Berlin, Germany
Phone: +49-(0)30-7007765-0

teNeues Publishing Company
7 West 18th Street, New York, NY 10011, USA
Phone: +1-212-627-9090
Fax: +1-212-627-9511

teNeues Publishing UK Ltd.
21 Marlowe Court, Lymer Avenue, London SE19 1LP, UK
Phone: +44-(0)20-8670-7522
Fax: +44-(0)20-8670-7523

teNeues France S.A.R.L.
39, rue des Billets, 18250 Henrichemont, France
Phone: +33-(0)2-4826-9348
Fax: +33-(0)1-7072-3482

www.teneues.com

ISBN 978-3-8327-9615-0
Library of Congress Control Number: 2012932117

Printed in the Czech Republic

Bibliographic information published by the Deutsche Nationalbibliothek.
The Deutsche Nationalbibliothek lists this publication in the
Deutsche Nationalbibliografie; detailed bibliographic data are available in the
Internet at http://dnb.d-nb.de.

MIX
Papier aus verantwortungsvollen Quellen
Paper from responsible sources
FSC® C005833
FSC
www.fsc.org

teNeues Publishing Group
Kempen
Berlin
Cologne
Düsseldorf
Hamburg
London
Munich
New York
Paris

teNeues